D1189756

Daughters of the State

Daughters of the State

A Social Portrait of the First Reform School for Girls in North America, 1856–1905

Barbara M. Brenzel

The MIT Press
Cambridge, Massachusetts
London, England

This is a publication of the Joint Center for Urban Studies.

This book was set in Baskerville by The MIT Press Computergraphics Department and printed and bound by Halliday Lithograph in the United States of America.

Library of Congress Cataloging in Publication Data

Brenzel, Barbara M.
Daughters of the state.

Bibliography: p.
Includes index.
1. Massachusetts. State Industrial School for Girls—History. I. Title.
HV9105.M42S733 1983 365'.97443 83-24986
ISBN 0-262-02194-3

For my mother and father
and the memory of my brother

Contents

Acknowledgments

This book is, in large part, the result of the help and insights of many people. I am, as always, indebted to my mother and father, who made social issues an integral part of my growing up. My late brother, Martin, through his work in the theater, provided an indelible example of the importance of paying close attention to the lives of others. It is to my family—their love, thoughtfulness, and integrity—that I dedicate this book.

Daughters of the State began as a doctoral dissertation; I am particularly grateful for Joseph Featherstone's unstinting help as my advisor. His conceptual judgment, ongoing assistance, and careful analysis were critical to my dissertation and to the work that built on it. My research began as a doctoral fellow at the Joint Center for Urban Studies at the Massachusetts Institute of Technology and Harvard University, where I was offered financial assistance and a stimulating environment in the beginning stages of this work. I am particularly grateful to Charlotte Moore, the center's director of communications, who urged me to publish my manuscript as part of the Joint Center for Urban Studies Series at the MIT Press.

Mary Jo Bane and Stephan Thernstrom continued to give me the encouragement and scholarly advice I needed in order to rework much of my dissertation into book form.

Michael B. Katz inspired me to pursue this study and for many years focused my research on aspects of social reform. Both he and Michael Frisch spent many hours in their Maine retreat analyzing and commenting on my manuscript. Their time, perceptive comments, and advice played a large part in shaping many of my ideas and interpretations. I also wish to thank these historians for their careful readings and comments: Robert Hampel, Marvin Lazerson, Robert Mennel, and David Tyack.

I was particularly fortunate in having the constant assistance of the Education Department at Wellesley College. My colleagues Barry Bull and Barbara Beatty read and commented on various aspects of the manuscript; Ethel Brown cheerfully typed early drafts and helped in proofreading.

I am grateful to Karla O'Brien and Jack Brenzel for early editorial assistance. And, of course, to Irene Goodsell, who not only typed the manuscript, but offered me wonderful meals and the hospitality of her and Lincoln's home. Thanks for researching parts of this study are owed to Barbara Craig, Terry Epstein, and Cindy Pratt. Patricia Nolan worked closely with me throughout the writing of *Daughters of the State*. Not only did she offer me invaluable research assistance, but her enthusiasm and sense of humor gave me the intellectual stimulation and levity necessary to complete this complex and often arduous task. I am not sure I could have done it without her. Earlier versions of parts of this book first appeared as articles published in *Feminist Studies* and *Harvard Educational Review* (see bibliography). It is with their permission that I have incorporated some materials from these earlier articles.

Obviously any deep understanding of an institution requires access to records as well as to the institutions themselves. Claire Donovan, former superintendent of Lancaster, now director of the Pelletier Center, was invaluable both in providing me with important data as well as helping me to understand Lancaster. Paul Jones, director of communications, Walter E. Fernald State School, provided me with documents of many of the girls sent to the Massachusetts Home for the Feeble-Minded, as well as unpublished materials written by Dr. Walter Fernald. Michael McCoy, director of the media center, Walter E. Fernald State School, supplied pictures for this book.

Special thanks are due to the late Paul David Birnbaum, who took pictures of the State Industrial School and captured the feeling of its original buildings and architecture.

My initial research was funded by the Canada Council for the Arts and Humanities. Continuation of the study was made possible by the generosity of Wellesley College, which gave me a year's leave of absence to pursue research and to write. I spent a wonderful year at the Bunting Institute, Radcliffe College, and the Henry A. Murray Center, Radcliffe College. The collegial and intellectual stimulation I experienced during that year made the tough task of writing much more pleasant. I am indebted to the National Institute of Education for summer funding and the Andrew W. Mellon Foundation for a year's financial support. This assistance made writing the book possible.

Many reference librarians, and especially Eva Moseley, archivist, Arthur and Elizabeth Schlesinger Library (Radcliffe College), and Claire Loranz, Margaret Clapp Library (Wellesley College), helped me to gather and to interpret important material.

As always, I feel particularly blessed by my wonderful friends who put up with my many moments of despair and were constantly available to offer care and reassurance. To them I offer deeply felt thanks.

September 1982
Cambridge, MA

Daughters of the State

Prologue

On Wednesday, August 27, 1856, Maria F., thirteen years of age, arrived at the State Industrial School for Girls in Lancaster, Massachusetts. Lancaster, the first state reform school for girls in North America, had opened the day before. To Maria, the first entrant, Lancaster must have appeared awesome but beautiful. From the railway station she crossed over the Nashua River through a covered bridge and entered the one hundred and ten acres of the school grounds, formerly the old Stillwell estate. Surrounded by large elms, three houses and a barn stood as the first buildings of the school. One of the houses, originally part of the estate, was over one hundred years old. This clapboard house was three stories high and provided impressive housing for Bradford K. Peirce, the first superintendent and chaplain. He was dressed like other clergymen of the day in a black frock coat, black knee britches, and black gaiters. Peirce and the massive grounds over which he presided were the first formal indications that Lancaster was indeed an institution to reform Maria and girls like her.

Maria, on the arm of a state agent, headed a long procession of inmates stretching to 1973, when the school closed as part of a new state policy to deinstitutionalize delinquent youth. Originally from New Jersey, she and her family had moved at least four times within New England, finally settling in Haverhill, Massachusetts. She was sent to Lancaster by the Haverhill Probate Court, following her mother's complaint of chronic disobedience. Her father, a housepainter, had left the family three years before and migrated to California, where he died. Maria remembered him affectionately as a pious man, loving his children and mindful of their religious instruction. In contrast, she described her mother as harsh; mother and daughter seemed utterly estranged. Lancaster's superintendent Bradford Peirce noted on Maria's record that "after her father's desertion, she had been sent out to work in families; sometimes her mother removing her from one place to another, and sometimes removing her residence without her mother's consent."[1] Maria thus became an active member of what nineteenth-century Americans called the "servant class," girls who were placed with various families with the expectation that they would aid in the domestic chores of the household and remain obedient and subservient to their acquired "families." Maria, however, was not compliant.

Bradford K. Peirce thought Maria's complaints about her family should be taken with a grain of salt, "as she appears . . . of a jealous and morose disposition, and is not careful always to state the exact truth." Maria's account according to Peirce went as follows:

> Her first temptation to do wrong was in Boston. She played truant and told her father a falsehood in reference to it: "and" she says quite frankly, "you know in Boston when one commits the first sin there are always persons ready to lead them on from one step to another." She afterwards took things from her schoolmates without their knowledge and consent, and finally in Haverhill, at the suggestion of a woman who was in the habit of stealing from the stores, she took a pair of shoes from a counter and would have been arrested if the officer had not judiciously interposed, and secured her apprenticeship to the state.

The intervention, noted Peirce, occurred at just the right time: "She says of herself, that she had been accustomed to go out evenings with older girls. There were six of them that met each other, and walked about. She says they were bad girls. They met no men, but wandered around, talking, singing, etc. She says, she was glad to see the officer when he came after her, because she knew that she would be ruined if she remained where she then was."

For Mrs. F., Maria's mother, the "straitened circumstances" resulting from her husband's desertion and death, combined with the uncontrollable behavior of her daughter, must have been hard. She complained of Maria as a "disobedient child, [who] refuses the reasonable constraint [she] endeavored to impose on her. . . . She goes where and with whom she pleases, and has left the several homes her mother had provided for her of her own choice and unsuitable ones . . . [and] she has been guilty of several acts of larceny."

Maria F. was labeled unmanageable, larcenous, and a potential prostitute, and so was welcomed into Lancaster. Considered deceitful by Bradford K. Peirce, and depraved by the police officer who brought her in, Peirce's discussion of her, nevertheless, was filled with great hope and a benevolent if patronizing concern. In a time of social enthusiasm and hope, it was assumed that Maria could be loved and guided into submission and virtue.

Maria's future might have been quite different had there been no Lancaster. Only a year earlier, there had been no facilities for girls like her. Without Lancaster, the most humane law officers would have ignored her, knowing full well that there was no decent place to send her. We know very little about the lives of girls like Maria, but the founders of Lancaster believed that the Marias of the world would wander the streets, likely to join the pernicious population, as a prostitute or as a criminal, in jail. Once arrested, Maria would have faced one of two fates: life with adult female convicts in Braintree or Tewksbury prisons or assignment to the almshouse, which had a nominally separate house of reformation for juveniles, but in reality was part of Deer Island, where juvenile inmates lived in the House of Industry along with adult "irredeemable vagabonds, common drunkards, and night walkers."

Thus Maria's future was imprisonment, or so the founders of Lancaster believed, and their beliefs shaped a part of the story we are relating. Superintendent Peirce discussed Maria with the ambivalences characteristic of Yankee reformers and child savers in the sentimental mid-century tone. He described her as "a pretty girl in the face . . . who sings quite well, and is very artless in appearance." Nevertheless, Peirce was aware that behind Maria's "artless" appearance, she was "deceitful, jealous, and quite corrupt in mind." She had already behaved in such a way that discipline was necessary. Peirce's report reflected his evangelical optimism. His firm belief in the inherent innocence of all children, and particularly girls, shone through his description of Maria: "Nothing touches her but the utmost kindness accompanied by religious motives. Under such an approach she has exhibited considerable sensitivity."

Peirce did not attribute Maria's sinfulness to her nature, but rather to her environment. "She is [therefore] to be sincerely pitied as her childhood has been sadly diverted from the path of obedience and truth, through the want of proper home cultivation." Peirce's optimism, his commitment to the belief that a rehabilitative environment could remedy the wrongs of Maria's childhood and reform her to her previous state of grace, was suggested in his comment that Maria had indeed given "evidence of [a] quite serious attempt to improve herself, and to conquer her peculiar temptations."

Maria, like many other poor and troubled girls in the nineteenth century, proved problematic to her family—which was clearly locked in a struggle to survive—as well as to the Commonwealth of Massachusetts. Wandering young girls like Maria were deprived and potentially dangerous. Families and the State worried about their welfare; they were also concerned about the moral and social implications of their "uncontrollable behavior."

Maria's story is only the first. Not unique in itself, it stands as an introduction to many aspects of nineteenth-century social history. She and poor girls like her were the subjects of an intense new concern at mid-century to create welfare policies in order to maintain social order. Because Maria was poor and a young woman, she was of particular concern to a host of reformers whose proclaimed mission was to preserve family stability. The threats of female vagrancy and prostitution loomed large in the reformers' eyes. Since they saw poor and seemingly unsupervised girls as potentially wayward, the futures of girls like Maria seemed ominous; their condition would not lead them to stable and virtuous womanhood. Saving young girls became a mission to the reformers in their zeal to maintain the woman's place in the family as a foundation of moral virtue and Christian industriousness. Bradford Peirce's voice again echoes a new nineteenth-century perception of woman as social savior: "It is sublime to work to save a woman, for in her bosom generations are embodied, and in her hands, if perverted, the fate of innumerable men is held. The whole community, gentlemen, personally interested as they are in our success because the children of the virtuous must breathe the atmosphere exhaled by the vicious, will feel a lively sympathy for you, in your generous endeavors to redeem the erring mothers of the next generation."[2]

Daughters of the State is a social portrait of the State Industrial School for Girls in Lancaster and explores the lives of many Marias. Like Maria, Lancaster is both unique and generalizable. Its history and its inmates illustrate in microcosm the intricacies, complexities, and dilemmas of nineteenth-century social thought. The school was intended as a model reform effort. It was the first "family-style" institution on this continent and embodied new theories about the reformation of youth. The story of Lancaster is the story of the origins of the institutional response to the young, especially the poor and delinquent young, and it provides us with a picture of the nineteenth century's attitudes toward females, particularly girls. No institution, in either the nature of its inmates or that of its program, can be fully understood without examining the context within which it functioned. It is treacherous to make causal inferences or to state with complete assurance and contextual fit between institutional changes as they occur over time and the contemporaneous external forces that may have brought them about. Yet it is critical to place Lancaster—or any institution—within its historical setting. Thus this book treats the historical and ideological currents from which the school emerged and attempts to weave the particular story of the State Industrial School for Girls, Lancaster, into its general social setting. I have chosen to study the first fifty years of the school. The examination of a reform institution during the second half of the nineteenth century reveals the devolution from reformist visions and optimistic goals at mid-century to pessimism and "scientific" determinism at the century's close. The mid-century ideal of rehabilitative care changed to the principle of rigid training and custodial care by the 1880s and remained so into the early twentieth century. Thus by studying a key nineteenth-century institution from its inception in 1856 to 1905, we can uncover the changes in ideology and practice from a period of hope to a time of disillusionment—in David J. Rothman's terms, from a period of "conscience" to a period of "convenience."

Historians concerned with the nineteenth century will readily recognize the forces within which Lancaster was created. At a time of rapid population expansion, the burgeoning of cities and the crystallization of social classes, fear of the urban poor mushroomed. This fear of the masses exacerbated the perception that the "criminal class" and its potential threat to the social norms had to be contained. In this atmopshere arose the perceived need to create an institution to re-form those girls who were considered potentially criminal women, and, therefore, probably prostitutes.

Several unifying themes run throughout this book. One is the critical influence of class, age, and gender biases on policies and programs for the reformation of the poor and potentially wayward. Another is the ideological bases for reform; the environmentalist vision of Lancaster's founders and the later hereditarianism that reverberated through the various documents of the commonwealth's reform institutions reflect the intellectual history of the nineteenth century.

Official statements made by the reformers of the day give us a wealth of information on these matters. The Massachusetts state records reveal the period's attitudes toward crime, institutions and welfare, and the causes of poverty and deviance. Additional sources are other public state documents; early reports by the Board of State Charities and Lancaster's trustees and superintendents; and similar reports submitted to the Massachusetts legislature by the State Reform School for Boys, Westborough, and other state charitable institutions. Many original case records and personal documents now housed at the Fernald School (formerly the Massachusetts School for the Feeble-Minded) also shed light on Lancaster. The tightening of the institutional web in which Lancaster existed supplies us with food for thought about what the state can and should do for the dependent now and what the consequences of such institutional actions might be.

Lancaster was treated as a model institution, a reform "first." Therefore it plays a special role in American social history. In its architecture as well as daily program, Lancaster was the first North American, "family-style," rehabilitative institution. It was hailed as a model for new family-style reform; its "homelike" milieu was to offer a complete therapeutic program that would give its girls the main thing missing from their wayward lives: Christian family life. The girls were to be bound "by cords of love" and were to learn, through example provided by surrogate family life, the desirable American virtues for young women of their station.

One of the main purposes of the book is to detail the various components that comprise an institution—in this case the State Industrial School for Girls, Lancaster. I was particularly fortunate to have an exceptionally rich source of data; the handwritten case records of every girl for the first fifty years of the school offered a vast store of information about the girls themselves. From these, I have selected a suitable sample and examined every entrant's record every fifth year for fifty years. (Because the record book for 1860 is missing, for the sample I had to substitute for it the year 1863.)

The Lancaster records supply the following information on each inmate: age, her and her parents' religious background, family circumstances, previous life beforing entering the school, alleged crime, reported complainant, and health and behavior at the school. We can also follow the lives of many of the girls after they left Lancaster because many of the records give various biographical details, such as indenture, employment, early death, marriage, and entrance into other institutions. Although the post-Lancaster data are not as accessible, there is still sufficient available evidence to allow one to draw conclusions about the impact of Lancaster on its wards. (I have changed the girls' names to protect their privacy, but in such a way as to preserve their ethnicity.)

Almost every case record is enriched by unquantifiable data. The attitudes and personalities of the superintendents and other officials toward the school and the girls are readily deciphered by a careful reading of the records. I assume that each superintendent expressed both his or her own biases as well as popular reformist thought of the time. The reports tell us, therefore, about those responsible for the girls as well as the girls themselves.

Although there is rich documentation on the girls at Lancaster, there are almost no letters or diaries by the girls themselves. It is always an act of presumption for one to speak for others, yet the qualitative and quantitative data available enable us to draw a fair and sensitive portrayal of the lives of girls who might otherwise have been forgotten. This book is intended to be more than an institutional portrait; I have tried to sketch not only Lancaster itself during its first fifty years but also the girls who went there.

The case records of the girls at Lancaster also tell us of the devastation and despair wrought by poverty. Poor and immigrant families were frequently the first to be ground down by economic hardship and unemployment. The children of such families, frequently labeled "street urchins," were often left to fend for themselves. Families had little other recourse. Nonetheless, one of the most critical discoveries of my study is the role the families of the girls played in using state institutions for their own ends. Almost no relief was offered to poor families, especially those with children to support, and, sadly, its limited availability forced them to represent dependence as deviance. In hard times, parents often sought the only relief available to them; in complicity with the law, they condemned their children and stigmatized them as stubborn and disorderly. In this light, it is not surprising that so many of the girls at Lancaster were there as a result of their parents' complaints. Regardless of historical changes and the many variables, one factor held constant: Except for one year, almost half of the girls admitted to the school during the time of this study entered as a result of their parents' complaints. The stories of the parents of the Lancaster residents are part of the story of Lancaster itself. They had learned to manipulate the system of admission to Lancaster to help themselves as well as their daughters. This phenomenon gave these poor families some control over their offspring. Their knowledge of the system gained for them whatever modicum of state aid was available, and in so doing they took into their own hands whatever decision-making power was possible. For some of these families, committing one's daughter to Lancaster and the state's care may have been a desperate but reasonable last act of parental responsibility. On the one hand, it provided emotional and economic relief to an overcrowded, impoverished home. On the other hand, it saved its daughters from joining the unspeakably squalid life for which the family was headed and guaranteed them food, shelter, job training, and future employment. Given that the "stubborn child" clause was removed from Massachusetts's legal dockets less than ten years ago, it is essential that we try to understand the reasons why parents committed their children to a state reform school and to think about present alternatives.

The parental decision to commit a daughter to reform school illustrates the extent to which certain cultural ideas dominated thinking in nineteenth-century North America. Nineteenth-century prescriptive literature informs us of the social expectations for women: As good wives and mothers—that is, as married women who are respectable, decent, and morally upright regardless of class, ethnicity, or race—women were to be society's protection against the onslaught of that immorality and rootlessness so feared as a result of rapid economic and demographic changes. For the Lancaster girls' families, living up to these expectations, regardless of class, was requisite for their daughters' future success and happiness. The girls' families, the trustees and administrators of Lancaster, and the state itself shared the view that the middle-class virtues of respectability and domesticity prescribed the steps to be taken to direct potentially wayward daughters. The haunting specter of prostitution loomed large for all three and resulted in the acceptance of an extremely narrow and conservative view of domestication as reform.

In spite of its peculiarities, however, Lancaster was also an integral part of an institutional network that had only partly begun to spread to include reformatories, mental hospitals, public schools, orphanages, and various urban missions.[3] Nineteenth-century Americans had reacted to the crises of urbanization, modernization, and immigration by seeking to create a web of institutions that would mediate between older values and the consequences of unchecked economic and technological change. Public schools were one such strand in this web. Lancaster was another. Although tied in with crime and poverty, Lancaster's uniqueness made it seem, at least at its inception, highly promising. It remains a wonderful window through which to examine institutional welfare rhetoric and actual rehabilitative practice.

This study of Lancaster is more than an institutional monograph on one key reform institution. It should allow us to examine nineteenth-century notions of social norms and therefore to comprehend better the period's efforts to correct perceived departures from them. And it can alert us to the various social and intellectual factors that continue to affect our reform institutions.

The story of Lancaster, and like institutions, may provide new insights derived from the glaring errors of the past.

1

Visions and Fears: Citizens and Strangers in Nineteenth-Century America

By the last decades of the eighteenth century, the village world was noticeably crumbling. Colonial life is presumed to have been a society in which formal institutions—apart from family, religion, and the state loosely conceived—were scarce. Had Maria F. lived in this earlier period, she would probably have been cared for as a dependent member of the community. There would have been no perceived need for a shelter such as Lancaster, nor would she have been labeled delinquent. Social problems were dealt with through the mechanisms of the family and community, and eastern seaboard communities were typically self-regulating and self-protecting.[1] An overly romantic literature describing life in these communities holds that the care of the dependent, the poor, and the deviant was integral to ideas of familial and community responsibility. According to this nostalgic vision, dependents in the village were often treated as poor cousins, and little effort was made to differentiate between types of needs, such as those of the poor, the old, the infirm, the insane, the widowed, and the unemployed. Part of the villagers' duties as interdependent members of a "collective family" insulated from the larger world was to care for their own—first within the family unit, then within the village. Dependents, therefore, were not seen as social threats, but simply as a particular segment of society in need of care. Outdoor relief—the practice of giving relief to the needy in their homes rather than in workhouses or almshouses—reflected this attitude. Aid was assumed to be the duty of the village, and the family was to be kept together if at all possible. Institutions for the dependent, in the few cases when they did exist, usually kept the family intact. Therefore families remained together even within institutions, especially in almshouses. In these, inmates of various ages with different infirmities lived together in a homelike setting within which they received supervision and sustenance. Dependent and orphaned children were usually placed with surrogate families.[2] This pattern of care was based on a firm belief that family life served as social bedrock and that small communities were obligated to provide family-style care whenever necessary.

This picture of stability and communal support is only partially true. To the extent that a colonial village was small and sufficiently insulated from other villages, relief through family structure was possible. Those receiving assistance were an identifiable part of the community. It was obviously easy to separate the deserving from the undeserving poor when there were only established residents living within the confines of the village. But often the poor were the itinerant poor, the sturdy beggars of England who threatened community stability at the time of enclosure and upheaval. The colonial villagers, like their British counterparts, were loath to support those they considered undeserving itinerant paupers, for it meant aiding and abetting strangers who were seen as threats to the social fabric. They were not welcomed into the community. Had Maria not been recognized as a resident of the community, she would have been "warned" out and forced to join the homeless poor wandering the countryside.[3] It was not within the realm of community duty to offer solace to the alien and stranger in their midst.

The problem for early-nineteenth-century Americans was that the number of strangers was increasing. As patterns of work changed, the sizes of communities increased, immigration mounted, and economic divisions of labor became more defined, the old relations between local communities and the dependent poor altered. Conscious efforts to care for and regulate the dependent—the threatening stranger—in larger, more heterogeneous social clusters required the invention of new mechanisms. What had been implicit became explicit; what had been informal became formal. The results were conscious social policy, new institutions, new definitions of "public" and "private," and new ideas about role of the state—in short, the emergence of the nineteenth-century liberal state.

Had one of the patriots aroused by Paul Revere's alarm visited his native land seventy-five years later, he would have been astounded by the major changes that Massachusetts had undergone. Foreign immigrants were pouring into the swelling urban centers. Increasing numbers of native and foreign-born were joining with rural migrants to create a new urban mass. This populace was dominated by young adults, of whom the majority was female.

The nineteenth-century American landscape was colored by a constantly moving population as streams of people shifted from rural hamlets to swelling urban centers and from foreign countries to North America. This immigration exacerbated a nostalgia for "the good old days" of stability and familiarity. The federal census figures affirm the emergence of a new rapidly growing and perhaps frightening America—one on the move. The 1800 census recorded 5,511,000 people living in the United States, a number that nearly doubled within two decades and had increased nearly fivefold, to over 25 million, by mid-nineteenth century.[4]

A constant flow of foreigners who had been uprooted from countries across the Atlantic and had come to settle in North America explains part of the tremendous surge in population. Upward of twenty thousand immigrants entered the United States in 1830 alone, nearly three-quarters of whom came from Western and Northern Europe. Economic hardship, like the well-known potato famines, resulted in large groups of Irish joining the steady stream of English, Scandinavian, and German foreigners as early as 1830. The fourfold increase in numbers of immigrants in 1840 over 1830 was, in large part, a result of Irish and German immigration. Immigrants continued to pour into the country, with 370,000 entering in 1850 alone. An overwhelming majority—83 percent—of these 1850 newcomers were from Northern and Western Europe, and more than half—58 percent—were English speaking.[5] Clearly, the effect of such an increase in a brief twenty-year span was that a substantial minority of the American population was foreign-born, or of foreign parentage (see table 1.1).

Most foreigners, even the English speaking, seemed peculiar to native-born Americans in physical appearance, dress, work habits, and speech. Also, newcomers with "different" religious affiliations, Catholics especially, were objects of derision and disdain. In 1853 Boston Brahmin Charles Eliot Norton decried the influx of foreigners as a "sea of ignorance . . . swollen by the waves of misery and vice . . . pouring from revolutioned Europe upon our shores."[6] A number of upper- and middle-class native Americans feared the dissolution of American life due to the overrunning of the republic by ignorant, poor outcasts from other countries. Mixed with this fear, however, was sincere pride in the hospitality and openness of the United States to other peoples. The vision of America as a melting pot that would benefit from the blending of various cultures coexisted with nativist concern over possible ill effects. Most Americans, including Norton and most if not all of his peers, approved of immigration and enthusiastically portrayed their country as one where liberty and democratic principles did and

Table 1.1
Immigration to the United States, 1820–1900

Year	Total US population (to nearest 1,000)	All countries	English speaking (England and Ireland)	Northern and Central Europe (Scandinavia, Benelux, Switzerland, and Germany)	Slavic and Southern Europe (Russia, Baltic, and Italy)	Other (Asia and North America)
1820	9,618,000	8,385	6,024	1,443	44	215
1830	12,901,000	23,322	3,874	3,300	12	172
1840	17,120,000	84,066	42,043	37,889	37	2,333
1850	23,261,000	369,980	215,089	91,955	462	9,973
1860	31,513,000	153,640	78,374	60,609	1,084	4,743
1870	39,905,000	387,203	160,573	158,119	3,798	40,877
1880	50,262,000	457,257	144,876	167,337	17,368	100,236
1890	63,056,000	455,302	119,349	52,148	87,601	3,833
1900	76,094,000	448,572	48,239	55,480	190,922	633

Source: Compilation of data from Bureau of the Census, *Historical Statistics of the United States*, part 1. Washington, DC: Government Printing Office, 1975, pp. 105–109.

should prevail. But as old problems persisted and new ones developed, the Yankee response toward immigrants and immigration became increasingly ambivalent. The United States continued to attract newcomers, who were both welcomed and feared, accepted and rejected.[7]

Each group of immigrants experienced prejudice, but during the pre–Civil War period, Catholics suffered particularly vehement attacks. Anti-Catholic societies multiplied in the 1830s in order, as stated in the Constitution of the American Protestant Association, 1843, "[to] awaken the attention of the community to the dangers which threaten the liberties, and the public and domestic institutions, of these United States from the assaults of Romanism."[8] Samuel F. B. Morse's book *Foreign Conspiracy against the Liberties of the United States*, addressed to fellow Protestants, typifies the propaganda consumed during this period. Reprinted five times in as many years, the tract called for an end to the immigration and especially the naturalization and enfranchisement of Catholics. "The serpent has already commenced his coil about our limbs," Morse warned, "and the lethargy of his poison is creeping over us; shall we be more sensible of the torpor that has fastened upon our vitals? . . . Because no foe is on the sea, no hostile armies on our plains, may we sleep securely? Shall we watch only on the outer walls, while the sappers and miners of foreign deposits are at work under our feet and steadily advancing beneath the very citadel?"[9] From New York's American Society for Promoting the Principles of the Protestant Reformation to Reading's Society for the Diffusion of Light on the Subject of Romanism, the various associations organized to spread the truth about American Catholics fostered hatred and fear of them. Periodicals of a virulently anti-Catholic bias, notably, *The Downfall of Babylon* and *The Protestant Vindicator*, printed, along with theological debates, lurid tales of convents rife with murder, promiscuity, barbarous rituals, and cruel persecutions in dungeons and lime pits. *The Vindicator*, alarmed at the growth of Catholic churches, pressed Protestants to join the war for justice. How could "delicate Christians," the editor asked in the June 24, 1840, issue, "stand by with folded arms and see the Jesuit priest enter their domicile, and use infinite pains to corrupt the minds of their children by papal idolatry and pollute their hearts by the obscenities and shocking vices of the confessional?" Nor were sermons and vituperative invectives the only signs of anti-Catholic fervor; often violence erupted, pitting Catholics against native Americans. Sentiment against the Boston Irish ran particularly high and led to several outbursts: the looting of homes and stoning of inhabitants of the Irish section of Charlestown in 1829 and 1833; mobs burning an Ursuline convent and a shanty housing thirty-five laborers, in the same area, in August 1834; rioting and fighting in the streets of Boston proper on two separate occasions in 1837.[10]

Spurred on by preachers and sensationalist writings, Yankees expressed their anxiety and dismay over their changing society in actions and words condemning anyone who was different—the stranger, the immigrant. Not all Americans espoused these views or applauded the agitators, but to an apprehensive populace in the midst of a transformation of its familiar world, the destitute and the foreign seemed logical targets for blame and recrimination. Ever mindful and proud of their own traditions of liberty and freedom for all, citizens nonetheless questioned welcoming those whom they considered the outcasts of other countries. The influx of "strange" people intensified the perception of the disintegration of face-to-face homogeneous community life. The presence of strangers in their midst had a tremendous impact on Yankee attitudes toward the indigent and consequently on the development of institutional responses to them.[11]

In addition to a tremendous population increase, another significant demographic trend irreversibly changed the contours of the American countryside; a noticeable shift in place of residence from rural to urban settings began as early as the formation of the Republic. The number of urban dwellers more than doubled between 1790 and 1800, with the proportion of the population residing in urban areas increasing from 5.1 to 9.5 percent. In both numbers and proportion, the urbanizing population grew steadily, so that by mid-century approximately one-quarter of the country was living in urban settings; by 1870, this proportion had increased to one-third. Other useful indexes of this shift in population concentration are the increases found in both the number and size of urban areas during this period. At the start of the century, only 6 cities in the United States had 10,000 or more inhabitants, and only 1 had 50,000 or more. Within thirty years, 23 cities had at least 10,000 inhabitants. By 1850 the number had grown to 62, of which 10 had more than 50,000 inhabitants; and in fact, 6 had populations of over 100,000. This trend, documented by official government figures, tells us of the dramatic yet steady increase of urban centers.[12] To many, even migrants who moved from rural areas were foreign; they too were different in their rustic garb and colloquial speech (see table 1.2).

Coincident with this rapid urban growth were significant changes in the age structure of the population. A declining birthrate, lower infant mortality, and decreased incentives for childbearing contributed to this shift. What we currently label "the youth problem" was likely

Table 1.2A
Trend toward urbanization: number of urban areas according to size, 1800–1900

Concentration of population	2,500–4,999	5,000–9,999	10,000–24,999	25,000–49,999	50,000–99,999	100,000–249,999	250,000–499,999	500,000–999,000	1 million or more
1800	12	15	3	2	1				
1810	18	17	7	2	2				
1820	26	22	8	2	2	1			
1830	34	33	16	3	3	1			
1840	46	48	25	7	2	2	1		
1850	89	85	36	16	4	5	—	1	
1860	163	136	58	19	7	6	1	2	
1870	309	186	116	27	11	7	5	2	
1880	467	249	146	42	15	12	4	3	1
1890	654	340	230	66	30	17	7	1	3
1900	832	465	280	82	40	23	9	3	3

Source: Compilation of data from Bureau of the Census, *Historical Statistics of the United States*, part 1. Washington, DC: Government Printing Office, 1975, p. 11.

Table 1.2B
Trend toward urbanization: percentage of population in urban areas, 1790–1900

Year	Percentage in urban areas
1790	4.3
1800	8.6
1810	7.6
1820	10.8
1830	14.1
1840	19.4
1850	25.9
1860	30.2
1870	35.6
1880	43.2
1890	37.8
1900	44.2

Source: Compilation of data from Bureau of the Census, *Historical Statistics of the United States*, part 1. Washington, DC: Government Printing Office, 1975, p. 12.

evident in mid-nineteenth-century urbanizing America. Whereas the group between the ages of fifteen and twenty-five represented only one-fifth of Massachusetts inhabitants throughout the first three decades of the century, by 1830 it accounted for 31 percent of the population. This figure held more or less constant until 1870.[13] During this time of course, the fear of unsupervised youth, especially those in urban centers, led to a desire for formal control. This call for supervision and control was addressed by various social architects. Some of these were involved in educational endeavors including common and reform schools.[14]

These various demographic changes in combination intensified the concerns of Yankee reformers. Adding to their distress was the predominance of females in certain regions. Although there were more males than females in the United States throughout the nineteenth century, there was an increasingly larger proportion of females than males from the colonial era on. Of significance to our story is that by 1850 there were more females than males along the eastern seaboard. These demographic changes had come about quite early in Massachusetts, where by 1800 females already outnumbered males by 6,000. This trend continued so that at mid-century females were 50.9 percent of the population, and by 1870 this proportion jumped a full percentage

Table 1.3
Population of Massachusetts by sex, 1800–1900 (in thousands)

Year	Male	Female	Percentage of females
1800	205	211	50.7
1810	230	236	50.6
1820	255	268	51.2
1830	298	312	51.1
1840	365	372	50.5
1850	489	506	50.9
1860	597	634	51.5
1870	704	754	51.7
1880	858	925	51.9
1890	1,088	1,151	51.4
1900	1,367	1,438	51.3

Source: Compilation of data from Bureau of the Census, *Historical Statistics of the United States*, part 1. Washington, DC: Government Printing Office, 1975, p. 12.

point, reflecting the surplus of thousands of women in Massachusetts: 17,000 in 1850; 50,000 in 1870[15] (see table 1.3).

These statistics provide more than interesting information about the demographic texture of the commonwealth. They throw light on the perceived need for a specially crafted youth policy. In particular, they help explain the pronounced fear of wanton women—of foreign women, of urban women, of young women, and of "surplus" women who had to sustain themselves without the support of a man and who would no longer provide the bedrock for stable families, so longingly and nostalgically called for by social reformers. They explain the vulnerability of Stephen Crane's Maggie and Theodore Dreiser's Sister Carrie, and they etch the background to Maria's lonely march up the steps of Lancaster.

The demographic changes also help explain the public outrage of antebellum America against crime and poverty. By the early nineteenth century, slums as well as pockets of crime had appeared in the rapidly growing cities. These impoverished, many of whom were women, were perceived as part of the army of itinerant poor threatening social stability and affronting Christian decency. Their haunts were brought to public consciousness by those alarmed citizens who felt compelled not to let their friends and neighbors ignore such wretched living conditions. For example, Bradford Peirce, the first superintendent of Lancaster and later of the New York House of Refuge, was given to quoting Charles Dickens. In *American Notes* Dickens had described the horrors of life in a well-known slum area in New York called Five Points:

> . . . narrow ways diverging to the right and left, and reeking everywhere with dirt and filth. Such lives as led here bear the same fruit here as elsewhere. The coarse and bloated faces at the doors have counterparts at home and all the wide world over. Debauchery has made the very houses prematurely old. See how the rotten beams are tumbling down, and how the patched and broken windows seem to scowl dimly, like eyes that have been hurt in drunken frays. Many of these pigs live here. . . . So far, nearly every house is a low tavern, and on the bar-room walls are colored prints of Washington and Queen Victoria, and the American Eagle. . . . What place is this, to which the squalid square conducts us? A kind of square of leprous houses, some of which are attainable only by crazy wooden stairs without. What lies beyond this tottering flight of steps that creak beneath our tread? A miserable room lighted by one dim candle, and destitute of all comfort, save that which may be hidden in a wretched bed. Beside it sits a man; his elbows on his knees, his forehead hidden in his hands. . . . Conceive the fancies of a fevered brain in such a place as this! Ascend these pitch-dark stairs heedful of a false footing on the trembling boards and grope your way, with me, into this wolfish den, where neither ray of light nor breath of air appears to come.[16]

The knowledge that these squalid conditions characterized sections of many American cities exacerbated fear of the unregulated poor and potentially criminal. The number of paupers and deviants alarmed native Americans, whose strong emotional response gave rise to various institutions intended both to protect and to preserve the social order. As early as 1821, Josiah Quincy, mayor of Boston and chairman of the Committee to Investigate Pauperism, formally voiced discomfort with outdoor relief, urging "that some usual and long-established habits of distributing public charity to the poor . . . be altered." He worried that outdoor relief encouraged sloth and dependence and therefore applauded his committee's conclusion "that the pernicious consequences of the existing system are palpable, that they are increasing, and that they imperiously call for the interference of the legislature. . . ." Rational and responsible legislative intervention was to be ensured by classifying and treating the poor as either impotent or able. The "impotent poor" were not deemed capable of work and were therefore deserving of aid. They were to be treated separately from the "able poor," who were capable of work. In spite of this effort to classify types of poverty, Quincy nonetheless acknowledged the difficulty in separating the two groups: "There always must exist, so many circumstances of age, sex, previous habits, muscular, or mental, strength, to be taken into account, that society is absolutely incapable to fix any standard, or to prescribe any rule, by which the right to the claim to the benefit of the public provision shall absolutely be determined." Noting this difficulty, the committee favored the distribution of public charity by the overseers of the poor in order to prevent benevolent "sentiments of pity and compassion" from encouraging "habits of idleness, dissipation, and extravagance among the class which labor." Concerned that humanitarianism might improperly promote charity, the committee called for the end of outdoor relief.

Their report endorsed policies to place all the dependent poor in houses and workhouses rather than to allow them to remain in the larger community. Thus dependents would be helped and the misdirected charity of the benevolent would be checked.[17] Although it is unlikely that indoor relief replaced less formal aid for most dependents, the belief in an organized and systematic system to dispense charity continued. In fact, by 1833 the *Report . . . on the Pauper System of . . . Massachusetts* rued the fact that the colonial method of "warning out" the indigent poor was no longer available.

Returns of the Overseers of the Poor systematically recorded the number and location of all paupers residing in the commonwealth and reported on their care. This penchant for sifting, sorting, and recording every detail underscored a conviction that the remedies to the state's plights could be found by thoroughly examining the prevailing conditions. This careful scrutiny indicated that more formal institutions were necessary because outdoor relief was proving itself to be less and less reliable.[18] Toward this end, efforts to implement and build on recommendations made by Quincy and other legislators resulted in policies that required each town to take greater responsibility for its own poor. Local communities began to dispense charity more and more and to have their roles formalized so as to be in greater control of those reform and custodial institutions within their jurisdictions. Among these institutions were almshouses, workhouses, asylums, and orphanages. Soon state efforts bolstered these local ones as prisons, charitable, and state hospitals were added to the list; significantly, by mid-century, so were reform schools.[19]

The commitment to systematic reports and records provides evidence of increasingly self-conscious efforts to deal with the growing numbers of unidentified poor. Throughout the century policies and institutions mediated between concerned but somewhat wary citizens and the dependent. As mid-century approached, many facilities for treatment and care had been created to serve what must have seemed a frighteningly large group of indigents. In fact, the 1846 returns of the overseers of the poor show that over 15,000 people in Massachusetts were "relieved or supported as paupers" that year. Of these, 7,022 were classified as state paupers, almost two-thirds of whom were foreigners. Aware of this preponderance of foreign-born almshouse residents, nativist writers blamed these dependents for the supposed disintegration of society. Fueling antiimmigrant sentiment, publications like *The Crisis, an Appeal to Our Countrymen on the Subject of Foreign Influence in the United States*, 1844, warned that pauperism, "fungus like, is rapidly growing by what it feeds upon; and it has now so fastened itself upon the whole body of the American people that it hangs a loathsome mass upon every community and corporation throughout our once pure and healthful community. Three-fourths of this pauperism is the result of intemperance, moral depravity and sheer idleness."[20]

The indigent poor, the insane, and the criminal were all treated similarly. In one form or another, all were culpable of social deviance, be they Yankees, rural vagabonds, or illiterates fresh from the ship. A substantial minority of each of these groups sought, or received involuntarily, aid from state and local institutions, both public and private. But the immigrants were singled out. It is not surprising that the majority of those incarcerated in 1860 in Massachusetts institutions for paupers and the insane were native-born white Americans, since it was they who were the great majority of the population; however, despite their numerical majority in these institutions, their proportion within them, only 56.8 percent, was substantially smaller than their proportion in the general population, 79 percent. *Returns of the Keepers of Jails and Overseers of the Houses of Correction* for 1846 in Massachusetts confirm both the alarming number of prisoners and the unusually low representation of Massachusetts natives; a sizeable majority of the over 6,500 prisoners were natives of other states or other countries. They were a striking presence, and it is likely that their poverty and foreignness combined to lead to their apprehension by the law and their placement in institutions set up specifically for social deviants. By 1860, in Massachusetts poorhouses, insane asylums, and prisons, foreigners comprised respectively 48.2, 37, and 49.8 percent of the inmates, even though only 20 percent of the commonwealth's inhabitants were foreign-born. Add to these statistics the following: Of those incarcerated in country jails, and in houses of correction and the state prison at that time, the overwhelming proportion was male. Furthermore, 40 percent of this population, or four out of every ten put away for criminal activity, were foreign-born males. This high proportion, four times as large as their representation in the general population, suggests unequal status, treatment, or punishment for native Americans and the foreign.[21]

Another related, and equally tragic, aspect of this story of public institutions for the deviant is the tale of immigrant women. Only slightly more than one in ten of the commonwealth residents was a foreign-born female, yet they comprised one in four of all inmates in both women's state almshouses and lunatic asylums. Since deviant women—both native and foreign—were more likely to be considered objects of pity or derision than hardened criminals, they were a small minority within the prisons where males predominated; most were institutionalized for dependence, not deviance. However, there was always a fuzzy distinction between dependence and wantonness. While the former condition might evoke pity, the latter ensured disdain and contempt. Deviant women tended to be placed in almshouses, workhouses, or asylums for the insane or destitute rather than prisons. The notion that most women were not capable of deliberate transgressions against the social good prevailed. And for those few deemed morally depraved or corrupt, no hope remained; whereas a man might benefit from punishment, once "lost" a woman could never redeem herself. The threat that dependent women would cross the fine line into wantonness led a segment of society to address the problem and to consider preventive measures. One result was the suggestion that the public domain treat girls tending toward deviance and "correct" them, thus preventing them from becoming criminal and, even more important than that, joining the increasingly visible, feared, abhorred, and shunned ranks of prostitutes.

The descriptions of the urban poor in novels, journals, and government documents alike, along with an evident increase in need for public aid and private charity, gave impetus to the search for remedial measures. The large proportion of the population in desperate circumstances, particularly those incarcerated in various institutions, were targets for reform policies and programs. Obviously many of the foreign-born ended up being "treated" or punished for events beyond their control. It is also quite probable that many among the native-born incarcerated were, in Douglas Jones's apt phrase, the "strolling poor."[22] Most dependents had probably left their homes—in the rural countryside or across the sea—in search of a more secure life, but instead had found themselves on the public dole. As we shall see, these unfortunates shared many of the characteristics of those families from which the girls at Lancaster came.

At least four major intellectual currents, all taking nourishment from Enlightenment rationalism, influenced social-reform efforts aimed at confronting the too evident threat posed by the urban poor: religion, environmentalism, increasing emphasis on the importance of the family, and a growing recognition of childhood as a separate estate. Complex motives underlay all these and other reform impulses. Social reforms were intended both to redeem the poor and erring and to secure social stability. The attempt both to care for poor foreigners and at the same time to keep them off the streets—the need for social control combined with humanitarianism—molded the reformist impulse.

Americans had always viewed themselves as having a special mission in the world: to set an example and, in Andrew Jackson's words, to help "extend the area of freedom." Both this missionary impulse and the Second Great Awakening encouraged people to create a "heaven on earth" and influenced reform efforts that well-meaning Protestants initiated to remedy social ills. During the first decades of the nineteenth century, religious revivalism, through camp meetings on the frontier, "protracted meetings" in the cities, and missionary, tract, and Bible societies throughout the land generated a resurgence of religious belief and intensity. The number of churches, denominations, and parishioners increased. Dissident sects multiplied as more Americans joined groups such as the Unitarians, Universalists, Transcendentalists, and numerous smaller, more transient groups, the most famous being the Millerites and the Oneida Community. Eager evangelicals, traditional and dissident, wished to usher in an era of goodness, and they oriented their work toward reform. Religious revivalism stressed redemption and salvation. This sentiment prompted engagement in humanitarian causes for a substantial segment of the population.[23]

The evangelical enthusiasm of the early nineteenth century, as well as religious changes best represented by the softening of Calvinism, influenced reformers to embrace a new social theory, one that preached the potential goodness in all, and this in turn led them to propose rehabilitative institutions. Unlike Calvinism, for which punishment was the appropriate response to sin and the threat it posed to social stability, nineteenth-century American reform efforts stressed rehabilitation and the return to society. As the millennial zeal of the Second Great Awakening spread and evangelical enthusiasm, rehabilitation, and salvation became components in the creation of the new order, the role of the good Christian, and especially the Christian woman, was to save the errant. The poor and the sinner were to be redeemed through Christian truth, care, and reformation. The threads of this evangelism were woven into the optimistic fabric of rehabilitative efforts. This religious enthusiasm was also tremendously influential in the establishment of many charitable associations, most notably missions, houses of refuge, asylums, and orphanages. Evangelism also reinforced the pious, messianic conviction that the sinner in jail could be redeemed and saved, not just punished and cast away.

The combination of religious revivals, millennial zeal, and a softened Calvinistic approach to personal behavior culminated in a wave of optimism and enthusiasm for the creation of a better world. The birth of the millennium depended on redressing pressing social problems. Rehabilitating the poor and the criminal and saving the innocent, especially the child, became the linchpin of reform during the first three decades of the nineteenth century.

A second intellectual current reflecting Enlightenment rationalism was a hopeful environmentalism. This current of thought may be best understood by contrasting it with antienvironmentalism, an early-nineteenth-century forerunner of Social Darwinism that argued for the heritability of weak character as the explanation for the relation between poverty and deviance. Typical of antienvironmentalism was Dr. Edward Jarvis's *Insanity and Idiocy in Massachusetts: Report of the Commission on Lunacy*, 1855, according to which "poverty is an inward principle, enrooted deeply within the man, and running through all his elements; it reaches his body, his health, his intellect, and his moral powers. . . . Hence we find that among those whom the world calls poor, there is less vital force, a lower tone of life, more ill health, more weakness, more early death, a diminished longevity." Jarvis refuted the possibility that poverty was solely an external circumstance. He went on to argue that although living conditions surely contributed to insanity, ethnic origins, intemperate habits, especially among the Irish, and inherent character weaknesses were the critical factors in the preponderance of insanity among the foreign-born.[24]

Environmentalist thinking, on the other hand, is found in Charles A. Cummings's review in the 1858 issue of the *North American Review* of *Social Statics or the Conditions Essential to Human Happiness Specified and the First of Them Developed* (1851) by the pre-Darwinist Herbert Spencer. Cummings found Spencer's work well reasoned but unacceptable. Cummings included in his review a positive account of the reform institutions both in Europe and North America. The reviewer's bias typically reflected early nineteenth-century social conscience—one that took a stand against theories of inevitability by hereditary predestination to argue for potential rehabilitation of the human soul and spirit especially of the young, who were still pliable in nature and not hardened of heart.[25]

In spite of a hereditarian undercurrent, reformist thinking in early nineteenth-century America fervently favored environmentalism and belief in potential change. The idea that people were shaped by their settings suggested an environmental approach to redeeming them; creating the correct context meant finding the right diagnoses for their ills. Reformers began to classify the types of need so as to effect correct treatment. No longer was it deemed acceptable to jumble people together and to offer them only immediate aid, food, and shelter. In particular, the almshouses, which accommodated what seemed a human "clutter" of disabled, insane, poor, and sometimes even the criminal, came to be more and more unwieldy and custodial.

The first step toward reform was classification by type of social deviance; each type was to receive its own appropriate rehabilitative approach. This trend toward differentiated treatment coincided with efforts to control the dependent and deviant and, together with a perceived threat of imminent social catastrophe, resulted in the development of an "institutional state": mental hospitals, insane asylums, and jails, a network intended both to treat and to redeem those judged to be in need of rehabilitation.[26] Parallel to the reformers' belief in redeeming the deviant was the belief of educational advocates in popular education as a preventive. Not only would potentially dependent and deviant children be re-formed and morally elevated, but they would learn socially useful values and habits of industry. In the words of a contemporary journalist, Stephen Simpson, education was to "change the whole face of society into one radiant smile of contentment and enjoyment."[27] Thus formal education was to provide the correct environment for socializing the young. Agitation for improved and expanded educational opportunity reflected the commonly held reformist assumption that human nature was malleable.

Increasing emphasis on the importance of the family as refuge, a third current, influenced how reformers designed institutional antidotes to the chaos and indifference of the new social and economic order. Family life came to be seen as the counterbalancing force to the unchecked economic changes by which the market economy and factory work in impersonal industrial centers were becoming the way of life for more and more people. Here the growing fear of social chaos and environmentalist thought were interwoven and yielded confirmation of the belief in the family as ballast against social disorder; the family would set the moral and religious tone for its members and secure them against temptation.

Women's role was newly defined in this expanded conception of the family. Now she was to be the domestic priestess. In addition to remaining in the home teaching and nurturing the younger children, she was to supply moral rejuvenation to her husband and older children, who were exposed daily to corrupting influences in the outside world. The family was to be an institution to discourage waywardness through precept and example. In a recently reappropriated phrase from Christopher Lasch, the family was a "haven in a heartless world."[28]

A fourth and related intellectual current also centered on children. It viewed childhood as a unique and distinct estate; the young in years were no longer small adults, but real beings with special qualities, including an innocence and potential that adults had shed. In concert with religious revivalism, this view produced a wave of schemes for child saving by institutional means: Sunday schools, common schools, houses of refuge, and so on. The familial spirit within these would make up for family deficits in the lives of poor children. By the 1830s, social policy aimed at placing every child into a family or a family-style institution of some kind.

In this spirit, Horace Mann, the "father" of the common school, stated that public schooling had to allow for state involvement in child rearing. The mixed motives behind common schooling of children and their subsequent socialization were stated thus: "After the state shall have secured to all its children, that basis of knowledge and morality, which is indispensable to its own security; and after it shall have supplied them with the instruments of that individual prosperity, whose aggregates will constitute its own social prosperity; then they may be emancipated from its tutelage; each one to go withersoever [sic] his well instructed mind shall determine."[29] Common schooling would teach the 3 Rs as well as industry, loyalty, and virtue.

For those children deprived of adequate family life and reluctant or unable to take advantage of public education, the state intervened as suprаparent. The teacher was mandated to act *in loco parentis*—in the place of parent—daily in the schoolroom; the state more completely displaced the natural family for those children in need of surrogate families. With this rationale, social reformers justified the creation of institutions for needy children, particularly reform schools. The story of Lancaster illuminates the state's efforts to merge their espoused goals: to offer family care and to ensure supervision and training of those considered deprived or potentially wayward.

In conjunction with this drive to place deprived children into family environments, penologists and reformers endeavored not only to classify adults but also to separate children from adults. As the optimism of the first three decades of the century faded, the wish to separate children from adults became more compelling. Not only was classification considered important for rehabilitation of adults; separation was also important as a way to save innocent children from them.

These four currents spurred reformers to create new forms of relief and treatment for the growing numbers of the poor and dependent as they swelled society. Their goal was to establish and to perfect institutions as physical embodiments of reformist enthusiasm within which the dependent and deviant would be rehabilitated. First, however, the dependent and deviant would be sorted out. Different institutions for the treatment of different types of dependents and deviants expressed the belief that it was possible and preferable to separate the indigent, the criminal, and the insane from both society and each other; this allowed specific treatment while guaranteeing society insulation from contamination.

No longer would acts of charity benefit the undeserving poor. Nor would they save the criminal from chronic evils or the child from the moral pollution of the city streets.[30] Lancaster Industrial School for Girls stands as a key Victorian mid-century innovation. It inherited a legacy from reform efforts of the Jacksonian era, particularly those to rehabilitate through institutional treatment programs.

2

From Punishment to Moral Therapy: The Half-Century Preceding Lancaster

Society, during the last hundred years, has been alternately perplexed and encouraged, defeated and successful, respecting the two great questions—how shall the criminal and the pauper be disposed of, in order to reduce crime and reform the criminal on the one hand, and, on the other, to diminish pauperism and restore the pauper to useful citizenship?

Dorothea Dix, *Remarks on Prisons and Prison Discipline in the United States*

Various policies and programs for the treatment of dependence and deviance were formulated in the first half of the nineteenth century. Three of these particularly influenced the birth of Lancaster: prison reform, houses of refuge, and the first state reform school for boys. Each was born out of the attempt to treat criminal adults, mostly men, and poor or wayward children by institutional care. By mid-century hope for rehabilitation had shifted from adults to children. The belief in the innate innocence of children—a belief that ran counter to rigid adherence to the Doctrine of Original Sin—made it important to separate them from the sources of "pollution": their environment, and more specifically, depraved adults.

Various attempts at penal reform brought to the Northeastern states international acclaim. In discussing their study of the penitentiary system, Gustave de Beaumont and Alexis de Tocqueville praised the ceaseless efforts of Americans to ameliorate their system and to initiate prison reform. "Whatever may be the difficulties yet to be overcome, we do not hesitate to declare that the cause of reform and progress in the United States seems[s] to us certain and safe."[1] This praise resulted from noteworthy American attempts to salvage the criminal and restore him to society. For the early colonists no individual was beyond redemption; and later Americans, building on this outlook, constantly devised new methods, new structures, and new ideologies in the hope of effecting it.

As early as 1801, Thomas Eddy, the American Quaker reformer, had encouraged penologists to overcome their tendency to consider criminals as depraved and morally incurable. Concerned with the reformation of the deviant, he encouraged a more humane approach and advocated rehabilitative treatment. He believed that convicts were not all of the same cloth and, indeed, that they could be broadly categorized into three types: those who were hardened offenders for whom there seemed little hope; those who were already of a criminal state of mind, but were considered suitable for rehabilitation; and those who were youthful offenders, many of whom had committed minor crimes and should not be treated along with the hardened and depraved. He wanted to see the criminal treated as an individual and classified as such. Eddy was convinced that if the celebrated Newgate Prison in New York attempted to reform the latter two groups by classification and treatment appropriate to the individual offenders, it would then "become a durable monument of the wisdom, justice, and humanity of its legislators, more glorious than the most splendid achievements of conquerors and king."[2]

Other reformers shared Eddy's belief that criminals could be saved by dramatic changes in penal institutions and their programs. Imbued with this ideology, organizations were formed in several states in order to hasten the progress of penal reform; the *Philadelphia Society for Alleviating the Miseries of Public Prisons*, founded as early as 1776 (under a slightly different name), was joined by the *Prison Discipline Society* of Boston in 1824 and the *New York Prison Association*, in 1844.[3]

As participants in this wave of idealism, penologists instigated reform programs at Newgate. Rejecting physical punishment as ineffective in preventing further crime and the inculcation of fear as fruitless in reforming the criminal, they introduced in their stead a rehabilitation program based on religious and moral training, a night school program for common education, and a strict routine of hard labor. They also took over the reform method of total solitary confinement practiced at the Walnut Street Jail, Philadelphia, as a rehabilitative procedure.

The myriad problems at Newgate soon aborted this rehabilitative effort. Constant administrative quarrels, overuse of harsh discipline—supposedly a means of reinforcing reform—overwhelming financial problems, and mounting overcrowding, especially after the War of 1812, made the new program increasingly difficult to administer. Additionally, in spite of Eddy's plea for classification, Newgate threw together adult males, adult women, juvenile delinquents, and the criminally insane. Furthermore, female inmates, considered the most depraved of all criminals, beyond redemption and social worth, were largely ignored.

Judges had hesitated to sentence women to prison on account of its lack of adequate provisions for them; the women at Newgate were there only because they were considered chronically sinful and wayward. Most were vagrant drunks, living lives of squalor and vice, in society's eyes the lowest dregs of humanity. Their presence posed special problems. Women were considered morally threatening to the male prison population; they were not only sexual temptresses, a view of women at least as old as the Old Testament, but both morally and sexually criminal.[4] This combined viciousness was considered the hardest to eradicate. An ex-inmate's indictment quoted by W. David Lewis reeked with the revulsion felt toward the wicked women in Newgate: "The utmost vulgarity, obscenity, and wantonness characterizes their language, their habits and their manners. . . . Their bestial salacity, in their visual amours, is agonizing to every fibre of delicacy and virtue."[5]

Although Newgate attempted to redress some of the harshest aspects of penal reform, to find innovative means by which the criminal could be rehabilitated, it was not really until the 1820s that penal reform became the rage of creative reformers. Their concern came to focus on deciding between two alternative approaches to rehabilitation: the segregate and congregate systems. The segregate system was popularized by the reform efforts made in Walnut Street Jail, Philadelphia. The Philadelphia system was based on Jeremy Bentham's model prison, the Panopticon. Its premise was that the way to rehabilitate the criminal was through total isolation. In solitary confinement he could no longer be tempted or be led astray by fellow criminals but, instead, would look inward and examine his soul, and in so doing save it.[6] Followers of Calvinist dogma believed that punishment and repentance in this world prepared the depraved for forgiveness in the world to come. Enlightenment thought, on the other hand, considered man free of permanent, irreversible sin; it encouraged the theory that man could be saved in this world and found in total isolation a way of forcing the depraved to concentrate on self-examination and thereby rediscover his soul. Although a great deal of criticism was leveled at the cruelty of total isolation, the non-Philadelphia reformers held firmly that their method was indeed the most effective; it gave the criminal the solitude necessary for his salvation. In addition, they rationalized their system as more humane since it required less supervision and less harsh punishment than the congregate system.

The congregate system was commonly associated with Auburn Prison, New York.[7] This system was a compromise between total isolation and the unclassified prisons of the eighteenth century. Inmates slept in solitary, but they went about their daily routines as a group. Strict rules of silence were enforced harshly; however, a marching procedure whereby prisoners marched and shuffled in line formation, heads averted, effectively stopped any social interchange between them when together. This assured penologists that the inmate was left uncontaminated by other criminals.[8]

Although frequent debates about the strengths and weaknesses of each program continued during the "reform" era of the 1820s to 1840s, there were constant arguments over administrative and financial procedures and accusations of overuse of harsh corporal punishment. Waves of optimism alternated with periods of pessimism.

By 1825 New York reformers had decided to replace Newgate, whose reform program had never been successful, and which was now old and overcrowded. Auburn, usually housing rural inmates, was also overcrowded. Sing Sing Prison—ironically first named Mount Pleasant—opened in 1825 primarily for the accommodation of urban felons. Sing Sing was particularly harsh and punitive, much more so than Auburn; fear and hatred of urban slum dwellers was the likely reason for this. Brutal flogging and frequent use of the shower bath—a punishment whereby prisoners were showered in great rushes of icy water, often resulting in drowning or broken necks–were common practices at Sing Sing. Although penologists continued to argue that a strict regimen of hard labor and rules of silence were essential to effective programs of reform, they made no claims for Sing Sing's rehabilitative value.

It continued to be the case that criminal women were excluded from prison rehabilitation programs. "The pessimism with which many New Yorkers viewed the reformability of the adult felon during the heyday of the Auburn system reached an extreme with regard to one specific type of offender: the female prisoner."[9] For almost fifteen years after Sing Sing opened, criminal women were left to roam the city streets. Prisons were for rehabilitation, but fallen women were considered beyond redemption. The popular view was that a fallen woman was the vilest and most corrupt of criminals. For women, jail was a place of incarceration, dehumanization, and total neglect: "Popular attitudes towards female prisoners were also deeply affected by a belief that the consequences of delinquency and sin were more dreadful for the woman than the man. Man had reason; woman depended upon feeling. Man was designed by God for a bold and adventurous existence; woman was created for more quiet pursuits and domestic cares."

Women offenders were doubly accountable: as women and as criminals. They repelled and at the same time confused reformers so that treatment for them had to wait until the 1830s. A few efforts to rehabilitate fallen women had already taken place, however. In England, Elizabeth Fry and some friends, organized as the Association for the Improvement of Female Prisoners at Newgate, had tried to influence British penologists to create a humane program for women convicts at Newgate Prison. It is likely that news of her work had some positive influence on American reformers. A wave of sentimentality toward women as well as a renewed concern with the role of the family also affected attitudes toward rehabilitation for female offenders.[10]

W. David Lewis's descriptions of the provisions for females at Auburn present a convincing picture of the reasons why penal reformers felt compelled to create more suitable quarters for females:

> In order to prevent any communication with the men, the windows of the women's quarters were kept closed at all seasons. The result was a dark, stifling, nauseating atmosphere in which as many as 30 women were crowded together without supervision or proper exercise facilities. Once a day a special detail brought necessary supplies and carried out refuse. Occasionally the chaplain or the prison physician put in an appearance, accompanied by the warden or his deputy. Otherwise the irredeemable were in a limbo all their own.
>
> The effects of such confinement upon women whose sentences ranged up to 14 years can be but dimly imagined. No attempt was made to separate hardened criminals from young delinquents serving their first terms; little protection was afforded the weak against the assaults of the strong. . . ."[11]

For a brief period, women were sent to Bellevue Prison, New York City, but by 1830 these accommodations were no longer considered adequate. Too many women were escaping. Trapped by the governmental policies to care for, to sentence, and to treat all deviants, Bellevue had become overpopulated as it frequently housed state convicts within the city prison. This practice was at the expense of more adequately accommodating the city's own depraved.

In a concerted effort to remedy this overcrowding and disproportionately male inmate population, New York commissioners decided to build new facilities for women convicts at Sing Sing. The women's jail, a separate building, was a marble fortress! But this mausoleum degenerated quickly to the conditions of the previous women's quarters. Rules of silence could not be enforced; therefore officers justified the frequent use of punitive measures. Pregnant women and new-born babies were so poorly treated that their neglect resulted in a high infant mortality rate. And soon it was also overcrowded. Discipline disintegrated. Therapeutic treatment was forgotten. Maintenance procedures became the overriding administrative concern.

In the mid-1840s, Sing Sing women enjoyed a brief period of relief when Eliza W. Farnham introduced phrenology into the program. Phrenology offered a complicated explanation for criminal behavior. It attributed most of it to deficiencies in certain areas of the brain. These deficiencies caused certain patterns of behavior to become distorted, and this distortion resulted in deviance. Unlike the hereditarians, however, the phrenologists refused to blame the criminal for misdemeanors. Instead, they joined with environmentalists in insisting that maladaptive habits could be treated—the environmentalists, by removing the errant from evil influences; the phrenologists, by altering the brain's composition. According to the phrenologists, as a result of various exercises and exposure to elevating circumstances in a pure environment, the brain would change, which in turn would have a profound and lasting effect on behavior; impulses and desires, originating in the head, would be altered permanently and the deviant would be literally a new person.[12]

For a brief period of time, Mrs. Farnham applied these principles to the women's program at Sing Sing. Regardless of the validity of phrenology, it gave Mrs. Farnham license to try to effect homelike alterations within the prison. Tremendous efforts were made to make the women's lives seem more domestic. Books, music, plants, household fixtures, and artifacts enhanced the women's quarters. The rule of silence was temporarily abolished in 1846 because it was considered antithetical to this new approach. But Eliza Farnham's efforts met the same end as the general optimism of the Jacksonian rehabilitative efforts. No more than three years after she had come to Sing Sing, a series of heated administrative arguments between her and more conservative penologists resulted in her having to relinquish certain key reform efforts. For example, the rule of silence was reestablished. By 1848 Farnham was forced to leave. With her departure penal reform efforts for women came to a temporary end.[13]

By the end of the 1830s, the reformist belief in the potential redemption of the adult criminal was on extremely shaky ground. Having failed at various rehabilitative programs, reformers began to consider the adult criminal irredeemable. The fatigue and disillusion felt by most reformers was echoed in the 1848 issue of the *North American Review*. In Francis Bowen's review of Gray's *Prison Discipline*, faint praise was made for efforts at penal reform. Indeed, harshness toward the criminal was justified by the assurance that "[s]ociety is not bound to reform the convict for *his own sake*; no one who has committed a grave offense against his fellow beings, can call upon them, merely to support him, but to find a cure for his hardness of heart and habits of self-indulgence which have betrayed him into sin."[14]

But reformers continued to hold that incarcerating youngsters with hardened older criminals was the first step in turning these youngsters into criminals themselves. By the 1860s, reformatories were being built within which new programs and procedures were to bring about reformation of first offenders or youthful culprits. Vocational training and reformation were stressed, and humiliation was to be avoided. It was a fond hope that the young offender treated with humane sympathy would turn from crime to become a respected member of society.[15]

Evangelical and egalitarian impulses to save children from lives of poverty, vice, and crime helped moderate the growing fear and distaste felt for urban street urchins. Prior to the establishment of reformatories, various philanthropies were created to protect and reform neglected and exposed children. Philanthropists wanted to control the lives of these neglected ones and make sure that they would be given some moral Christian example to guide them. Frequently the programs offered through philanthropies such as orphanages, homes for children, and Catholic charity associations were a way to shore up what was perceived as the irresponsibility of the urban poor and/or immigrant families. For example, the Sunday School Movement and the New York Free School Society[16] were two efforts made by the Episcopal Church in the 1830s to offer schooling to children of the poor. This schooling was to educate poor children in Christian habits and morality. Certainly these programs were part of increasingly popular public and state efforts to reform children. Common schooling was both a right of children and a social necessity. Sentimentality toward children as well as a strong belief in common schooling reinforced the charitable impulse to ensure that poor children have some schooling for both their own and society's benefit.

Many children remained untouched by any reform efforts, however; these were the dependent, neglected, and vagrant who, though regarded as criminals (truants, vagrants, or petty thieves), were frequently dismissed by judges, since jail was considered harmful to them. But juvenile delinquency was an increasing urban problem, one with which reformers had to contend. Unsupervised poor youth wandering about with no discernible purpose was a visible threat to a well-ordered urban environment. In an effort to find a solution to this pressing problem, John Griscom, an American Quaker active in penal reform, went to Europe to study some efforts there to reform refractory children. On his return to the United States, Griscom presented his findings to the Society for the Prevention of Pauperism, an association which, not surprisingly, shared the concerns of the 1821 Massachusetts Committee to Investigate Pauperism. He convinced the society that it should concentrate on caring for juveniles. In 1824, the Society for the Reformation of Juvenile Delinquents was formed, and it was decided to move hastily in order to create a suitable institution for the education and reformation of juveniles, one that might offer reformation, not mete out punishment.

As a result of this activity, the New York House of Refuge was created in 1825. This institution was praised by Governor Clinton as one of "the best penitentiary establishments which [had] been conceived of by the genius of man, and instituted by his benevolence." De Beaumont and de Tocqueville also lauded its opening in 1825: "There exists no establishment, the usefulness of which, experience has warranted in a higher degree. . . . Misfortune is particularly dangerous for those whom it befalls a tender age; and it is very rare that an orphan without inheritance and without friends, or a child abandoned by its parents, avoid the snares laid for his inexperience, and does not pass within a short time from misery to crime."[17]

The House of Refuge opened to offer care and supervision to juvenile dependents and delinquents of both sexes. Unlike jails and earlier almshouses, it was especially for youth—both those in need and those seen as youthful offenders. Girls were assigned to live in a separate house, thereby making it virtually impossible for the two sexes to mix. The program at the House of Refuge was intended to aid in the protection and reformation of the juvenile. Under an old legal theory, *parens patriae*, the state could stand as guardian or supraparent to all minors. Although the House of Refuge was a private philanthropy, the state granted its managers legal rights over the children they housed. Thus this doctrine of *parens patriae* gave the House of Refuge legal charge over its wards until their adulthood or suitable placement and supplied it with a legal justification for removing children from parents who, in its view, contributed to their children's depravity. In practice, parents had little recourse, for even when counteraction was legally possible, their straitened circumstances forced them to accept the transfer. And so for poor parents responsibility for their children paradoxically came to be exercised by relinquishing such responsibility to the state. But the act of intervention by which the state justified the creation of child-centered, formal institutions eventually tipped toward punishment, not only of seemingly inadequate parents, but also their offspring.[18]

But the confusion of purposes of the House of Refuge, made evident in its statement of purpose—to protect, to reform, and to punish youthful dependents and delinquents—bore the seeds of its own failure. The idealism of the founders of the New York House of Refuge soon eroded, and the refuge became known as a punitive jail for delinquents. *Parens patriae* was increasingly abused as a hostile act against poor parents and an excuse to incarcerate indeterminately rather than to shelter youth.[19]

Similar efforts to rehabilitate criminals and reform juveniles were being conducted in Boston. The Charlestown jail experimented with various attempts at rehabilitation programs for criminal adults. Like their New York counterparts, commonwealth penologists became disillusioned. And like their New York counterparts, Massachusetts reformers became increasingly concerned about children and youth sharing jail with hardened adult offenders. The New York House of Refuge seemed to present a good solution to this pressing problem. The Bay State reformers believed that a Boston House of Reformation would be suitable for treating juveniles. Learning from the mistakes of the New York experiment, however, they decided to house and to educate only juvenile delinquents.

Josiah Quincy and Louis Dwight were heavily involved in these efforts to create a quasi-public municipal program for youth offenders. Josiah Quincy, the reformist mayor, established by Quincy Report of 1821 his advocacy of institutionalization. Louis Dwight, founder and secretary of the Boston Prison Discipline Society, had studied various aspects of the program at the New York House of Refuge and felt they were worthy of adoption in an attempt to reform Boston youth. He "observed that the workshop routine, together with Sabbath instruction and a few hours of daily school" provided the milieu in which characters would be formed for usefulness.[20]

In 1826, under the auspices of Quincy and Dwight, the Boston House of Reformation for the Employment and Reformation of Juvenile Delinquents opened. It differed from the New York House of Refuge in that it was solely for youth already convicted of criminal behavior. The courts had state jurisdiction to send both boys and girls directly to the House of Reformation, which was separate from, although physically next to, the adult house of correction. Unlike the New York House of Refuge, the Boston House of Reformation was to avoid blurring dependence with delinquency and to concentrate its efforts solely on rehabilitating the young offender.

The first superintendent, Reverend E. M. P. Wells, an Episcopal minister, was optimistic and enthusiastic. Under his direction, 1827–1832, the Boston House of Reformation seemed to offer a promising program. Unfortunately, Wells, like his New York City counterpart, Joseph Curtis, was at the center of a political struggle with a more conservative faction. Criticized for what was considered his overly idealistic commitment to academic, rather than vocational, training, he was forced to resign from his superintendency. With his resignation the emphasis shifted away from education and reformation.[21]

The dream of Quincy and Dwight degenerated quickly. By 1841 the Boston House of Reformation was considered a punitive junior prison, like the New York House of Refuge. In an effort to save the program at the Boston House of Reformation as well as to economize, the Boylston School and the Boston House of Reformation merged in 1841. The purpose of the Boylston School had been to shelter and to protect orphaned and neglected children; it was not considered a place for reformation but rather a refuge for children in need. Thus its merger with the House of Reformation ended the brief period when the reformers deliberately separated poor from delinquent children; while the toughest children were still sentenced to a penitentiary, the less hardened delinquents as well as the dependent were sent to the House of Reformation. The New York story was repeated.

Two other key institutions for the care of young boys fared slightly better. The Boston Farm School had been founded in 1832 to offer rural life to destitute boys. Under the auspices of Boston's Episcopal minister to the poor, Reverend Joseph Tuckerman, the school did provide adequate care. However, its success was due in large part to the paternalistic supervision of Tuckerman, who saw the school as preventative rather than reformative or punitive. The Boston Asylum for Indigent Boys was also concerned with the wayward and homeless. It too was privately funded and run for city boys. In 1835 both of these institutions were beset by economic trouble. As a consequence they merged to become the Boston Asylum and Farm School at Thompson's Island. The new institution, which was also private, fared better financially than the House of Reformation. There are at least two possible explanations for this. It may be that as a private school it was not subjected to the whims of the public or the constant shifting of economic priorities. Or it may be that it continued to care for poor, orphaned, and neglected children, not confusing them with juvenile delinquents or punishing them for their poverty.[22]

By the mid-1840s many cities, including New York and Boston, faced mounting pressure to deal with increasing numbers of urban children. It was generally agreed that problem children should be treated separately from adult criminals, and this consonance of views was reinforced by the increasing commitment to common schooling as both a right of and a means to provide moral example for all children. European and American reformers were also able to draw on utilitarianism, most clearly defined by Benthamite ideology, and romanticism, an attitude associated above all with the poet Samuel Coleridge. While the utilitarians rationalized the growth amd expedience of policies that resulted in the creation of social institutions and laissez-faire economic policies, the romantics yearned to recover the pure and pastoral.

The Westborough State Reform School for Boys, founded in Westborough, Massachusetts, in 1847, making it the first school of its kind in the United States, in keeping with the romantic stream of thought, was to be a rural retreat for boys exposed to the evils of the city streets, a bulwark against urban corruption and ignorance.[23] Funded partially by the state, partially by private donations, it was to be a state-run accommodation with the mission of compulsorily detaining the commonwealth's boys for the purpose of reforming them; schooling was to be a critical aspect of the reformation program.[24]

The school, a landmark in the history of institutionalization, was considered critically important for the "future prosperity and moral integrity of the community"; its mission was to take "neglected, wayward, wandering, idle and vicious boys with perverse minds and corrupted hearts, and cleanse and purify, and reform them, and thus send them farther, in the erectness of manhood, and the beauty of virtue, educated and prepared to be industrious, useful, and virtuous citizens." This view was iterated by one member of the Foster Committee, who believed this reform goal would be achieved through good teaching and intellectual stimulation:

> I apprehend that very few human minds can be found that have not a natural craving for knowledge. A teacher, even of depraved boys, may win their affection, in some degree, if he succeeds in revealing to them their own capacities of enjoyment in the pursuit and attainment of knowledge, or in the imparting to them a single new idea . . . a teacher who has acquired influence over his pupils by exciting his intellectual powers, or furnishing his mind with stores of valuable knowledge, has peculiar advantages for inculcating the truths of religion and morality. . . .

Moral instruction, the 3 Rs, and vocational training were interwoven. It was hoped that employers would hire Westborough graduates, who would be good farm, mechanical, and domestic laborers, both hard working and virtuous.[25]

Within this reform school, boys were to be treated with love and guidance rather than harshness and the threat of punishment, as if in a family environment. Because they were sentenced to Westborough under the doctrine of *parens patriae*, the state was to assume the role of parent. The administrators, all male, were supplemented by matrons hired to work in the school and sweeten the atmosphere with their "loving" temperaments; their tenderness of manner was expected to calm the urban delinquent and assist in his education.

Unfortunately, the legacy of the New York House of Refuge prevailed; the State Reform School for Boys ended up housing and reforming both the deviant and the dependent. Although Westborough was to have a family atmosphere, the physical plan of the school as well as its program defied this possibility. The building was large, centralized, and dismayingly jaillike. The boys there lived and worked in a congregate style, and although the school lacked the rule of silence, the daily routine of the boys was frighteningly reminiscent of Auburn Prison in most other ways. By the early 1850s the school had already become a junior prison.[26]

In spite of these reform efforts, at mid-century both girls and adult women were still being overlooked. They may have been neglected because it was assumed that there were many more male delinquents than female. It may also have been that it seemed too difficult to treat females; they were considered prone to hysteria or, if already tainted, beyond the pale of treatment. The earlier experiments at Sing Sing had been left to die. However, by the 1850s the "women problem" had to be faced straight on. Many women were living neither in domestic "bliss" as wives or daughters nor employed in acceptable jobs. Some women participated in illegal liquor trade, others in petty crimes, such as fencing, forgery, and stealing. Even more repugnant were those women who, flaunting all religious, social, and moral tenets, were streetwalkers and prostitutes. The untouchables of nineteenth-century life, prostitutes, were considered beyond human understanding or compassion. Fallen women were seen as victims of their own immoral characters. In society's eyes they, more than other deviants, threatened the already shaky foundations of modern life.

By the third decade of the nineteenth century, social reformers and concerned citizens felt compelled to acknowledge the existence of these women. Some of them, like John R. McDowall, whose 1831

Magdalen Report numbered 10,000 prostitutes in New York City, considered these "depraved and abandoned" females a threat to male society. Others, in contrast, regarded young wayward women as victims of society. For example, those involved with the New York Female Reform Society, founded in 1834, expressed concern for the young women corrupted by lustful and irresponsible men. Although these women continued to be general objects of disgust throughout the century, some reformers echoed the sentiments expressed by the New York Female Reform Society that prostitution was not always caused by the wicked characters of women, but rather resulted from poverty or male exploitation. Dr. William Sanger surveyed 2,000 prostitutes in New York City jails and concluded that economic desperation had forced these women onto the streets. Consequently in the 1850s Sanger sought reform of those laws that severely punished prostitutes. Virginia Penny also argued that the economic vulnerability of women was a primary cause for prostitution. She urged that all girls be trained to earn a decent wage so that they would not have to resort to life on the streets. Both Sanger and Penny were environmentalists who believed in the possibility of the prevention of waywardness. They, like the founders of Lancaster, felt that external circumstances, not human nature, determined behavior, especially that of the poor and potentially deviant. Most nineteenth-century Americans, however, feared and loathed wanton adult women.[27]

Troublesome and devious women had always posed problems to society, but in earlier times such women, for example, Nathaniel Hawthorne's heroine Hester Prynne, could be supervised and punished without complicated legal mechanisms. In urbanizing America, however, Prynne's counterpart became a frightening symbol of rampant and uncontrollable evil. And while women were seldom formally charged with crimes, being considered less likely to engage in criminal behavior, women found guilty were not spared prison, especially in the latter half of the nineteenth century. Indeed, they were often imprisoned in greater proportions than men. Examples of this tendency to punish women severely for straying from their appointed path may be found in nineteenth-century Boston's court records. Barbara Hobson's study of prostitution in Victorian Boston, "Sex in the Marketplace: Prostitution in an American Victorian City, Boston, 1820–1880," cites proof of discrepancies in treatment of males and females brought into court on charges of immoral behavior. Greater numbers of females were found guilty and, upon sentencing, a larger proportion were imprisoned; men were more often fined. Women brought to trial were overwhelmingly accused of moral turpitude; they were tried for offenses

Table 2.1
Charges against women appearing in Middlesex County Superior Court, 1850–1905[a]

	Liquor (selling and licensing)	Petty crimes (larceny, etc.)	Other property crimes (burglary)	Social behavior (vagrancy, lewd and lascivious behavior, common drunkenness, nightwalking)	Sex related (adultery, fornication, house of ill fame)	Assault	Serious
Number of cases	276	71	44	145	157	81	7
Number punished	62	21	19	57	65	11	0
Percentage punished	22.5	29.6	43.2	39.3	41.4	13.6	—
Number imprisoned	24	17	16	46	54	7	—
Percentage imprisoned	8.7	24	36.4	31.7	34.4	8.6	—
Percentage imprisoned of those punished	38.7	81	84.2	81	83.1	63.6	—

Source: Middlesex County Superior Court Criminal Dockets, 1850–1905.
a. The figures are drawn from the dockets at five-year intervals.

against the public order more often than they were charged with crimes against persons or property. It is also clear from Hobson's work that impoverished deviant women suffered more than their more well-to-do sisters in the criminal world. "High-class" brothels and prostitutes were usually ignored by police; houses of ill fame in poor and immigrant sections, on the other hand, were periodically raided. Clearly, the underclass generated more fear than the upper class.[28]

A study of both Middlesex County Superior Court criminal dockets and Suffolk County Court dockets of the second half of the nineteenth century underscores this great disparity on the law's part in the treatment of men and women. Additionally, differences in types of alleged crimes committed by men and women are revealed. Men were generally held for property crimes and assault; women, for immorality and unlawful "social behavior": disorderly conduct, drunkenness, fornication, vagrancy, and running houses of ill fame[29] (see table 2.1).

The role of the nineteenth-century woman was to stabilize the family, for as cities grew, families were looked to to buttress the social order.[30] Particular attention need be paid, therefore, to the social upbringing of girls in order to avert catastrophe. It was from this fear of social chaos, therefore, that by mid-century had grown the conviction that girls could no longer be left out of reform efforts. This conviction was reinforced by Victorian egalitarian impulses (for example, girls were to receive common schooling along with boys) and worries about the consequences of imprisoning youth with hardened criminals. But the danger to girls was seen to exceed the danger to boys, since girls had a special role as future mothers of the Republic. This worry further increased public demand for appropriate provisions for delinquent daughters in order to stay their waywardness.

Painfully aware of the weaknesses already apparent at Westborough, and determined to create a reform school that would be truly in keeping with the reformation of the "gentler sex," the Massachusetts legislature created the Fay Commission in 1854 to decide where and how the commonwealth could best establish the first state reform school for girls. Composed of well-established legislative reformers from the commonwealth, the commission decided to study thoroughly the problem in order to make recommendations for the creation of a reformatory for females. Along with investigations of similar efforts in this country on behalf of boys, they would examine closely reform efforts in Europe. The creation of this commission heralded a new beginning for delinquent women.

3

In Search of a Solution: The Fay Commission

The Massachusetts legislature's "Resolves for the Establishment of a State Reform School for Girls" of April 12, 1854, entrusted to the appointed commissioners the task of doing all the preliminary research and planning for a Lancaster and presenting an actual proposal to this effect to the legislature. The leaders of the commonwealth—evangelicals, reformers, and legislators—had committed themselves to an experiment in social improvement and control. In historical perspective, we may view this commitment as the culmination of several other reform initiatives and an expression of prevailing ideology and sentiment.

In 1854 distress over the lack of rehabilitative care for girls resulted in a Commissioner's Report recommending the following: "A sense of great impropriety, if not even injustice, of such practical provisions on the part of the State, pervading the people no doubt, induced the Legislature of 1854, on the recommendation of the Governor, to make provision for an institution for girls, similar in purpose to the State Reform School for Boys at Westborough."[1] The mechanism for creating a girls' school was complicated and dramatically self-conscious. Driven by deep-rooted concern that this school be a model, the commissioners became the social and programmatic architects for the State Industrial School for Girls, Lancaster.

Using the method of funding the establishment at Westborough as a guideline, $20,000 were appropriated to open a state reform school for girls. As at Westborough, an equal amount of private money was expected to be donated prior to its planning. Once the money was collected, the governor appointed three commissioners to begin working toward the creation of Lancaster.

Francis Ball Fay, John W. Wilkins, and Henry B. Rogers recognized the gravity of their task and thoroughly researched the precedents in reformatory institutions. Sincere participants in the reform endeavor, these three men were all worthy citizens, interested in the community, with records of social service. Francis B. Fay, the most prominent member of the commission and the man for whom the commission was named, had served as a member of the United States House of Representatives, as well as in the Massachusetts General Court and Senate, and later as mayor of Chelsea. Described by a contemporary as a "Whig of little education but a man who got the unheralded things done," he engaged himself completely in the tasks of a commissioner. After this duty had been fulfilled, he then served as trustee and treasurer of the school he had helped found. In fact, Fay retired at 65 to South Lancaster, "that he might be near the institution: in which he felt totally invested."[2]

Such personal devotion to a cause was characteristic of many "do-gooders" of the period. The commission's mission was just that: a mission, a task both personally and socially motivated. Although a community consensus no longer characterized the governance of society, care for the poor, particularly children, was still regarded with respect as paternalistic benevolence. Social reformers wanted to do more than build cages in which to confine society's problems; they sought a means of solving the problems or curing the afflicted—in this case the morally afflicted. The methods embraced, therefore, by those working in prisons, the temperance crusade, and orphanages, as well as children's reformatories, invariably incorporated evangelism, the Protestant work ethic, and faith in domesticity. Lancaster was in complete accord with the reformist creed: to legislate the creation of an environment, albeit an institution, that would provide for deprived girls.

The Fay Commission's mandate, as set forth in the Congressional Record, was threefold: "To select and determine the location, and prepare plans and estimates of the buildings, necessary for the institution, and a system for its organization and government, to be submitted to the next legislature. . . ."[3] The first task, the selection of a suitable site, touched off a philosophical debate about the nature of progress and perfectability, in which the Romantic ideology was the winner.[4] It was decided that the perfect environment to cleanse the girls, who were considered polluted by city life, was the country, where the purity of living with nature would inspire the redemptive and healthy growth of the potentially wayward child. Consequently, the commissioners rejected any site within a fifteen-mile radius of Boston. But since a state school had to service the needs of the whole state, it could not be too distant from the most heavily populated areas.

Therefore preference was given to a rural estate with cultivated farmlands but easy access. To this end, the commissioners advertised for a suitable site in these words: "The lot must contain at least 50 acres; must include, or border upon, a pond, river, or unfailing brook, must be partly woodland, or interspersed with trees. A southerly aspect is very desirable, if not indispensable." After inspecting many parcels of land, the commission finally settled on a site donated by a local gentleman.[5]

Next the exact structure and program had to be worked out. To do so, the three commissioners made trips to several juvenile reform institutions in the Northeast, including Westborough as well as ones in New York and Philadelphia. They also held numerous discussions with like-minded reformers; indeed, they looked into all the available resources on both sides of the Atlantic. Among other things, they sent out a questionnaire to various American officials concerned with juvenile delinquency and reform, including George Matsell, Chief of Police for New York City; John D. Russ, Superintendent of the New York Juvenile Asylum; and G. W. Pearcy, Assistant Superintendent of the Asylum at Five Points.

The questions they asked and the replies they received cast light on the reform thought of the period. More to the point, this thought influenced the Massachusetts Resolves of 1855, which sanctioned the creation of Lancaster Industrial School for Girls. The commissioners' questionnaire asked the following:

1. What class of girls should be admitted to the proposed school?

2. What should be the limit of age as to admission—how young, and how old?
For how long a term should the girls be sent—for their minority or for a shorter period?

3. What should be the principle of classification, and how far is it advantageous to carry it?

4. Are there advantages in providing separate buildings, with separate yards and grounds, for the different classes of girls?

5. Should each girl be provided with a separate bed and bedroom?

6. What shall be the treatment and discipline?

7. What instruction—intellectual, moral and religious—should be given?

8. What kinds of work—in-door or out—can girls profitably pursue?

9. What amusements should be provided?

10. How long should girls be retained at the Institution?

11. Should the main object be to apprentice the girls as soon as possible, under the idea that the chances of reformation in a good

family in the country are greater than at the Institution? Should the chief reliance for reformation be placed upon the Institution?

12. How, and by what authority, shall girls be sent to the Institution, and especially those who have not been guilty of any criminal offense, but whose idle and vicious practices are corrupting their own morals and those of the community, and placing them in imminent danger of falling into crime?

13. What should be the general plan of the buildings?[6]

Similarities in the responses indicate ideas shared by mid-nineteenth-century social reformists. One such point of agreement was that girls should be about seven years old to qualify for entrance to Lancaster and should remain in custody of the state until early adulthood—specifically, ages sixteen to eighteen—because girls between these ages were considered most receptive to rehabilitation. Further, it was generally held that the doctrine of *parens patriae* legitimatized the State's assumption of the role of responsible parent for these girls. The staff of the school would then serve *in loco parentis* to the girls during the pre- and postpubescent years. Also, sentences would be indeterminate regardless of age or offense; girls considered to have acted without discernment would remain at the school. Since *parens patriae* was considered protection rather than punishment, such compulsion was regarded as not only the girls' legal due but an act of love.[7] In addition, the respondents agreed that admittance should hinge on whether the girl seemed capable of reformation. Here differences emerged; however, all assumed that at least some of the population could be saved. All also assumed that sexual experience—although defined slightly differently by each respondent—was a cutoff point; violence was abhorred in boys; wantonness in girls.

The viewpoint of George Matsell, Chief of Police for New York City, reflected the attitudes of those reformers who believed that most wayward young girls were children to be helped:

By no means admit those who have been convicted of criminal offenses by a court, unless you determine to confine your Institution entirely to that class of girls, as experience abundantly testifies to the impolicy of connecting in the same Institution persons who have been convicted of criminal offenses, and those who, through poverty or the reckless indifference of parents or guardians to the morals of children under their care, allow them to run in the streets and form vicious acquaintances and habits, thus gradually leading them on to acts of moral turpitude. . . .

These remarks do not apply to those whose chastity has been successfully invaded, unless they are confirmed prostitutes, or evince such a vicious disposition as to show an unconquerable innate depravity.

An even more tolerant view was expressed by John D. Russ, superintendent of the New York Juvenile Asylum: "No girl should be admitted under ten, or over sixteen years of age, and between these ages, the thief, the pickpocket, the obdurate and the disobedient, the liar and blasphemer, and, should there be opportunities for complete isolation of classes, the youthful prostitute (should be admitted)."[8]

What is important here is that despite these differences, all believed that some girls suffered from a poor environment rather than irreversible and inherited viciousness. It was on the basis of this shared assumption that reformation was made the major goal at Lancaster, to be brought about by providing what the home had lacked: loving yet firm guidance for a moral and industrious life. None of the reformers advocated a juvenile prison. Partially in reaction to the obvious disasters of such congregate juvenile reform schools as Westborough, every respondent gravitated toward some idea of a rural, family-style institution, one where girls would be far from the temptations and vices of the city. Although the terms "family" and "cottage style" were used interchangeably, "family style" expressed more specifically the goals of those men. In keeping with this rural ideal of a family-style institution, a farm would be part of the school grounds, so that both agricultural and domestic training could be integrated into daily work routines.

George Matsell advocated a plan whereby separate buildings would house fifty girls apiece. Each girl would have her own room with space for certain toilet articles and personal belongings. The girls were to be chastened by reason and, when necessary, deprivation of privileges. No corporal punishment was to be used. As in a loving family, the girls would not require more severe punishment. Their goal would be to please their "parents." "The treatment of the pupils should conform as far as possible to the treatment given by a *judicious parent* to *children*, so that the pupils would be led to love and regard it as a home. It is well known, to those who have given any attention to the female character, that the *love of home* is the most predominant and lasting feeling of their hearts; and if the pupils can be led to regard the Institution as a *home*, in truth and in fact, the discipline becomes comparatively easy."

John Russ, superintendent of the New York Juvenile Asylum, expressed reluctance to give the girls their own rooms because it was important that they be "safeguarded" against "secret vice." He strongly opposed physical punishment, which he viewed as expedient, but not rehabilitative. In addition, he advocated that the school keep the girls in small groups, so that they could be offered proper care:

Strict discipline has been accepted as a substitute for reformation, and a subjection of the muscles for a change in the heart. One man with the whip can bring a hundred into order easier than he can radically change the purposes of one, fifty, sixty, and even one hundred, are sometimes placed under the direction and charge of one person. These must be subjected; and thus their management falls into a certain routine, which serves the purpose of outward show, while but little is done, or can be done, to implant those great principles of virtue and morality, which are alone necessary to their future welfare and usefulness. No school or institution can be considered truly reformatory where more than thirty pupils are subjected to the control of one person; and even a less number would give better chances for reformation, as it affords a better opportunity of studying their tempers and dispositions.

The respondents also agreed that both intellectual and moral training should be part of Lancaster's program, in keeping with the American belief in the moral efficacy of common schooling. Therefore the girls would not only be taught to perform household tasks but receive instruction in reading and writing and in religion; education and moral training were seen as mutual reinforcements:

Intellectual development exalts the moral; and although order and more direct appliances may be necessary to complete its culture, still, when you open the avenues to knowledge and supply the mind with healthy food, it ceases to long after the garbage which works such mischief with those who have nothing else to feed on. The cultivation of *self-respect*, besides the inculcation and enforcement of those great moral truths which it is the business of society to develop and to cherish, should be carefully attended to.

The germ of all morality lies in self-respect; and, unless you have sufficiently stimulated and excited this, all your efforts will be as "sounding brass: or a tinkling cymbal.[9]

Confusion over the methods and implications of classification was noticeable in the responses. On the one hand, the respondents espoused rehabilitation by means of the creation of surrogate families; wayward girls should be housed together as sisters, that is, grouped as if one big family. On the other hand, some respondents thought that the girls should also be grouped according to prior behavior. The unresolved question was how to provide familial love while enforcing institutional discipline.

Clearly, the greatest fear of the reformers was the further degradation of girls after admission. It was assumed that most young children, even the deviant, would grow up virtuous and responsible citizens if given proper care and love. But certain youngsters were considered beyond salvation and so not fit for admission; indeed, by their very presence they would contaminate and lead to doom girls otherwise redeemable. In particular, promiscuity, because perceived as voluntary, was considered both undeserving of pity and untreatable. Indeed, in the eyes of many of the respondents, the abhorrence of unchaste behavior and prostitution overrode any objections to classification. Classification in these instances, they held, was best for all the girls and in keeping with the primary object of the school: rehabilitation of potentially wayward girls. For example, Frederick A. Packard wrote, "It is my firm conviction that no girl whose chastity has been successfully invaded should have the opportunity, in such an institution, of intercourse or communication with those whose virtue is unimpeachable; and hence it seems to me that in any refuge or school of *reform* where girls of a tender age are confined for delinquency, such as indicates an evil temper, a vagrant disposition, disregard of parental control, or even where an older and more depraved class are received who have maintained their chastity inviolate, none should be admitted who have lost it." One would think upon reading these statements that loss of chastity was a highly contagious disease, easily caught by mere proximity. The major question facing the founders of Lancaster was that voiced by many other reformers: When was a young girl too sexually experienced so as to no longer qualify as an innocent child to be redeemed?

Even in this matter, however, distinctions were made by some for the sake of reform: Any girl who willingly engaged in sexual activity was forever lost, in both this world and the next, but those who acquired sexual knowledge unwillingly, although morally tainted, were not irreversibly sinful. Russ and Matsell were even willing to accept the sexually "deviant," meaning sexually active, girls, though in a separate category. In fact, it is their sole qualification for classification; the promiscuous must be isolated from all other entrants. Similarly, the Reverend Edward E. Hale advised that he would admit everybody who applied, "then separate most carefully girls who have been in licentious life from other[s]. . . ."

In their effort to create a model reform institution for girls, the Fay Commission also looked to Europe. This was not a surprising part of the planning process; institutional responses to modernity—urbanization, industrialization—were very much a transatlantic phenomenon. A sense of social crisis prevailed on both sides of the Atlantic, but perhaps not with the melodramatic extremes of boosterism and anxiety that accompanied the American response.

By the time the Fay Commission began its work, reformist theories and programs had existed for over a century in Europe. Indeed, there had already been lively transatlantic discussion of reformist concerns for at least five decades prior to the opening of Lancaster. As early as the 1830s de Tocqueville and de Beaumont had visited New York and Philadelphia prisons and had written an extensive report in an effort to influence the French government to make changes they thought valid in light of what they had seen. American reformers felt comfortable with European reformist ideology. Both groups favored Enlightenment over Calvinism. Both were committed to social benevolence, which, they hoped, would establish a Christian kingdom on earth and would extend love and charity to all "brethren."[10]

British Quakers, who influenced Eddy and Griscom, were particularly concerned to alleviate human suffering. They regarded industrialization as both good and bad, a source of both material goods and new forms of poverty. To aid the urban poor, British Quaker reformers created missions and relief programs, particularly in London, Manchester, and Liverpool, which had become centers of rapid industrialization, urban blight, and human suffering. American Quakers—for example, Thomas Eddy, the penologist and principal founder of the New York Society for the Prevention of Pauperism in 1811,[11] and John Griscom, the founder of the New York House of Refuge[12]—aware of these efforts, borrowed and traded ideas for building similar institutions in the United States.

More secular British minds had also given thought to the general issues of penology and reform. For example, Jeremy Bentham, a well-known British Utilitarian, discussed issues of poverty and welfare at the same time as he was promulgating a theory of tough-minded individualism based on free trade and laissez-faire. In *Tracts on the Education of Youth* and *Tracts on the Means of Supporting the Poor and Preventing Idleness and Vagrancy*, he outlined the application of these ideas to the corrective treatment of criminals, juveniles, and the poor. Contributing to transatlantic exchange, Bentham requested Patrick Colquhoun, an English police commissioner who corresponded with Thomas Eddy, to send these treatises to Eddy. In 1792 Bentham created a philosophical and architectural "vision" for effective treatment—the Panopticon—which had been inspired by the state penitentiary in Virginia as well as by several other American prisons. The epitome of rationalism, the Panopticon was meant to be the perfect institutional response to the deviant and the dependent. It was a particularly harsh and inhumane "reform" that placed inmates under constant one-way surveillance and was characterized by maximum control and rigid supervision:

> Invisibility is a guarantee of order. If the inmates are convicts, there is no danger of a plot, an attempt at collective escape, the planning of new crimes for the future, bad reciprocal influences; if they are patients, there is no danger of contagion; if they are madmen there is no risk of their condemning violence upon one another; if they are school children, there is no copying noise, no chatter, no waste of time; if they are workers, there are no disorders, no theft, no coalitions, none of those distractions that slow down the rate of work, make it less perfect or cause accidents.[13]

By mid-century, European reformers had already become convinced of the necessity for separate and distinct institutions for youthful offenders, thus paving the way for Lancaster.[14] Samuel Gridley Howe, Charles Loring Brace, and many other American reformers were greatly influenced by European developments along this line. They also found congenial their European counterparts' faith in cottage-style reform, that is, institutions to rectify the evils of industrialism and family life by acting as surrogate homes. In addition, they accepted the European assumption that education was a major function of these institutions, providing along with school, family, and church the instruction necessary for averting social chaos. But while Europe tended to be more legalistic and concerned about enforcing the law and preserving order, America put more emphasis on common schooling and the family.

There were strong ideological reasons why Americans emphasized educational institutions so much, even when speaking of public order. Reluctant to let their world become as formalized as the one from which they had fled, they preferred to let existing facilities take on additional social functions. Also, schools were viewed as the answer to American social stability. For unlike the Europeans, Americans could place the blame for social ills on foreign immigrants, whose Americanization at school would thereby solve American society's problems. The Boston School Committee voiced this ideology in 1847: "Our schools are our hope—we look to them, and their effects upon the intelligence of our citizens, as the Ark of Safety to our institutions."[15]

The members of the Fay Commission examined European precedents, then, to perfect America's reform system: to learn why reform schools like Westborough failed to rehabilitate, to apply this knowledge to the creation of a successful system of reform schools, and to extend this system so as to include girls.

Encouraged by Samuel Gridley Howe's earlier reports, the commissioners examined the German reform movement. Prussia, in particular, had developed a strong system of charity, including educational institutions, in response to the needs of the poor caught in the midst of rapid industrialization. The Germans, like the Americans, considered the family the best environment for good Christian upbringing, so that failing this ideal, surrogate arrangements would be of great benefit, albeit second best.[16] Two brothers, Karl and Christian Zeller, formed group houses called *Bueggen*, later known as *Rellingshauser*, in which they housed, educated, and cared for children. The thoughts of Johann Pestalozzi reinforced the work of the Zellers. His pedagogy encouraged and reinforced the new, more "child-centered" and optimistic approach to child saving. Recognizing their ideological affinities with the Germans, the commissioners carefully scrutinized the program instituted by Johann Heinrich Wichern, the "father" of the family-style rehabilitation center. Wichern, who had witnessed the effects of modernity on poor city children, offered as a countereffect a model of family-style institutional life, the Rauhe Haus. In 1783, Wichern bought a thatched roof cottage in Horn, near Hamburg, and began there a home for twelve boys, all of whom had been beggars in the slums. Wichern's goals for this "rough house," considered "the most influential social enterprise in Protestant Germany . . . an enduring symbol of the purpose of religion in the world," were to train these destitute street children to be good Christian workers and staunch religious family members. Wichern provided family life for the boys; he, his immediate family, and a few lay assistants supervised, taught, and offered them religious instruction. The staff encouraged them to supplement their rigorous work and religious observance with simple pleasures, such as tending their own small gardens and celebrating special occasions. By deliberately avoiding training them for menial work and, instead, encouraging their learning various crafts and trades, Wichern hoped to make them more self-sufficient adults. American reformers, and particularly the Massachusetts commissioners, were greatly impressed by Rauhe Haus and its successful blend of school and family. However, the overt Protestantism of German philanthropy could not be wholly grafted onto American models.[17]

Inspired by, but not entirely satisfied with, German reformism, the commissioners also studied the French. The land of liberty, equality and fraternity was beset at this time by the same upheavals and economic disorder caused by the growth of cities and the demographic shifts resulting in concentrations of dislocated urban poor. Paris, "Sin City," epitomized Americans' worst fears of urbanization. Like other continental philanthropists, the French plunged into institutional reform. A wave of Romantic enthusiasm for reform swept over intellectuals, judiciaries, and government officials. As always, this romanticism was dampened by the persistent need for social control. Nevertheless, benevolence prevailed and led to some changes in criminal law and the reduction and softening of corporal punishment. In addition, reformers, particularly Villermé, wrote political tracts to expose the inhumane working conditions in factories in order to effect some alleviation of laborers' dire working conditions. Child labor laws were passed to limit the legal age of employment for children. (This was only in part an effort to protect poor children from exploitation; it was probably also intended to protect jobs for older people.)[18] As in the United States, many of the socially prominent considered illiteracy a serious cause of unemployment and crime. A weaker version of the American commitment to common schooling led the French to adopt limited educational reforms, such as the Guizot law of 1834, which established by edict that primary education be offered in each commune throughout France.

Like the American evangelicals, the French humanists were influenced by Rousseau. It was Rousseau who had most forcefully set forth the view that understanding the nature of the child gave insight into the nature of the adult, especially as he might have been had he not been "polluted" by a corrupting environment. Rousseau had advocated rural life for children so that they could retain their innocence and, in the absence of the corrupting atmosphere of the city, learn the true nature of the universe and acquire basic survival and educational skills. Rousseau's thought was to play a central role in the Romantic current, whose impact on American reformers has already been noted. It was in this vein that writers like Victor Hugo contributed to the pressure for penal reform by arguing that man is inherently good and should not be brutalized by his circumstances and environment.[19]

The French humanist reformers, among whom were de Tocqueville, de Beaumont, de Metz, and de Courteilles, were quite active in improving social conditions in France, especially for the children. One notable result of their involvement, L'Ecole Agricole at Mettray, France, was very much a product of transatlantic exchange; their work in turn was to have an impact on the Fay Commission.[20] De Metz's enthusiasm for American missions, which he had studied at first hand, had led to a glowing report to the French government proposing them as a sound alternative to the French system of youth reform.

De Metz later cofounded La Société Paternelle, which was to create a family-style reform school in rural France devoted to the care of dependent and delinquent French youth (*detenus*). "His active, original mind at once devised a plan combining the German and American

An 1845 engraving of La Colonie Agricole Pénitentiaire de Mettray, Ecole Agricole, Mettray, France.

systems, and grafting upon them military disciplines peculiarly adapting to it the taste and character of his own country." He retained the labor, educational instruction, and close supervision that he had seen in the American houses of refuge, but adopted Wichern's cottage-style accommodations for the boys at the colony, and on this he superimposed the strict French military-style discipline, severely rigid but justified by its proponents as therapeutic treatment.[21] Ecole Agricole was founded by de Metz and M. le Vicomte de Courteilles on the latter's estate at Mettray, a rich agricultural area through which the Loire River flowed. The colony was perfectly situated for farming and was surrounded by small French farms and other estates. The American reformers were impressed by the French version of a fairly large family-style reform, one which avoided the crowded dormitories and congregate style of Westborough. In many matters Mettray offered a viable alternative both to the obvious pitfalls of Westborough and the religious emphasis of Rauhe Haus.[22]

As it was critical that the Ecole Agricole give the spirit of family life to the *colons* who lived there, the physical structure as well as the actual program was of tremendous significance. On either side of a large green square, the colony was composed of two rows of stucco cottages—*pavillons*—in each of which forty-two boys and a supervisor lived. Each *pavillon* served as a home for the boys. Hammocks were

An 1845 engraving of a workshop for making cord, Mettray, France.

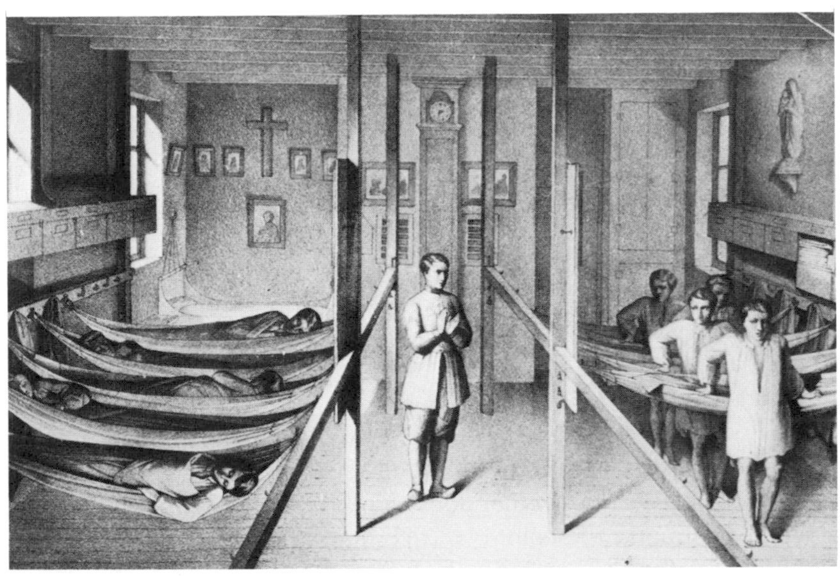

An 1845 engraving of regimented reveille, Mettray, France.

stretched across the room by night; these were rolled up and pinned against the wall during the day so that the cottage could be used for "family meals" and recreational activities. At the end of the square, firmly placed between the rows of *pavillons*, was the church. A room for solitary confinement was at the back of the church and constructed in such a way that the penitent could see into the church and thus receive moral instruction. However, like a segregated prisoner searching his soul, the *colon* was invisible to his fellows. On either side of the church were *ateliers*, where the boys were taught hand skills such as woodworking and rope making. Surrounding the school and large barn were fertile rolling hills, which the *colons* planted and tilled. Their major activity was to learn agricultural skills; it was hoped that these boys would become competent farm laborers and fill those labor needs in rural France made severe by the massive movements of youth into the cities; Paris, like Boston and New York, was looked on as a wicked lure whose fatal attraction would lead to labor shortages on the farm and corruption of innocents in the city.[23]

Most of the inmates were young boys who had been accused of real crimes, such as petty theft and arson, as well as status offenses, such as begging, vagrancy, and vagabondage—another instance of a juvenile reform effort blurring the distinction between poverty and delinquency. While these boys were to live family style, it must be kept in mind that family style at Mettray (as at Westborough) did not mean genuine sentimental affection as much as a certain arrangement of the physical plant. The regimen of Mettray was harsh and militaristic. Not only did *colons* wear uniforms, but their daily lives were extremely tightly organized. Punishments were harsh; solitary, flogging, a diet of bread and water, confinement to quarters, and return to jail did much to guarantee a well-run colony under tight-fisted control.

Similarly, rewards bore little resemblance to warm family encouragement. Good behavior was recognized by the inscription of one's name on the honor roll. Although a large percentage of boys qualified—at least in the early years—the threat of having one's name removed for various minor infractions was constant. In addition, the extraordinary frequency of punishment made the requirement that three punishment-free months elapse as a precondition for name inscription on the honor roll difficult.

To the physical and militaristic exercises and training in various occupational skills were added the constant presence of the Sisters of Charity and the Church and enforced church attendance. This was the French formula for reformation. In the final analysis, Mettray was simply the application to new problems posed by industrialism and

An 1810 engraving of new children being received by a master and a matron, Southwark, London, from pamphlet *The Royal Philanthropic Society's School: Redhill, Surrey*, p. 3.

its consequent demographic changes of earlier religious and military institutions.[24]

The Fay Commission found unacceptable Mettray's harshness and Catholic and militaristic emphases. Once more, the commissioners turned to Britain, where concern for reform extended to females[25] and was actively supported by many notable personages.[26] Five of Britain's institutional responses were of particular interest to the commissioners: Parkhurst, Isle of Wight; Aberdeen Industrial Feeding Schools, Scotland; Kingswood and Red Lodge, Bristol; and Redhill, run by the Royal Philanthropic Society. This last made the greatest impact. Redhill was instigated by the moral crusades of prestigious British reformers including Jeremy Bentham, David Ricardo, Elizabeth Fry, and Lord Gladstone. Unlike American efforts at reform, which called for public policy and funding, Redhill was privately regulated and financed.

The forerunner of Redhill began in 1829 as a home for reform in a small house in Hackney, London, with twelve children and a matron who served as a surrogate mother. Not surprisingly, this home was soon overrun with masses of poor children and forced to expand. In

An 1840 engraving of trained printer-boys showing their work to visitors, Southwark, London, from pamphlet *The Royal Philanthropic Society's School: Redhill, Surrey*, p. 3.

addition, the district of Hackney was rapidly decaying, and most considered the location of the home to be the cause of these children's depravity. In an effort to retreat to a less congested area of London, the home was removed to St. George's Field, Southwark, in 1833. There youths lived in a cluster of small houses enclosed by a high wall, and were trained in various occupational skills. Girls were totally segregated and lived in a separate building. Most of these girls were children of prisoners and considered dependent, not delinquent. The treatment of females was not totally ignored, unlike in America at that time.

It was the British custom to treat public problems by private philanthropy. The Royal Philanthropic children came to the reform institutions by recommendations made to the society, usually by wealthy and well-connected members of the Establishment. Unlike the American preference for public policy to regulate the poor and dependent, the British continued to rely on noblesse oblige—a contrast of philosophical as well as practical ramifications.

Entrants to the home were of two types: dependents who had lost criminal parents by execution or "transport" (removal to a British

The original receiving quarters, built 1848, of the Royal Philanthropic Society's School, Redhill, Surrey.

colony, a fairly common custom in England then); and criminals themselves, but considered reformable. Criminal children were first to be punished by imprisonment; only then, if they demonstrated worthiness of reformation, were they to be transferred to the home. There children were to be reformed by a combination of religious instruction, education, and occupational training within a supportive but firm familial context:

> The religious and general education of the child with his practical instruction in some useful branch of industry, that should enable him to maintain himself in afterlife by his own honest exertions. The end to be attained is to awaken in him the practical sense of error and the evil of his former career, which may make him ready, really wish to abandon it, and exchange it for a better and happier course; to accustom him to that personal self-control that steady constraint and mastery of his wandering and dishonest propensities, which may make it comparatively easy for him to put his better resolutions into practice;—to give him that knowledge of some useful branch of industry which may enable him to support himself by honest means; and to start him to live under such protection, and with such safeguards

The remaining original cottage, built 1848, of the Royal Philanthropic Society's School, Redhill, Surrey.

around him, as may keep the temptations to relapse into his former habitat a distance from him, during the first and most dangerous years of his new career.[27]

In spite of many boys' first stint in prison, the Royal Philanthropic claimed they tried to achieve these ends by minimizing punishment and instead rehabilitate children with affection and parental-like guidance. Punishments similar to those meted out in Mettray were used to control the "inmates" at the home; nonetheless, rhetoric did indicate that the British were acting on sentiment and espoused theories of good family life, though, gentle rhetoric to the contrary, occupational training—for both sexes—took precedence over familial protection and love. Indeed, like Mettray, the home saw much of its reform mission in vocational terms. Children were trained in occupations considered most likely to give them easier access to trades once they left the home. Shoemaking and printing were considered particularly appropriate for boys, both because they could be offered at relatively little expense to the Royal Philanthropic Society and because apprenticeships in these trades were difficult to secure. It was expected that boys would be apprenticed to tradesmen, in either Britain or the colonies; girls were to be trained and indentured as domestic servants.

Farmland (above and page facing), part of the Royal Philanthropic Society's School, Redhill, Surrey.

In 1849 the Royal Philanthropic Society moved its reform school to the rural countryside in Surrey, a few miles away from the city of Redhill, and became a farm school solely for boys; the trustees did not feel themselves adequate to the task of treating girls, whose potential hysteria, they said, frightened them. Like the Continental schools, especially Mettray, Redhill's location had been chosen on the premise that a rural retreat away from the perversity of the city streets would help rehabilitate and uplift dependent and criminal boys. Strongly influenced by the family system at Mettray, the self-sustaining farm school consisted of a series of small houses; at the time of the Fay Commission's study, the 230 inmates there were divided into six families; each family lived in its own house. No walls or bars restrained the boys' movements. The pastoral simplicity was to encourage the boys into wanting to live at Redhill—and presumably to choose to remain at the school out of a sense of well-being. (But practically speaking, Redhill, like Mettray, was too far a run from the big city.) Here again we see the mid-century nostalgia for the pastoral.[28]

The Fay Commission's preparatory studies suggest how much early- and mid-nineteenth-century reform was transatlantic in nature. Both

Western Europe and America were confronted with the same problem—industrial capitalism. Their responses overlapped and were communicated to each other. Accounts that focus only on North American reform betray parochialism and ignore the dialogue that shaped it. Like their European counterparts, the Fay commissioners desired both to protect and to rehabilitate children, and, like their counterparts, in doing so confused dependence and deviance. There were differences too, of course. The European schools were privately funded and operated, for example. However, they were still accountable through various legislative links to the general public. In the United States, the new laissez-faire orthodoxy required, curiously enough, state action in education and welfare.

Other differences are evident in the Fay commissioners' assessments of European family-style models of reform. For example, the sentiments of Wichern, his desire to bring abandoned children "to know and feel the blessings of *domestic* life, and to bind them with the magical cords of a warm, Christian home," was of course one with which the Massachusetts commissioners were in sympathy. But Wichern's school was not specifically geared to the reformation of girls. In addition, the emphasis of his program was based more on sectarian religious practices and vocational training than education; American reform, however, was supposedly nonsectarian and emphasized education.

Mettray was also considered admirable but not totally desirable. Its approach to family-style reform certainly offered a coherent alternative to Westborough. To the commissioners, however, it was too militaristic—certainly too militaristic for girls. Americans viewed common schooling in the way the French viewed military training: a method for learning self-discipline and moral accountability. Also, the Americans considered agricultural vocational training, which was central to Mettray's reform program, secondary to education.

Much of the commissioners' criticism of the British schools centered on their attitude toward Britain's use of its colonies as future homelands for reformed youth. This, of course, was not a real option for the Americans, although Brace did ship homeless New York children to the western part of America. However, their discomfort with many of the British models went well beyond this. Except for Redhill, the English seemed unable to choose between saving society and saving the criminal. As a result, two systems had sprung up: penal reformatories and industrial reformatories. No institution other than Redhill strove to be protective and preventative at the same time. But the Americans had serious questions about Redhill as well. They were dismayed at its insistence on punishment—in prison, sometimes with adults—preceding rehabilitation: "These children are placed in these schools upon the presumption that they have committed crime *without discernment*, and that jail would only ruin them. Why, then, this happy and hopeful training should be preceded by incarceration for even a short period does not seem apparent. If it is to warn others *from* crime, it fails; if it is to punish the criminal, then it asserts the falsity of the decision that the act was committed without discernment; for certainly a *guiltless* child however criminal should not be punished."[29]

The Massachusetts commissioners had been appointed to create a state institution. Yet some Americans at this time began to wonder whether additional institutions should be built at all. Ironically, anti-institutionalists like Charles Loring Brace were now joined by some of the previous advocates of reform institutions, particularly Samuel Gridley Howe. Disillusioned with the failures of reform institutions, especially Westborough, Howe petitioned the commonwealth legislature to desist from further institution building; he specifically petitioned against the reform school for girls. He was more sympathetic to Brace's Children's Aid Society, a program whereby New York urban slum children would be transported west to live with rural farm families, which both men considered the most efficacious means for moral reform.[30] In spite of such mushrooming antiinstitutionalism, the Massachusetts legislature felt compelled to redress the wrong against girls: their exclusion from reform schools; and cognizant of the reasons why men such as Brace and Howe were opposed to institution building, but convinced that a more comprehensive reform plan could meet the requirement of the commonwealth and also serve as exemplar, the commission remained dedicated to its task.

The commission's report to the legislature recommended unanimously the cottage-style institution for the reconstitution of potentially wayward children, especially girls. Furthermore, the report supported programs to involve all inmates, regardless of gender, in domestic training to equip them for their adult lives. All this seemed natural and appropriate to Americans, and the report generated enthusiasm and support.

Broadly speaking, the Fay Commission report suggests that Americans, although sympathetic to the reform efforts in Europe, were gentler and more sentimental. They tended to take a softer, more "educational," line. Perhaps Americans were more egalitarian, and therefore more inclined to believe in the rehabilitative power of education. That they seemed more intent on rehabilitation is not surprising, however; their cultural background was less hierarchical and certainly less militaristic. Thus Americans were more preoccupied with educational uplift than occupational and practical training. Moreover, American egalitarianism ruled out Europe's institutional paternalism, by which the aristocracy and settled governmental elites traditionally arranged quasi-government action for the social good; this pattern of deference had been virtually destroyed in America during the Jacksonian era.

Americans then—as now—felt it made their institutions distinctly American. Having evaluated both at home and abroad various institutions and having thoroughly read the responses to their questionnaires, the Massachusetts commissioners decided to create their own—the first—family-style institution in America, and at the same time the first state reform school for girls, a hybrid of the best Europe had to offer and the best America could invent. As a result of the Fay Commission's recommendations and of the Commissioner's Report, January 1855, the Resolves to establish the school were passed in the Massachusetts legislature in 1855. Lancaster's first superintendent was Bradford K. Peirce, who served from 1856 to 1861. When Peirce left in order to work with the New York House of Refuge, he was replaced by Marcus Ames, who served from 1861 to 1875. Ames resigned due to a disagreement with the trustees—most of the matrons and staff resigned with him—and was replaced by Loring Lothrop, superintendent from 1875 to 1878. Lothrop also resigned, due to failing health, in 1878, and was replaced in that year by the following interim acting superintendents: Miss Proctor (superintendent's assistant, February 14–March 16); Francis B. Fay (chairman of the Board of Trustees, March 16–August 9); Joseph A. Allen (trustee, August 9–September 12); and again Miss Proctor (September 12–October 1). The acting superintendent for the period 1878–1885 was N. Porter Brown, who on resigning was replaced by Luann L. Brackett (1885–1910), the first woman to serve officially as superintendent.

4

Lancaster, an Academy for the Poor: Its Opening Year

> We have reports from the different police districts in Boston, which show in that city after an examination not very thorough, that there are 230 girls who do not attend school and are not under the control of parents or guardians. . . . these girls are surely tending to ruin. In other countries of the State, especially in those having the large manufacturing towns, it is the same; and nothing but the prompt interposition of the Commonwealth can save this unfortunate class from falling. And why should the State not interpose? Not with lagging service, but heartily, promptly! Those whom the world gives up, why should not the State take up? Why should not the body politic of a Christian community redeem those who are just overhanging the fatal fall?
>
> Massachusetts Public Document 24, 1858

The resolves of 1855 to open at Lancaster the first state industrial school for girls realized four reformist dreams. First, the school was to be created and operated on state initiative. Therefore it would be nonsectarian, although obviously, like public schools, Protestant. Second, it was to be an instrument for social reform. Third, it was to offer common schooling and also training in skills and work habits. Fourth, it was oriented toward meeting the unique needs of women.

The resolves set forth Lancaster's theoretical basis and justification in these terms:

> The title of the Resolve under which the Commissioner act is, "Resolves for the establishment of a State Reform School for Girls." *A State Reform School for Girls!* Every word is significant and suggestive. In the first place the institution established is to be a state school. . . . Its establishment and maintenance will certainly affect the material interest of every citizen; and its beneficial operation will as certainly it is hoped return a manifold recompense, purifying in its nature, into the bosom of society.

Original house on Stillwell Estate, State Industrial School for Girls, Lancaster, Massachusetts.

> In the second place, it is to be a *reform* school. . . . It aims to be the means, under the divine providence and by the divine blessing, of reconstructing . . . of rebuilding . . . of re-forming. . . .
>
> In the next place, it is to be a reform *school.* It aims to accomplish its object in and upon its subject as pupils. It aims to enlighten the understanding, and to mend and regenerate the heart, by teaching the pupils what is true, and by training them to think and speak it, and by showing them what is good, and by leading them to act and do it. . . .
>
> And, finally, it is to be a school for *girls*—for the gentler sex. . . . This circumstance is an important one, and enters into and modifies the plan of building and arrangement of rooms, with all the details relating to employment, instruction, and amusement, and, indeed, to every branch of domestic economy.[1]

Lancaster, the site for the model school, was a beautiful rural area of Massachusetts, about fifty miles west of Boston, nestled in hilly farmland away from the evils of the city. The adjacent farm and landscape afforded the rusticity and tranquility desired. A two-story frame house already existed on the property and became the superintendent's residence. A small stone chapel was built at the center of the grounds. Unlike the superintendent's residence and those in the neighborhood, the original "cottage," as well as those built subsequently, was a fairly large red-brick building, more an academy than a home. In an obvious effort to lend a flavor of domestic tranquility

First cottage (Roger House), State Industrial School for Girls, Lancaster, Massachusetts.

Church, State Industrial School for Girls, Lancaster, Massachusetts.

Ironing room, State Industrial School for Girls, Lancaster, Massachusetts.

Barn, State Industrial School for Girls, Lancaster, Massachusetts.

and to make the buildings "homey," small white embellished porches and handrails were added to the entrances. The architecture and spatial arrangements of the school revealed the mixed goals of the founders: to bring about moral reform through institutionalization. Its pastoral simplicity, deliberate imitation of family life, and consciously protective, idealistic atmosphere revealed the founders' source of inspiration: nineteenth-century reform thought. Within the confines of this institution without gates or walls, girls were to be sheltered, educated, trained, and tenderly incarcerated.

The rooms for the girls were small and placed on either side of a long, narrow corridor. Each girl had her own room, although their size and layout made them seem cell-like. No bars were at the windows, however, and each room contained a cot and small table for toiletries. The matron's room was off the same corridor. Each cottage had a kitchen and ironing room large enough to train the girls as well as to provide for the daily needs of the inmates. A living room with an ornate fireplace functioned as a place for meetings and recreation. In contrast to the living quarters on the first floor was a basement room used for solitary confinement. The square red-brick buildings appear less like the neighboring homes and more like the New England academies of the era. The school's capacity was relatively small; according to the Board of State Charities' Reports, the number of girls in residence at any one time averaged between 90 and 120. On the average, there were 69 entrants per year.

Both as the first reform school for girls and the first family-style institution, Lancaster was to be a model. The superintendent, acting as a kind but firm father, would live apart from the girls' cottages in a large old house on the school grounds. As in many traditional nineteenth-century families, the superintendent was to act as the paternal surveyor of the whole family. The matron would act as a mother and live in the cottage. She was to be, in Peirce's characterization, loving, kind, and flexible. She was to consider each daughter as an individual and, like a natural mother, adapt her discipline to the capacity and disposition of each inmate, thereby enhancing her power and success.

Under this loving, maternal guidance, no more than thirty girls were to live in the same house under one matron. Furthermore, girls were not to be classified according to age. Instead, they were to live together as sisters, the younger to be gentling influences on the older, who in turn were to act as big sisters. According to the commissioners, the arrangement was to be familial: "The idea of a family is elevated and made perfect by a variety in age and stature, as well as by diversity of disposition, habits and acquirements." A heterogeneous face-to-face community was thereby created. It was one in which "sisters" of varying ages and backgrounds were housed together, hopefully in harmony. As at first there was only one cottage, previous discussions of classification were overruled by physical reality.

Operating principles for the new institution reflected the recommendations made in the responses to the aforementioned questionnaire: Girls were to be sent to Lancaster by a judge of probate or a commissioner of the state appointed especially for this purpose; the judge or commissioner decided suitability for admission; age of eligibility for entry was to be between seven and sixteen. Since the purpose of the school was for "the instruction, employment and reformation of exposed, helples, evil, disposed and vicious girls," sentences were to be indeterminate. The school was to be a training ground and refuge during the vulnerable years of inmates. It admitted two varieties of girls: those charged with criminal acts and those in a condition of want and poverty. Delinquency and poverty, in other words, were merged. The sentiments expressed in the act make obvious the extent to which the reformers of the day confused being poor with being criminal:

> Whenever any girl above the age of seven and under the age of sixteen years, shall be brought by any constable, police officer, or other inhabitant of the city or town into this Commonwealth, before any Judge of probate or commissioner . . . upon the allegation or complaint that the said girl had committed any offence . . . punishable by fine or imprisonment for life, or that she is leading an idle, vagrant and vicious life, or has been found in any street, highway, or public place within this commonwealth in circumstances of want and suffering, or of neglect, exposure or abandonment, or of beggary, it shall be the duty of the judge or commissioner aforesaid, before whom the said girl is brought, to issue a summons. . . .[2]

The founders of Lancaster were self-consciously determined to create what they believed would be the ideal reform school. In this spirit they chose one of their fellow Yankee reformers to be—significantly—both superintendent and chaplain. Bradford K. Peirce epitomized the goals and values of his fellow founders. Born in Vermont and graduated from Wesleyan College, he had been ordained by the Conference of the Methodist Episcopal Church, had been active in editing various religious journals, such as *The Sunday School Teacher* and the *Sunday School Messenger*, and had written several books, including one entitled *The Eminent Dead or the Triumphs of Faith in the Dying Hour* (1848). In 1855 he had become a member of the Massachusetts Senate, which post he had to leave in order to become trustee, superintendent, and chaplain of Lancaster.[3] Peirce played an active role in Lancaster's creation. He had been in close contact with the Fay Commission and knew many of the details of the family-style reformatories in Europe. He had spoken eloquently about the cottage-style institutions and their emphasis on industrial training for rehabilitation. After careful analysis, however, he too had ruled out for Lancaster aspects of these establishments that were not American.

The educational program at Lancaster embraced the ideology of the common-school movement. Common schooling was believed to pave the path to virtue. At Westborough, for example, the combination of the 3 Rs and vocational and religious training had been expected to create a stalwart man. Since the recipients at Lancaster were girls, their training would also teach them how to become women, the type demanded by society. Educational theorists earlier in the century had preached that women's education should be gender specific. Pioneers in the fight for formal education for women, including Emma Willard, Catharine Beecher, and Mary Lyon, acknowledged the importance of a specifically female education for domesticity: "[It] is to *mothers* and to *teachers*, that the world is to look for the character which is to be enstamped on each succeeding generation, for it is to them that the great business of education is almost exclusively committed. And will it not appear by examination that neither mothers nor teachers have ever been properly educated for their profession. What is *the profession* of a *Woman*? Is it not to form immortal minds, and to watch, to nurse, and to rear the bodily system."[4]

Not surprisingly, this educational philosophy expressed by Beecher influenced Lancaster, where education would be geared specifically to the task of saving the future generation of mothers. Peirce used similar words in his report to the legislature several decades after Beecher: "Passing the argument of Christian duty and humanity, does not public security demand that those who will become the women of the country should receive the protection, the training and the culture of the State? As are the women so are men of a nation; refinement, dignity, modesty of women are equally, by an alternate action, the cause and the reflex of those traits in a people. Her life and conduct give tone to the family circle, and by a thousand influences make the character of the young and so of the race."

Here Peirce was echoing the common mid-century American notion that somehow women were the bedrock of social stability. Hence the reformers' emphasis on domestication and the institutional educational program designed to accomplish it. The comissioners' and Peirce's belief in reform through domestication was shared by common-school advocates and juvenile reformers alike. They believed strongly that teaching girls domestic skills was critical for social cohesion, and concomitantly that egalitarianism, which had prompted both the common-school movement and the foundation of Lancaster, should be upheld on principle. Therefore, popularizers of public education indicated concern that girls follow both the common curriculum and in addition those areas of study most appropriate for the socialization of females, particularly the young and poor. Like the commissioners, they believed that education of poor young women should include vocational training and instruction in motherhood. The 1867 Boston School Committee Report was simply expressing these common notions when it made the following declaration:

> Boys graduate to prefer . . . the sea or the farm, of little taste or qualifications for household duties. . . . [Girls] are not fitted to be poor men's wives; they know not how to prepare the family repasts or make neat the family garments—possess aptitudes to make home attractive. If their training had prepared them to become intellectual, cheerful and amiable companions . . . and [gave them] a competent knowledge how to discharge with graceful propriety and skill, housekeeping obligations, more limited means would admit of family ties, the meagre and deteriorating discomforts of boarding house life would be escaped and happy homes be more numerous than they are.[5]

The trustees of Lancaster held the same sentiments: "Almost every woman is destined to have a leading or subordinate part in the management of a family. Preparation for the ready and intelligent performance of household duties, the lowest as well as the highest, is therefore, of the first importance. Now, as perfect cleanliness is essential to health of body and of mind and to cheerfulness, all the arts of washing and scouring should be early learnt and practised, so as to form and fix the habit of doing them well, thoroughly, rapidly, and willingly."[6]

In brief, Lancaster sought to blend reformism and the social ideal of womanhood through a healthy balance of religion, common schooling, and domestic training. Cognizant of the pressing problems of poverty-stricken women, whether unmarried, married, or widowed, the school also sought to provide its girls with an opportunity to earn a living. In keeping with these goals, the Lancaster program culminated in a two-year indenture under the aegis of the state. Regardless of age at entrance, at sixteen girls were to leave for indenture to suitable families, where they would remain in service under the supervision of the Board of State Charities until age eighteen. Initially, at least, the trustees were adamant that the program at Lancaster precede indenture regardless of placement opportunities. Their position rested on their view of the importance of the religious and vocational training. They saw Lancaster's program as "missionary work of the noblest character; a Christian devotion, prompted by love, benevolence and humanity, and a spirit of patience and forebearance"; they worried that the girls would be matured before they had sufficient time to "eradicate their idle, vicious, propensities and habits and to establish those of truth, virtue and industry."[7] They also felt that part of their mission was to protect their charges from the "sordid or selfish motives" of certain employers who would overwork the girls and neglect their moral training. Those not indentured because of poor health, behavioral problems, or lack of a suitable place would remain at Lancaster or be transferred to another institution until they could be discharged at eighteen. Some families petitioned for their daughters' release; in these cases, the state often did decide that the petitions were reasonable and released the girls to return to their families. A condition of indenture was return to the school at any point during the "indenture years" if the families of placement were dissatisfied or unable to keep them or if the girl made complaints of bad treatment to one of the visiting trustees. The indenture period was the most vulnerable part of the program because it depended upon prior training at Lancaster, a welcoming climate outside, and the prevailing job market.

Not by coincidence, of course, did the training at the school address the needs of the labor market. The founders of the school knew full well that domestic servants were always likely to be in demand and hired if adequately trained. Labor statistics indicate that the majority of available jobs up to and including 1879 were domestic in nature.[8] Anyway, regardless of general economic need, women were pressured to find work considered acceptable, that is, work consonant with the belief that women should be submissive, pure, and domestic: domestic service, textile work, home-style industries (dressmaking, laundering, and so forth), and teaching. Except for teaching, these jobs offered women safety, shelter, and supervision in urban areas, thereby safeguarding their reputations and guaranteeing a measure of social stability.

Through 1870 national census figures list domestic service as employing nearly half of the female labor force. Initially the largest group of women in service came from Yankee Protestant homes. By mid-century, however, when Lancaster's first "class" enrolled, it was becoming Irish Catholic. Many scholars have debated the positive and negative social aspects of employment in service. It must be kept in mind, however, that such work was frequently only temporary for young girls; although low paying it offered them the benefits of room and board, ready-made families, and the home environment in which to learn or practice domestic skills for their futures as wives and mothers.

Notwithstanding these benefits, there were drawbacks to life in service. Many young women complained of the lack of privacy that a totally supervised life necessitated. Their duties gave them little control over their own time. Class differences between them and their employers made it difficult for the girls to find in this home environment much support or sympathy; rather, domestics were frequently subjected to the moods and whims of their employers. Regardless of these disadvantages, however, domestic service remained the most available and—perhaps not by coincidence—chosen category of employment up to 1900. The administration at Lancaster recognized that shelter, supervision, and family-style living, combined with the continuing labor demand, made domestic service a very desirable source of employment for its girls.

The First Annual Report of the superintendent and chaplain, Bradford Peirce, describes the daily life of the Lancaster girls:

> The chapel bell rings at six, at which time or before, the girls rise, and put themselves and their sleeping rooms in order, and prepare the breakfast; at seven this meal is eaten. Housework is attended to until nine, at which time the chaplain comes, to take the direction of the morning devotions. Labor holds as many as can be spared from domestic duties in the workroom until dinner; this occurs at twelve. School is held from half-past one until half-past four; supper at five; and sewing, knitting and reading in the work-room until evening; prayers at eight; after which the girls are dismissed for bed. During the day sufficient time for exercise is allowed in the open air.[9]

This first report rings with the confidence of success. The girls are well adjusted to their new home, and their caretakers' optimistic faith in their redemption runs high. Discipline, when necessary, could be administered without recourse to physical violence; stern chastening or, if absolutely necessary, isolation and a "light diet" for a few days usually sufficed. When several girls attempted to escape, the threat of expulsion was a traumatic event within the "family." The drama of the event is described as follows:

> The whole matter was discussed before the family; the case of the three girls, it being understood would be referred to the Trustees;

they had voluntarily left us, and now they must remain in their rooms until it was determined whether they would be permitted to remain.

The three girls were brought before Mr. Fay and their case was seriously and kindly considered. The superintendent expressed a desire that they might be reinstated as members of the family. After appropriate counsels and warnings, they were permitted again to enter the family circle on probation.

Col. Fay writes to me in a letter subsequently: No scene has given me so much gratification, so much hope and confidence, to me, as that between Mrs. C. and the returning prodigals . . . her arms encircling them all at the same time, caressing them, expressing her joy that *her children* had come back again; not a frown, not a word of reproach, but every look a smile, every word tempered by kindness and affection.

Peirce believed strongly in the efficacy of religious services; religious conversion was, in his view, the hallmark of reformation. In one section of his report, "An Affecting Scene," he describes how some of the girls were so moved that they confessed to their sinfulness and repented:

At the evening prayers conducted by the matron, one of the little girls expressed her sorrow that she had not always been a good girl, and desired to know how she could have her sins forgiven, and go to heaven when she died. She began to cry quite bitterly. The other girls, partly through sympathy, perhaps, and in some degree, we hope, from a personal consciousness, followed her example of confession and contrition. The grief became quite distressing. . . . After a short conversation, in which I sought to turn their tenderness of heart to the best practical account, and an explanation of the divine plan of forgiveness, the family joined together, in a subdued voice, in singing the hymn commencing, "I want to be like Jesus," and then joined in prayer.

Lancaster, a model for all juvenile training schools, was to save the children from "perversion through conversion" and, through loving care and an atmosphere free from the sins and temptations at existing institutions, redirect the lives of the girls so that they could be redeemed. Bridget O'M., the thirteenth entrant at Lancaster, was placed there on the recommendation of a probate court judge, who removed her from the house of correction. The superintendent of Lancaster lamented Bridget's unfortunate original sentencing: "What could this have done for her, but ruined her?" A place for girls like Bridget—young, needy, and reformable—finally existed and promised restitution to innocent victims of poverty and urban corruption.

Lancaster's first year seems to have justified Peirce's enthusiasm. This is the conclusion of a detailed study of the lives of the first years' ninety-nine inmates before they came to Lancaster, during their years in the school, their indenture years, and their lives subsequent to their discharge. This study also confirms many of the findings of the social historians of nineteenth-century institutions.[10] Only 53 percent of the girls were American-born; this group was primarily white. Of the foreign-born, more than half were Irish. More than 47 percent of the girls were of immigrant status, since few of the parents were American-born. Almost all, however, spoke English. This fact is not surprising considering that parental complicity was necessary in order to commit a girl; it is unlikely that parents would seek out the probate court unless they felt themselves competent to communicate with it, nor accept its procedures unless they had lived in America long enough to internalize the norms of the white Anglo-Saxon society within which they had to function. Ninety-four percent of the parents were foreign-born. Almost three-quarters of them were Irish, many of whom had immigrated as the result of the Irish potato famine of 1845. By the 1850s, more than half the population of Boston was foreign-born, and mostly poor Irish; the daughters of most immigrants were very poor indeed.

Thus the overwhelming number of Lancaster's girls were Irish Catholics. It is considered unusual for such a large group of Catholics to be in a Protestant institution, except by force. Certainly by 1840 Catholics had issued public complaints against public schooling. In New York, for example, Catholic immigrants, through the efforts of Bishop Hughes, fought for public money to start their own schools. Catholic parents opposed the use of the King James version of the Bible and the lack of catechismal instruction in the classroom, as well as the Protestant insistence that schools be nondenominational. According to Carl Kaestle, many of the textbooks used in public school exacerbated this situation by containing anti-Irish slurs. In short, Catholics regarded the policy of the public schools as, in effect, Protestant and, ipso facto, anti-Catholic. Catholic parents exhibited great hostility toward institutions that they saw as undermining their own religious and ethnic identities. Understandably, their greatest hostility was directed toward schools and other institutions that cared for their young.[11] In light of antagonism between Catholics and Protestants, it seems peculiar that Lancaster was so heavily Irish Catholic, particularly since, as we shall see, most of the girls were there with parental complicity.

Much more significant than the girls' religions, races, or places of birth, however, was their overwhelming poverty. By the most modest estimate, more than 75 percent of their fathers worked in low-ranking, mainly unskilled, occupations. Most of their mothers did not work at paid jobs; The 17 percent who did performed such menial tasks as taking in washing, mill work, and domestic labor, or they worked in brothels. Most of the mothers who worked were widowed and were obviously doing all they could to provide some means of support for their children.[12] Poverty forced some girls, or their parents, to seek help from the state's institutions. One example from the schools' records shows clearly the meagerness of such family resources "[Hahnora] says she told her mother 'that she would come to the School so that the rest of the family would have more to eat'. . . . she slept upon a comforter on the bed-cords and told her mother it was softer to sleep upon the floor. . . . she never was in such a placement home, where they had such good things and such a kind mother. . . ." Given the social and economic mobility of the time—both upward and downward—the fact that so many fathers of Lancaster girls were in the lowest occupational ranks is noteworthy. While other men changed their financial positions, they were in a permanent state of poverty.[13]

The Lancaster girls experienced not only economic devastation but also internal family chaos. Death had forced changes in family life for most of the inmates. In fact, two-thirds of the girls had at least one deceased parent; and in at least two-thirds of these cases, the deceased parent was the mother. Fourteen percent were without parents at all. These girls had been living either with relatives, surrogate families, or in orphanages. This points up a noteworthy fact: Most girls at Lancaster in its first year came from a family environment of some sort. But a more noteworthy fact is that the absence of a natural mother seems to have been the most common factor precipitating a girl's entrance into Lancaster in its first year; this goes far to explaining Bradford Peirce's hope that the state would serve the girls "as a mother—not a stepmother."

Lancaster, then, offered alternative shelter for daughters of poverty-stricken and perhaps jobless and widowered fathers, for stepdaughters of harrassed and overburdened stepmothers, and for orphaned girls. Here they would be fed, clothed, and properly supervised. To the poverty-stricken and perhaps foreign or Catholic parents, left alone with several mouths to feed, and with work to find, unable to supply their children with adequate care and supervision, even a Yankee Protestant reform school must have seemed a desirable option. For them, it was definitely better that their daughters be Protestants than that they become prostitutes, and better that they be judged delinquents so long as they were well cared for.

The Lancaster girls' families did a good deal of moving about. Approximately two-thirds of the girls experienced at least one major move—that is, a move out of their home towns. Seventeen percent had moved two or three times; 10 percent, more than four times. Sarah H., for example, in addition to having been taken from Ireland to America, had been placed first with relatives and then with various families. Although she was recorded as having made only one major move, in reading her case it is obvious that she experienced considerable physical dislocation.[14]

In spite of the difficulties of their families, two things apply to the girls at Lancaster in its first year: They had not spent much of their lives in and out of "custodial" institutions; nor were they a group of chronic "welfare" poor. For most of them, the Lancaster experience was their first brush with the state's institutional response to poverty and deviance. Only 9 percent of them had ever previously experienced custodial care—3 percent in orphanages, 5 percent in almshouses, and 1 percent in houses of refuge. Four percent had experienced punitive institutionalization. However, 7 percent of their mothers and 3 percent of their fathers had been institutionalized prior to their stays at Lancaster; and only 2 percent of their mothers and 1 percent of their fathers during their stays at Lancaster. It is also significant that 6 percent of the girls had sisters at Lancaster; 2 percent had brothers at Westborough.

One of the speculations voiced by the superintendent, and echoed in many statements printed in the reports made to the state, indicates that the reformers were not unaware that many of the charges brought against the girls by their parents were, if not fabricated, certainly exaggerated. The following excerpt from the superintendent's report indicates that he was aware that many girls came from poor homes and that he thought it likely that the lure of having the state care for poor daughters was a major factor in parental complaints:

> The child [Hannah] says her birthplace was Northampton, where her own mother died three years since. The family lived in Braintree, and now her parents reside in Worcester. Her father is a carpenter. Her parents sometimes attended the Baptist Church, until her mother became sick—she is still an invalid. Hannah has a brother and two sisters—one of the latter is an infant. The other sister is the oldest child of the family and Hannah speaks of her as talking very unkindly and improperly to her mother. . . .
>
> We learn incidentally from [Hannah] that the circumstances of the family were somewhat straitened, and we have supposed this fact might have some weight in inducing the parents to relieve themselves from her care and expenses. We see no good reason why this pretty little girl may not be a substantial comfort to anyone who will carefully train her.

Hannah's father turned her over to Lancaster because she was, he said, a chronic masturbator. Although almost upon her arrival at Lancaster she was shown to be morally "clean," nevertheless she was allowed to remain there as a dependent of the state for eight more years. She then was indentured under the supervision of the state for another two years. Her continued incarceration may have been due to the sympathy of the authorities; it may also have been a result of their fear of what might befall a poor girl from a disrupted home. In the trustees' eyes, she was still considered potentially deviant.

The case of Elizabeth T., brought to Lancaster at the request of her guardian, provides further evidence of the desperation that compelled poor parents and surrogate families to turn to institutionalization as both the solution to their economic problems and the remedy for their fears for their children's futures at a time when state welfare policy gave them practically no other option:[15]

> [Elizabeth] is about ten years of age; her father is dead, and her mother is an intemperate woman now in the House of Correction. The mother gave her daughter, about two years since, to Rev. W. T. Sleeper, then City Missionary in Worcester, now the Chaplain of the State Reform School in Westborough; and he was appointed her guardian. Not being able to provide for her in his own family, he placed her in, as he supposed, good homes. She was found to be capable, quick to apprehend, and generally well-behaved, but not always to be trusted—addicted to falsehoods. This unfortunate characteristic of the child rendered her services less desirable, and she was changed from one place to another. Finally, it was thought best to place her where she would, at once, be removed from temptation, and brought under the regular discipline of a kind, constant and religious training. The ground of complaint was the habit of deceit referred to above, and so with a little wooden box, containing a few trifles, she has come to rest awhile upon the heart of the State—as a mother. I trust it will not prove a *step*-mother to her.

The following examples drawn from the first year's case records illustrate that for certain children, Lancaster was their only opportunity. Therese M. entered Lancaster at age 13 through the efforts of the Christian Friend Society, which had charge of her. Daughter of a "depraved and abandoned woman . . . and a dissolute man," she attended Lancaster but ended at an almshouse, where she died at 19. Anne H. was also placed by a benevolent association, the City Missionary in Salem, after service placements failed. The product of "supposedly" married parents, her father had deserted to marry a 15-year-old; her mother, "ignorant, without ability to mother," received "visits from sea captains." Lucy E., whose mother had died and whose father had no interest in her, was sent to Lancaster by the Overseers of the Poor. Peg W. found her way to the school thanks to a truant officer. The school thought her lucky and definitely better off as an inmate than as a wandering waif: "With the streets for her only home, with beggary as her only means of support, and with intemperate parents as her only guardians, what must have been her fate if the State or the City had not interposed for her rescue?" Isabel J., like many of the girls, was a victim of physical abuse and brutality, as well as poverty and intemperance. The school records show many instances of violence within the family. Isabel J.'s parents, for example, had inflicted injury on her in the past, and upon entrance, Isabel J. bore "a mark upon her head, of a blow, from an axe, struck by her aunt," with whom she lived.

Parents and outside observers frequently agreed that the best interests of the girls lay in taking them away from home, that in view of the cruelty of a pauper's existence a better life could be found within the confines of Lancaster. There is little evidence in the early Lancaster records to substantiate the image of the mean and hard-hearted officer lurking behind the bushes waiting to snatch up street urchins. The girls at Lancaster do not appear to have been brought in at the initiative of the impersonal and bureaucratic state. In fact, a conservative estimate indicates that at least half of the 1856 girls were brought to Lancaster as a result of actions taken by relatives, mainly on charges of uncontrollable behavior. This estimate is conservative since the complainant was recorded as a relative only in cases where there was a direct statement of this fact. In some cases, no complainant was named; in others, the complainant was a town official, but the prose suggested that he may have been acting on the request of the family. During Lancaster's first year, the complainants were family members for 41 percent of the entrants; the state for 32 percent; good citizens for 6 percent; and other agents for the remaining 21 percent. This last category included such parties as school officials and neighbors who were acting at the behest of the parents. Fathers, mothers, stepfathers, and stepmothers were primarily responsible for sending girls away. Other relatives sometimes did so, particularly when the parents' whereabouts were unknown. And third parties, besides family and the state, intervened as well: "Three little Irish girls rescued from the streets and from the depraving society of their homes by Miss Briggs, one of the teachers in the Sabbath School of the Church of the Advent, of which Bishop Southgate is rector."

The actual case studies bear witness to the salience of ethnicity to the school's administration. Often references to the girls' and/or their parents' origins were derogatory, clearly influenced by a prejudice against immigrants, especially the Irish: "Her person and dress were loathsome in the extreme when she came. She may make an excellent servant and will be indeed, 'a brand snatched from the burning.' . . . She is thoroughly Irish, with a strong brogue, sadly ignorant, and bearing manifest evidences of neglect . . . undoubtedly from a miserable, intemperate family." But the Irish were not the only objects of ethnic prejudice; a German entrant was said to "bear all the characteristic marks of her nation." Many of the girls were Catholic, and in the school's view, Protestantism in large doses was the antidote to the girls' "Romanism" and at the same time the key to their assimilation.

Most of the girls sent to Lancaster had been accused of moral rather than criminal offenses. In fact, 68 percent of the inmates in the opening year were accused of "crimes against morality"—vagrancy, beggary, stubbornness, deceitfulness, idle and vicious behavior, wanton and lewd conduct, and running away—that is, threats to social and moral order, not crimes against property or people. Twenty-nine percent of the inmates were accused of petty larceny; however, the girls so accused were like Maria, the first entrant, whose forays into stealing were relatively innocuous, but whose behavior seemed uncontrollable, or were like Hannah, whose charges were trumped up or inflated so that they could receive shelter at Lancaster. It is interesting to note that "crimes against morality" included juvenile misdemeanors such as stubbornness and running away as well as crimes frequently leveled against adult women—beggary, wanton and lewd behavior, and vagrancy; but this confusion of juvenile misdemeanor and adult crime was justified by the notion that the one led to the other.[16] In the final analysis, the crime of most Lancaster girls was poverty. Their problems were the outcome of their families' destitution; poverty's attendant consequences were the reason for the actions that led to their placement at Lancaster.

Let us again consider the case of Hannah K.: "The complaint, made by her father, is to the effect that she is constantly guilty of self-abuse; that they cannot restrain her—that if they tied her hands, she polluted the bed in her obstinate resistance; that she is so vulgar in her habits that she cannot be kept at either a public or a private school; that she is disobedient to her parents and altogether uncontrollable." Hannah's case provides rich evidence of what was deemed morally deviant. Masturbation was viewed as a moral crime, and great relief was expressed when the matron discovered Hannah to be suffering from a chronic rash rather than immoral conduct.

> Upon inquiry it was discovered that she had been subject to erysipelas, which of itself, will account for all the physical phenomena, which in the testimony against her was attributed to moral causes. The child is evidently rather to be sincerely pitied than to be blamed; and to be most carefully guarded and aided with such medical appliances as her diseased system requires.
>
> Since writing the above, I have learned, that one morning before the child was fairly awake, the Matron noticed a movement, such as was referred to in the complaint. She immediately addressed and thoroughly awakened the girl, who at once, and with perfect simplicity and confidence, answered her question, as to the meaning of the movement. 'She itched,' she said, 'dreadfully.' 'Sometimes,' she said, 'it felt so bad, she couldn't hardly bear it.' There was no appearance of animal excitement, no perverse resistance, no apparent moral feeling excited—simply a physical irritability, readily accounted for, and imperatively demanding involuntary relief. The child only requires kind medical and physical treatment. The question is only one of health, not morals.

State and parents agreed that the onset of sexual maturity was a particularly vulnerable time for young girls already in some sort of trouble. Regardless of provisions for housing younger girls, the institution offered refuge to pubescent and postpubescent girls whose ages and circumstances made them seem potentially morally and sexually deviant. Approximately 75 percent of the girls were twelve or over.

It must be kept in mind, however, that poverty was looked on as a cause of moral and sexual deviance. Indeed, social theorists of the time had trouble distinguishing between the innately vicious and the poor. But this line of thought led, on the part of the staff, to pity rather than to blame the girls. Regarding Sharon and Lynn, two sisters brought to the school in its first month, of the elder it was written that "one can readily imagine that certain ruin would be found in the path of such a girl, in such a village, and so unhappily situated at home," while her sister's record of wickedness was accounted for by her home environment, where she was "unaccustomed to restraint": "It is certainly not the fault of the girl that she is uncouth and uncomfortable in her temper." Another girl, who had been beaten on occasion by her drunken stepmother, was tenderly described as "the poor child [who] has, from her earliest hours inhaled a pestiferous atmosphere living in a house of ill fame, and breathing pollution daily."

Another likely reason why certain families turned their girls over to the state was the general unavailability of medical facilities. Lancaster seems to have been used by some families, particularly those who were the complainants, as a place to care for the consumptive, sickly, and seemingly unbalanced. The case of Hannah would indicate this. The cases of Kathryn N. and Amanda N. provide ample evidence that at least some of the girls required medical aid. Kathryn N., upon arrival at Lancaster, was described as seeming mentally unbalanced:

She is but eleven years of age; short; with jet black hair and eyes; incessantly in motion; causing her hair to float around her face; suggesting at once to the observer the probable presence of some disease in her system; her trains of thought change instantly, and switch off upon other tracks, often becoming laughingly grotesque from their suddenness and strangeness. Thus upon giving a proper and reverent answer to a religious question, upon the same half expended breath, she will make a remark without a change of countenance, upon the most foreign matter conceivable. She talks and hums continually, but readily accords for the moment to any expressed wish in reference to her behavior. In the next moment, involuntarily, there is a new development in this state of unrest.

Amanda M. came to Lancaster in obvious need of physical care:

She has worked at service since she was nine years of age, in different places; at one place . . . she was cruelly overworked, and suffered as a result such physical injury as many terminate in a permanent weakness, and perhaps shorten, very materially, her life. Her shoulders have been drawn out of shape, being bent inward to the serious threatening of her lungs. The slightest exertion causes a painful disturbance in her heart. [Amanda] is very hard of hearing; she cannot understand ordinary conversation and it requires a very loud tone of the matron's voice to reach this feeble sense, when she is at a little distance.

Five percent of all inmates' records alluded to insanity; 21 percent cited some physical frailty or chronic illness. Although no mention was made of either mental or physical health in most cases, and the school did function primarily as a reform institution for physically healthy girls, for over one-quarter of the girls the school staff took on itself the role of provider. For children like Amanda, "Our institution . . . must assume rather the form of a hospital and asylum than that of a reform or industrial school."

It is difficult to assess with much accuracy the level of education most of these girls had received before they entered Lancaster. However, the superintendent frequently made reference to the matter of literacy in his records. A rough estimate of educational attainment gathered from Bradford Peirce's records indicates that 35 percent of the girls were illiterate, 44 percent had very slight reading ability, and 19 percent had some mastery of reading and writing. Only 2 percent were fluent in both. We may assume, then, that the overwhelming majority had had little exposure to schooling. Lancaster housed a group of girls who were not only poor but unschooled as well.

To the Lancaster reformers, education was the path to virtue. To what degree did Lancaster follow through on its education program? This is hard to answer. Certainly common schooling occupied the girls' afternoons—but industrial training in the form of housekeeping, religious training, and prayer meetings occupied the largest proportion of "school" time. What can be said, then, of the results of Lancaster's education program? For this, we may turn again for information to the reports of the superintendent. Here, by careful reading, we can get some idea of how Lancaster educated, how the Lancaster girls fared during their stay, what experiences they had during their indenture years, and what became of them later on. Consider the case of Abigail F.:[17]

> Her parents died when she was a little child, and she was taken home by her grandparents who now reside in Whitinsville, and lived with them until within two or three years. They being poor and becoming old, could not properly provide for the girl, and she was taken by the overseers of the poor, of Uxbridge, and placed in various families. But having been, probably, indulged by her grandparents, she did not satisfy her employers; and was also, in the habit of running away. She was complained of as a vagrant and a stubborn child and upon a warrant to this effect was sent to our school.

When Abigail turned sixteen, she was indentured; at eighteen her indenture expired, and we have no further information about her until July 20, 1871. It reads as follows: "She has done well, borne a good character, united with the church and has recently been married."

Maria M., brought to Lancaster when she was nine years of age, had a similar background, but was a less fortunate "product" of the school: "She is an illegitimate child . . . born in the poor house of Harvard, where her mother was living at the time of her entering our school. The overseers of the poor have placed the little child at service in several families, but fault was found with her. She was considered to be stubborn and disobedient." Maria was indentured at sixteen, but returned to the school, having been found "unsuitable." At eighteen she was discharged. In February 1871 the following was reported: "C. S. Gerry Ch. of Overseers of the Poor, Harvard, writes that 'she had entirely abandoned to the care of the overseers of the poor, an illegitimate child (daughter) now nine years of age. She was an inmate of the Harvard Almshouse at the time of its birth. When last heard from she was at . . . N.H. at work in a mill." From there, she was reported as being employed "at service."

Both Abigail F. and Maria M. worked in service before coming to Lancaster; unlike them, Margaret S. did not. Half the entrants had worked before coming to the school, most in menial jobs. Of those who had been employed, more than half had been placed with families. Only 5 percent had worked as mill girls. Most of the girls at Lancaster, then, were part of the servant class: those who would be placed out with other families and were expected to perform domestic tasks in return for food, shelter, and supervision. One wonders whether the girls who had been placed out were, in fact, as unruly and insubordinate as they were described to be by their employers, or whether their employers simply were unwilling to assume responsibility for their safekeeping, even if it meant sending them back to a reform school. From the records it appears that 65 percent of the girls were compliant and responsive at Lancaster; 35 percent presented noticeable "behavior problems," and only 5 percent tried to escape.

Margaret S. must have been considered a major success for Lancaster:

She has a beautiful eye, an inviting expression and altogether a noble presence. Her parents are poor, respectable people; attended the Baptist Church and are willing to aid as far as they are able in the support of [Margaret]. She has, until two or three years, attended the Grammar School in Salem and was esteemed a good scholar at that time. She says her first loss of self respect was occasioned by her being placed in the school with the boys as a punishment. She has a powerful will; and evidently became utterly unmanageable at home. She fell into the lowest company and into the violent habits. 'There is no sin,' she says, 'that I did not commit.' She would drink to intoxication, has been carried home drunk, and frequented the lowest restaurants in the city of Salem. Her family and the City Missionary, Mr. Bale, were very anxious that we should make the attempt to save her; she was therefore committed to our care. She was profane, coarse, impure, affected by sexual desire, brought a bottle of rum with her, but with all this there was something very attractive about her.

The report goes on to outline the rapid and steady improvement that she made, especially after the matron and superintendent decided that she would improve best if given a lot of responsibility. Instead of being placed in domestic service during her indenture years, Margaret was sent by the state to Framingham Normal School; after her training, she was hired by Lancaster to serve as matron in one of the cottages. From this position, she then went to San Francisco to become the principal at the Protestant Orphan Asylum. The final entry concerning the success of Margaret S. is a news clipping glued into the record book. It reads as follows:

> LANCASTER
> In a San Francisco paper a few weeks since, appeared the following marriage notice and communication. The lady referred to was once an inmate of the State Industrial School at Lancaster, and afterwards a teacher there.
>
> MARRIED—In this city, September 27, 1870, at the Second Congregational Church by the Rev. E. G. Beckwith, Mr. Julius F. Rapp to Miss [Peggy];
>
> To this announcement a young and grateful pupil of the bride adds: 'It is worthy of special mention that the recent Miss [S]—now Mrs. Rapp—has been a good and faithful servant for over six years in the capacity of principal teacher at the Protestant Orphan Asylum of this city, where she was universally beloved for her intrinsic worth, and as a kind and tender friend to the little orphans placed under her care. Her pupils were present at the marriage ceremony, and it was a beautiful sight to see the dear little children clustering around their much loved (though to them now lost) teacher proffering, with throbbing hearts and tear-stained cheeks their little tributes of bouquets and wreaths of flowers. Mrs. Rapp has reason to feel grateful to God for such a treasure as the guileless affection of these innocent little ones, which, it is hoped, may prove an omen of happiness to one who has been faithful.'

These records of so many successes, of generally happy and hard-working inmates, raise several questions. Did the girls become compliant because of their kind treatment or was their treatment harsher than reported? Were really difficult and unhappy girls underreported, perhaps by matrons who feared losing their prestige or jobs? Were girls falsely charged as being difficult and unhappy in an effort to gain them shelter? The data on the indenture years of these girls provide some of the information necessary for at least beginning to answer some of these question.[18] Forty-eight percent of the girls were indentured successfully; that is, they were placed in and completed their two years of service before being discharged by the state at eighteen. Sixteen percent were reported as not having successfully completed these two years. They were returned to Lancaster either at the request of the families or by the girls themselves. (It is a positive comment on the school that some of the girls felt they could return if they were harshly treated elsewhere.) In addition, 5 percent of the girls escaped.

Nine percent went to other institutions, namely, hospitals and asylums. The remaining 23 percent stayed at the school until they were discharged, died, or escaped before placement. Two percent enjoyed special consideration, such as that given Margaret S. It is safe to say, therefore, that by sixteen to eighteen at least half of the girls were engaged in the positions for which they had been trained.

It is necessary to look at what happened to the girls in their postindenture years before assessing the results of Lancaster.[19] After indenture 41 percent of the inmates returned to live with their relatives or the complainants with whom they had lived previously; 9 percent became servants; 38 percent were married. Thus 88 percent of the girls were living in a family shortly after leaving Lancaster. Another 4 percent died or were in institutions. It is important to note that not all of those who had been recorded as institutionalized remained so. It is known that many, like Abigail F., returned to a "welfare" institution on a temporary basis or were ill and temporarily hospitalized.

We have information on the work after indenture for only 20 percent of the first-year's entrants. Some remained at home with their families and did not work; some were institutionalized; some escaped; and some were lost to history, their lives no longer reported. Of the 20 percent about whom we have information, 75 percent were engaged in menial but respectable work, 15 percent seemed to have prospered, and only 5 percent were reported as living lives of "ill fame." The remaining 5 percent were in an institution.

No more than three years after the first postindenture report, the superintendent attempted a second follow-through and found that 10 percent of the girls were living with relatives; 15 percent were living with another family, either working for them or nearby; and 56 percent were married. In short, more than three-quarters of the girls were living in a family context. The balance had shifted from living with a family to having a family of one's own. The remaining 25 percent had escaped, were institutionalized, or had died. The number in the last two categories, although it had doubled from the first follow-through, was still relatively small—15 percent.

From these details we can see that the early childhood of Abigail F. was fairly typical of Lancaster's first-year entrants. She and Hannah K. fared about the same as more than half of their comrades. Maria M. represents the small group of "failures." Unfortunately the case of Margaret S.—truly a success story—was not frequently repeated. On the basis of its first year, however, it seems that Lancaster succeeded in preventing poor young women from falling into lives of vice and crime. Although it did not send them on the road to fortune, it enabled them to travel the path common to their class—and to do so with respectability.

At least in the beginning, for the most part the girls ended up where one might have expected them to. Only a small number of inmates rose above or fell below their previous stations; they remained in the class into which they had been born. They found employment in predictable positions and lived predictable lives with the sort of husbands they would have married had they not been sent to Lancaster. It would seem, then, that the school served as a way station for the adolescent daughters of the poor—and as an employment agency.

However confused the motives of the original reformers may have been, however ambivalent their feelings toward the poor, and toward pubescent and seemingly deviant girls, and however strong their fear of social chaos, they were in earnest. The family-style reform school, with all its careful plans to protect and supervise its girls, seemed able to bind the girls with "cords of love" and in this gentle, loving, but firm, context redirect them to the path of virtue. Lizzie L.'s case may be taken as representative. Sincerely believing that Lancaster would benefit her, the administrators wished ardently for her salvation. "Nothing but her prompt removal from her mother and her home saved her from a certain and an early ruin. . . . We have good reason to hope that the school will become to her a house of redemption." Whether their hope was realized is a matter of opinion, since Lizzie did spend time in an asylum and a jail. Afterward, however, she married and went to work, and there was no further evidence of criminal behavior on her part.

In its opening year, Lancaster Industrial School for Girls had accomplished some of the things for which its founders had hoped. It had separated the girls from the influences thought to encourage promiscuity—and if the records are accurate, it had done so without being overly harsh. One way in which the school reached this goal was by maintaining strict control over the girls once they were in the school and watching carefully lest already "lost" girls—in particular, the older ones from the jails and workhouse—pollute others. The trustees remained wary of older girls. In the first year, only two girls, originally accepted although feared to be wanton, were discharged from the school. Supposedly fifteen years old, but of a "more mature" appearance, both were removed as unsuitable: one upon the discovery that she was pregnant; the other, after an attempt to induce others to escape with her to a "house of ill-fame." The skepticism regarding the ages of the two expelled girls is an indication of how strongly the trustees were attached to the assumption that only women could be judged irredeemable, whereas all children could be taught righteousness and morals.

The first full year of Lancaster's operation gave cause for celebration and discouragement. Lancaster succeeded in sheltering the "exposed"; its cottages were rapidly filled with poor girls from urban streets. Superintendent Peirce and his staff could congratulate themselves on providing obviously needed refuge to the girls placed under their care. Furthermore, most of these girls eventually attained respectability. But Lancaster could not claim unqualified success in uplifting and transforming near-wanton urchins into models of virtue; almost none of the first year's entrants could be so described.

The true test for Lancaster would come only with the passage of time.

5

Change, Control, and Order: Lancaster's Historical Context

The story of Lancaster is not one of a dream come true. The commissioners' lofty aspirations soon collided with the reality of its social, political, economic, and institutional context. Peirce's First Annual Report, so full of glowing optimism, became an artifact of mid-century reformist zeal. By 1865 the Second Annual Report of the Massachusetts Board of Charities was full of pessimism and voiced an insidious and popular bias against those whom the Fay Commission had considered worthy candidates for reform: poor, dependent, and wayward children.

The Second Annual Report of 1865, coauthored by Samuel Gridley Howe, president of the newly organized Board of State Charities, and Franklin Sanborn, secretary of the board, was to become a landmark in reformist thought. It reveals the change of attitude among the reformers, marking a profound shift away from "sentimentalism," from environmentalism to hereditarianism. This shift was in some measure due to contemporary social science, whose influence on the Second Annual Report is made explicit in the section of the report entitled "The People's Own Work": "A body made up of men who had studied physiology, and little else, would make sorry work at legislation; but one made up of men who knew the general rules of physiology and of social science, as well as of political economy, would save both money and human suffering by preventing a growth of social evils, instead of waiting until the evils are full grown, and then striving to lessen or suppress them."

Ironically, Howe had originally been an especially influential and active institution builder. He had founded in 1829 the New England Asylum—later known as the Perkins School—and in 1847 the Massachusetts School for Idiotic and Feeble Minded Youth, had supported Horace Mann's campaign for common schooling, was a staunch supporter of the Walnut Street jail, and endorsed vociferously the commonwealth's plan to create a state reform school for boys at Westborough. By 1856, however, a shift had occurred in Howe's thinking. Now he fought strenously against Lancaster. His reasons for opposing Lancaster were based on "biology." It was in the nature of the biological family to ensure the piety of its members; any alternative to the natural family, such as the surrogate family, would necessarily fail to secure this end. So strong was Howe's belief in this argument that he lobbied for direct placement of girls with good families. It should be pointed out, however, that his loss of faith in artificially created families, and therefore in Lancaster, had not yet detracted from his firm belief in the potential redemption of all children.

But a decade later Howe and his coreformer Sanborn were no longer voicing the belief that all children were salvageable or that placement in a good family ensured reformation. Optimistic environmentalism was rapidly being superseded by hereditarianism. The focus of the Howe-Sanborn report is not on reform and restoration but on the social burden of children and the elderly ("who are under or over the period of life during which men earn more than they consume, so that they, too, have to be added to the greater burden") and on classification by type of depravity. What concern there was for reformation was expressed in a hereditarian context. Deviance was traced to two types of "inherited organic imperfection": vitiated constitution and poor stock. Reformation was more likely with the former, it was believed, than with the latter. But, the report went on, it was impossible to distinguish between them, so that it was virtually impossible to institute a suitable system of correction.[1]

To the authors of the Howe-Sanborn report, intemperance was a cause of hereditary weakness, social chaos, and moral slackness.

> The use of alcohol modifies materially a man's bodily condition and so far as that affects him individually, it is his own affair; but if it affects also the number and condition of his offspring, that affects society.
>
> If its general use does materially influence the number and condition of the dependent and criminal classes, it is the duty of all who have thought and cared about social improvement to consider the matter carefully; and it is the special duty of those having official relations with those classes to furnish facts and material for public consideration.[2]

The officers and trustees of Lancaster agreed with this report; alcohol was an easy scapegoat, a much easier target for blame than the profound nineteenth-century problems of poverty and social inequality.

The temperance crusade, into which the Howe-Sanborn report may be fitted, found intellectual justification in hereditarianism; drunkards were expected to reproduce weak stock: "Any morbid condition of body, frequently repeated, becomes established by habit. Once established, it affects the man in various ways and makes him more liable to certain diseases, as gout, scrofula, insanity and the like. This liability, or tendency, he transmits to his children as surely as he transmits likeness in form or feature."[3] Hereditarianism is also evident in the report's discussion of the tendencies transmitted to children by their parents inebriated at the time of conception: "It is known to physiologists that if a man's system is once tainted with certain diseases, the taint remains, a black drop in his blood for life. Every outward symptom may have gone, never to reappear in him; but children born to him years after his apparent cure may show that black drop in some of the protean forms of scrofula."[4] The report elaborated on the theory that "the unfavorable condition of parentage may not be intensified during one life, and, therefore, one generation of children may escape; but the abnormal tendency exists in the stock, and it may crop out under favoring circumstances in the second or third generation." The authors then cited Edward Jarvis's research on the infant mortality rates gathered from data on the headstones in a wealthy Cambridge cemetery, Mt. Auburn Cemetery, and in several immigrant, Catholic, and working-class cemeteries in the area. Jarvis found that infant mortality was higher among the foreign population and concluded in support of the message in the Board of State Charities report that vitiated stock "must go on deteriorating."[5]

It should be emphasized that Howe's pessimism was not universally shared. In particular, Sanborn continued to argue that redemption was still possible: "In a few generations, with temperate life and wisely assorted marriage, the morbid conditions disappear."[6] It was Sanborn's belief that although some children may be irreversibly tainted by poor stock, others can be rehabilitated given the proper environment and treatment—which, Sanborn steadfastly maintained, was family-style care.

A major effect of the Howe-Sanborn report was to lighten the burden of responsibility placed on the officers of Lancaster, for if some children were unsalvageable, the school could not be expected to achieve success with everybody. But, chiefly through Sanborn's efforts, the report did assign to Lancaster a continuing role in reform efforts, since in its view a good family life and education remained the best weapons against vice: "We find in our public institutions, that, other things being equal, the nearer they approach the family system the better and the contrary."[7] Even Howe, despite his leanings toward hereditarianism, allowed the weak and the poor a way out: "[If they] live a temperate life and marry appropriately there is still a chance."

The Howe-Sanborn report reflects a shift in reformist ideology brought on by general historical forces and events: the Civil War, industrialization, the associated rise of labor organizations, urbanization, and immigration.

The society that reformers like Howe and Sanborn had been struggling to improve had expanded and changed; the social, economic, and political developments only hinted at at the beginning of the nineteenth century were in full swing by its last decades. In the post–Civil War period the trend toward city living intensified, so that small communities lost even more of their autonomy. Small businesses gave way to an early form of Big Business. Science was playing an ever larger role in determining the shape of the future. The landscape and complexion of the population was changing drastically as Slavs and Southern Europeans flowed into already crowded cities. Another very critical aspect of this changing landscape was communications. Railroads doubled and tripled their mileage; telephones entered into every town; and newspapers appeared throughout the land. Society was expanding rapidly beyond the boundaries of the frontier, creating a vast and rich country truly spanning the continent. The "distended society," as historian Robert Wiebe has labeled it, appeared stretched to the breaking point.[8]

Perhaps it was simply an attempt to get a handle on these confusing and changing times that some reformers claimed to see in intemperance the root cause of all social problems.[9] Believing that eradicating liquor from society would fundamentally ennoble it, self-appointed crusaders fought for temperance legislation, in the belief that national abstinence was the only cure. Indeed, in the latter half of the nineteenth century, temperance was a national movement, in which the Lancaster reformers were able to fit themselves quite comfortably. Actually, the Lancaster reformers already had a lot in common with the temperance advocates. The fears that had motivated the former to reform delinquent girls also spurred the latter to reform delinquent adults. Lancaster's objects of concern were mostly the daughters of poor, first-generation immigrants; temperance crusaders aimed their righteous appeals at the Irish and other immigrants and at the laboring classes. As we know from Robert Hampel's study of temperance activity in antebellum Massachusetts, inebriety was assumed to be disproportionately high among laborers, especially the Irish, who were thought to possess a genetic predisposition to alcoholism.[10]

As economic expansion continued unabated and good work habits were pushed as the key to a strong national destiny, the evil of drink came to be looked on, as Jesse Goodrich, a staunch Massachusetts crusader, put it, as the great hindrance to the triumph of "Capital—Enterprise—Industry—Morals—and Religion."[11] Reading over the categories invoked by Goodrich to define success and comparing them to those embraced at the State Industrial School for Girls can only reinforce the argument that the thinking of the Lancaster reformers was consonant with that of the temperance leaders. But examined in this light, the intense fight for abstinence was motivated less by religious conviction than by a desire to ensure a sober, productive labor force, and the urge to sober up adults and straighten out young girls was a corollary of the assumption that individual prosperity and order rested on social prosperity and order.

It must be understood that reformers were reacting to social realities, not only fears or prejudices. A clear indication of instability may be seen in the population statistics and demographic trends for the United States at that time. Both show increasing urbanization and economic expansion, and the processes by which America's agricultural colonies were becoming an industrialized and urbanized nation were both welcome and disconcerting. The population in the United States swelled by more than 35 percent from 1840 to 1850, and again by the same amount during the next decade. Even in later decades, when growth had slowed, the increase remained quite high—for instance, 25.5 percent from 1880 to 1890. And this at a time when the frontier was closing and the amount of available land shrinking. As in the past, a large part of the expansion could be traced to immigration. Starting in 1850 the number of immigrants exceeded 100,000 in a single year. After the Civil War, immigration surged; in 1870, 387,203 immigrants entered, and approximately 450,000 in the first year of each of the next three decades. These foreigners, in addition to straining the resources of all the states and every large city, increased their numbers rapidly and, it seemed to some, with abandon. The fertility rate of American-born women started to drop, but no such reduction was noted among the newly arrived; there was a fear that the good native Yankee stock would be swamped by foreigners and strangers[12] and that pure Yankee America would be no more.

Where did the swelling native population and the recent arrivals go? They poured into existing cities and created new ones out of towns, villages, and crossroads. From 1850 to 1860 alone the number of urban areas with a population between 2,500 and 10,000 increased by 72 percent, from 174 to 299. Larger cities multiplied by 50 percent,

Table 5.1
Proportion of Massachusetts population in urban areas

Year	Percentage
1800	16
1810	21.5
1820	23
1830	32
1840	38
1850	50.5
1860	64
1870	67
1880	74
1890	81
1900	86

Source: Compilation of data from Bureau of the Census, *Historical Statistics of the United States*, part 1. Washington, DC: Government Printing Office, 1975, p. 29.

from 62 to 93. In 1880 America had its first city of over one million inhabitants; within just ten years there were two more urban areas of that size. In 1850, 24 percent of the nation was urban; by 1880 38 percent was. By 1850 the majority of the citizens of Massachusetts lived in cities. And within a few years after the opening of the State Industrial School for Girls at Lancaster, fully 64 percent of the commonwealth lived in cities. A decade after this the percentage of Massachusetts citizens defined as urban, 67 percent, was double that of the United States as a whole, a ratio that was to hold up to 1900, when fully 86 percent of the citizens of Massachusetts lived in cities[13] (see table 5.1).

Having built institutions to counteract the unwelcome effects of modernization, Massachusetts reformers must have wondered whether their efforts could keep pace with the inflationary growth in population. Hordes of strangers, whether foreigners or transients, served as a constant reminder that the good old days of informal community life were disappearing and that in their stead were confusing new days of frenzied energy, accompanied by potential anarchy. Although still proud of their heritage and tradition of extending opportunity to all, many Yankees, acutely aware of their crumbling old world, were disturbed by both the demands and the needs of immigrants. Consequently, at the same time that some Americans were adjusting existing institutions like Lancaster to fit the changing world, others were contemplating how to stop the processes in motion. For example, we see now the earliest legislative efforts to restrict immigration—in which efforts Boston was the leader. We see also nativism and eugenics sweeping the nation. The popularity of Reverend Josiah Strong's *Our Country* testifies to this emerging xenophobia. Strong listed immigration, Romanism, intemperance, socialism, and urbanism as the major perils to America, and he linked them all to the immigrant, typically "a European peasant, whose horizon has been narrow, whose moral and religious training has been meager or false, and whose ideas of life are low. Not a few belong to the pauper and criminal classes." Strong was only echoing widely held views when he characterized foreigners as polluting influences, "smitten with the blasts of temptation," which could not be withstood by weak creatures.[14]

Fears that unrestricted immigration were ruining the country were exacerbated by economic reversals to the new industrial order. In 1857 and 1858 there was a short, but very severe, depression. Blaming the poor was one outlet for the anxiety caused by this economic uncertainty. In straitened times, the poor, the criminal, and the immigrant were convenient and easily identifiable scapegoats for the fear and rage brought on by hardships. And of course the girls at Lancaster were but one of these groups caught in this policy of "blaming the victim." Not by mere coincidence therefore was the trustees' report from 1857 fraught with confusion over the characters of and appropriate treatment for poor girls already tainted by criminality. The trustees asked whether "when the criminal desire has developed itself into the criminal act . . . is there any prospect for permanent reformation?"[15]

Many of the emotional conflicts resulting from economic upheaval continued into the Civil War. This war made clear that no part of the Union was free from the devastation of national catastrophe. Although the commonwealth incurred fewer direct losses from the war than other parts of the country, knowledge of the draft riots, many of them instigated by the Irish, and other reported civil disorders reinforced Massachusetts reformers' belief in the need for more stringent controls. The trustees' report of 1863 illuminated this fear of disaster and the need for counterchecks to social turmoil. Occurrences like the draft riots and war dislocations both were to the moralizers proof of family decay. They proclaimed, "Let the families of the land be homes of ignorance, vice and immorality, and we shall find ourselves in the midst of confusion, bloodshed and anarchy, and daily with scenes like those so recently enacted in our chief commercial city."[16] Nor were immigrants and labor organizers considered the only cause of civil disturbance; the same report holds women and girls particularly responsible for the turmoil of 1863: "Remember you not that women and girls were most faithful allies in that work of pillage and death? Indeed it was one of the saddest features of that mob, that it was composed so largely of women and children. Boys and girls in throngs, we are told, helped to tear down the buildings, pulling the ropes and lighting the fires."

Along with a hereditarian argument to explain the deviance of children, an antifemale sentiment was also evident. For example, it was believed that mothers had relinquished home responsibilities and lost or given up control of their children. In response to newspaper accounts reporting that "women, the mothers of these children, were seen urging on the rioters and, making the air resound with their shrill voices . . . ," the trustees voiced consternation that "*such* are some of the mothers and children in our land." The terrifying behavior attributed to these women and their obvious unwillingness or inability to function as mothers to the republic, now in dire need of moral guardians, justified their preemption of responsibility for errant and neglected children. In this way the trustees also rationalized the crucial role Lancaster played, in heroic terms: "As lovers of the country, then, and desirous to promote her welfare—to make her the home of freedom, justice and purity, where peace, prosperity and happiness shall prevail—an asylum for the oppressed—a blessing to the nations of the earth and the glory of all lands, we shall labor to imbue each one of our inmates with the spirit, and train each to the practice of those habits and virtue the possession of which will insure this desirable result."[17] War intensified the fear of social turmoil, the horrors of unsupervised youth; the potential or real absence of a male family member to give guidance to children brought to the forefront all the biases against women alone. The state had to step in to replace absentee men and fathers. The social chaos of the Civil War exacerbated the reformers' fear of the poor and the uprooted. The death of over half a million men left many poor girls unsupervised, roaming the streets and often homeless.

This visible threat in the midst of general turbulence of the postwar years as well as the simultaneous expansion of the urban population meant that cities had to deal with tougher, less controlled girls, many of whom would be the perfect clients for Lancaster. As a result, there was increased pressure on the school to expand to receive more inmates.[18] Ames, superintendent in 1866, ascribes to the demographic changes in New England an increase in girls needing the type of reformation provided by the school, a process interrupted but not changed by the war. "In all our cities, large towns and manufacturing villages, there are numbers who are falling under corrupt influences, and are being led astray. . . . Association with evil companions on the street, and in saloons and various public places of amusement, and even in some of our public schools, has proved and is proving, occasion of ruin to many."[19]

The war and postwar years were marked by a period of increasing productivity and a general upswing in the economy. However, a reversal jostled the postwar complacency. In 1873 the country was thrown into an economic panic. Fears and insecurities were thereby intensified and were to get worse during the downward trend, which lasted until 1878. One result of these economic difficulties was labor unrest. The Molly Maguires, the Homestead strike, and the great railroad strike all contributed to fear of mob disorder more than they garnered sympathy for the poorly paid and badly treated workers. Labor statistics show mounting unemployment and help to explain both dissatisfaction among labor and fears of social chaos among the general public. In 1876 from 12 to 14 percent of workers could not find jobs; nearly twenty years later, 1894, this figure had risen to 18 percent.[20]

The civil disorder and numerous riots associated with the troubled economy prompted upright citizens to call for brute force to keep the masses in their place. For example, the *Independent*, a religious journal, condoned violence as perhaps necessary to subdue hostile crowds: "If the club of the policeman, knocking out the brains of the rioter, will answer, then well and good; but if it does not . . . then bullets and bayonets, canister and grape . . . constitute the one remedy . . . Napoleon was right when he said that the way to deal with a mob was to exterminate it."[21]

Upright, moral citizens clamored loudly for order and control by any possible means at the disposal of the state. Abhorrence of labor unrest took precedence over the principle of granting to the troublemakers due process. The division between owners and workers was being crystallized during this time. Company-instigated massacres of unorganized miners and the use of scab labor to replace those fired for protesting were management policies used in the postwar world; the emerging entrepreneurial class could not meet the mounting demands of the workers upon whom they depended for their accumulation of wealth.

The poor foreigner had become the object of universal derision and dread. The Reverend Austin Phelps, author of the introduction to Josiah Strong's *Our Country*, was expressing a widely shared fear when he cautioned that the "foreigner" would destroy the country and advised Americans to take strong hold of their heritage:

> Fifty years ago our watchful fathers forecast the future of the Republic. The wisest among them even then began to doubt how long the original stock of American society could bear the infusion of elements alien to our history and to the faith of our ancestry. . . .
>
> Fifty years of the most eventful history have been piling up the proofs of our national peril, till now they come down upon us with the weight of an avalanche.[22]

Fears of social chaos spurred late-nineteenth-century Americans to latch onto "scientific" theories claiming to have the solutions to rising crime, poverty, and social disorder. In particular, the publication of Charles Darwin's *Origin of Species* in 1859 was seized on by social theorists and reformers to justify hereditarian attitudes—this despite the fact that Darwin himself had limited his inquiries to animals. Sir Francis Galton was instrumental in transforming his cousin Charles Darwin's work into "social Darwinism." Galton's hereditarian beliefs, outlined in *Heredity, Genius, and Inquiry into Its Laws and Consequences*, claimed to demonstrate "that a man's natural abilities are derived by inheritance. . . . Consequently . . . it would be predictable to produce a highly gifted race of men by judicious marriages during several consecutive generations." Galton attached little significance to the environment's role in the shaping of character and ability. So convincing were Galton's scientific claims for eugenics that Darwin's later work, *The Descent of Man*, 1871, echoed many of Galton's ideas on the hereditability of talent and intellectual capacity.[23]

Subsequent works in both Europe and the United States outlined biological explanations for the perceived differences between economic classes, ethnic groups, races, and genders. Herbert Spencer's account of these differences played a major role in the debate of the 1870s and 1880s. Deploring state intervention in the form of poor laws, public education, and state-supported institutions, he echoed Jeremy Bentham's utilitarian belief that nature, unimpeded, would eventually lead to the disappearance of evil and predatory behavior and allow the development of human perfection. In Spencer's recasting of this idea into the language of survival of the fittest: "[If people] are sufficiently complete to live, they *do* live, and it is well they should live. If they are not sufficiently complete to live, they die, and it is best they die."[24]

It is difficult to appreciate the national impact in this regard of the American William Graham Sumner, but by translating these theories into a seemingly reasonable rationale for conservative ideology, he was able to turn many against the fundamental democratic ideal of equality for all. Survival of the fittest implied unequal abilities. Natural selection would, of course, eliminate the feeble. Legislative efforts in behalf of human welfare contravert "natural" laws; since intelligence and character are innate, trying to alter social conditions to affect human circumstances must fail. Logically, legislation should be formulated for the "fit" by those who are "fit." In Sumner's words:

> With savages, the weak in body or mind are soon eliminated; and those that survive commonly exhibit a vigorous state of health. We civilized men, on the other hand, do our utmost to check the process of elimination; we build asylums for the imbecile, the maimed, and the sick; we institute poor-laws; and our medical men exert their utmost skill to save the life of everyone to the last moment. . . . Thus, the weak members of civilized societies propagate their kind. No one who has attended to the breeding of domestic animals will doubt that this must be highly injurious to the race of man. It is surprising how soon a want of care, or care wrongly directed, leads to the degeneration of a domestic race; but excepting in the case of man himself, hardly anyone is so ignorant as to allow his worst animals to breed.[25]

To the biological determinists, then, poverty and suffering were ordained by nature. No one deserved special treatment; the fit would survive, and the unfit would die out. Social welfare was against nature. Biological determinism fit in nicely with the conservative romanticism of reformers like Sumner who advocated that man should be left to "make himself," thereby legitimizing the failures of social reform. A similar devaluation of social reform is found in the work of the noted criminologist Cesare Lombroso, who claimed to demonstrate that criminals were members of an inferior subspecies, characterized by a smaller brain and incomplete physiological and evolutionary development. Others used the same methodology to prove the intrinsic unworthiness of women, certain ethnic groups, the poor, and all nonwhites, all of whose brains were held to be smaller and of lower quality.[26]

Social Darwinism had its impact on Lancaster. The 1869 Annual Report hinted that the faith of the school's officials had started to ebb, that "many were certainly saved" but some would "after all . . . be lost." The 1871 report talks of the girls' "inherited tendencies," which lead them to commit offenses against morality. Although still considered deserving of pity, love, and support, the girls were increasingly characterized as unfortunate recipients of "bad" genes. As early as 1866, inherited viciousness is a concern of both superintendent and trustees:

"Unless the present generation reform[s] its own habits and enter[s] upon the virtuous living, it may expect to find that the next generation will present a still larger number of inmates for our reformatories and prisons: for as is the mother so will be the daughter, and as the father so the son, and with increased intensity of perverseness and wickedness."[27] It should be noted here that the romantic environmentalism of the early reformers was not complete behavioral environmentalism. Although it presumed that all children possessed a basically innocent and good character, despite protestations to the contrary, it did not totally rule out the possibility of innate "badness," so that when improvement was slow or nonexistent, romantic reformers sometimes assumed innate character as a cause of failure. Social Darwinism, therefore, was not alien to earlier reformist thought; there were grounds for its acceptance.[28]

In addition to the hereditarianism, another issue of concern to Lancaster was social purity. The social purists' goals, which overlapped Lancaster's, were to establish a single standard of sexual purity for men and women, to eliminate prostitution, and to exalt motherhood—in a word, to control sexuality. Not surprisingly, purists also used social Darwinism to underscore the righteousness of their cause. Consider, for example, these words by the activist for social purity Elizabeth Evans: "If women had their own way in the matter this physical intercourse would take place at comparatively rare intervals, and only under the most favorable circumstances. . . . Such an arrangement would be in infinite benefit to the race: men would preserve their vigor, and women their beauty and spirits, and though fewer children might be born, their quality would be improved."[29]

Statements of this sort reflect the conviction that women are directly responsible for "future generations." For the Massachusetts legislature, this idea had meant the allocation of funds for a female reform school. For Evans and her group, this belief meant women should take a more active role in ensuring the continued improvement of the human race through a form of selective breeding. It included as well efforts to regulate prostitution and to support a woman's desire to say "No" to marital relations and their consequences. Unnerved by a rise in unwanted pregnancies and induced abortions, fighters for this cause also pushed legislation limiting the availability of birth-control information and devices. The Comstock laws, passed in 1873, had classified such material as obscene and prohibited its distribution through the mail. Any further discussion of the Comstock laws would take us too far afield. It suffices to note that the underlying reasons for such legislation overlap those for the continued existence of Lancaster, namely, curbing socially threatening sexuality. More generally, we may note that the various post–Civil War reforms, the efforts of that period's activists and charity workers, were intended to offset the effects of the modern world; Lancaster's emphasis and near obsession with the chastity of its girls derived from the same attitude that spawned the drive of the social purists against prostitution.

At this time there arose debate over the need for new formalized structures to run the modern world: its business, its politics—and of course its social welfare, of which Lancaster was one element. As Melvin Dubovsky has stated, "community tended to succumb to society, the personal relationship to the bureaucratic one, the human to the mechanical."[30] Americans found themselves in the midst of a seemingly irreversible progression from the old world to something new and strange. Free and open marketplaces were yielding to monopolies, and ties to family and community to formal relations to an impersonal technological bureaucracy. And in this changing world, moral reformation for the poor was gradually replaced by a systematic study of the causes of poverty and criminal behavior and by bureaucratic solutions based on such study. Having failed to stem the tide of immigrants, or to halt these foreign and rural newcomers flooding cities, or to prevent the "contagion" of pauperism, criminality, and moral turpitude from spreading, vigorous reformers turned to "modern" methods of investigation, selection, and systematization; routine record keeping of those receiving aid and organized charity were the new hallmarks of reform. Not surprisingly, these methods borrowed their rhetoric and models from business. Institutionalization had not been discounted, but its belief in the inevitability of success through the establishment of surrogate families had become anachronistic. The need now was to organize and to control.

"Modern" scientific philanthropy gained great popularity. Charity organization societies sprang up in the last two decades of the nineteenth century to "promote co-operation and higher standards of efficiency among the older relief-dispensing agencies." Through systematization, reorganization, and the provision of self-help services—day nurseries, kindergartens, workrooms, and training—rather than money, organizers hoped to correct past reform failures through the application of the scientific method. As part of this increasing need to manage services, the Commonwealth of Massachusetts moved to place the governance of institutions for the care of the dependent under public jurisdiction. State governance and dispensation of treatment, it was now argued, would be more efficient, consolidated, and "scientific."

Due to this mood, there was increasing tension between the state and the governing officers of Lancaster on how best to serve the state's charges. While the superintendent and trustees continued to view the school as their private responsibility and domain, the commonwealth organized and reorganized in such a way that bureaucratic procedure conflicted with the paternalistic patterns of trustee governance. As the state centralized its bureaucratic procedures, state governance became increasingly distant from the individual institutions. The state occupied itself with the more judicial and managerial aspects of running reform institutions and left the individual institutions to function more independently, but under its aegis.

In 1865, in an effort to centralize the administration and supervision of the various state charities, the Massachusetts legislature created the Board of State Charities, appointing Samuel Gridley Howe as the first chairman and Franklin B. Sanborn the first secretary. This new attempt to systematize charitable care was a significant and progressive act, appropriate to a rapidly modernizing society. By consolidating state charities under one board, the legislature hoped to guarantee a more equitable redistribution of public resources, an objective held worthy by Howe, Sanborn, and many other reformers. The same current of thought was having an impact at this time also on the public schools, whose officials were busy formulating a common curriculum and centralizing school administration.[31]

Part of the Second Annual Report was a detailed critique of institutional effectiveness: "Danger of misdirection in this process and benevolent work is that two false principles may be incorporated into projected institutions which will be as rotten pile in the foundation and make the future establishments deplorable, defective, and mischievous. These are first close congregations and second the life-long association of a large number of idiots: whereas, the true, sound principles are: separate idiots from each other; and then diffuse them among the normal population." The report even questioned the potential rehabilitative value of family-style living: "We might as well try to imitate within a house sunshine and rain, and clouds and dew and all the shifting scenery of nature, as initiate in a reformatory the every varying influences of family life. . . . We have at best a make believe society, a make believe family and, too often, a make believe virtue."[32] Ironically, although reformers embraced science and "system," they now advocated a simpler and more nostalgic treatment for wayward youth: direct placement on rural farms in morally upright families.

Recognizing that suitable placements had to be found and then supervised, the State Visiting Agency was established for boys in 1869, and for girls one year later. Gardiner Tufts, formerly an agent of the US Sanitary Commission during the Civil War and a proven able administrator, was appointed the first visiting agent. His appointment was also part of the commonwealth's effort to make public services more systematic, efficient, and thus more equitable. Tufts shared Howe's and Sanborn's belief that family life could not be replicated by any institution regardless of its program and structure. He supported Howe and Sanborn in encouraging direct placement as the only really preventative measure and discouraged judges from sentencing all but the most hardened to reform schools.

Through the actions of these men resulted certain key legislative changes, specifically sections 8 and 10, chapter 359, Acts of 1870, which allowed the visiting agent of the Board of State Charities to attend trials and to oversee placement once the girls received their sentences. By this act the agent could direct older girls to the school and place younger, and seemingly more innocent, girls directly with families. This, of course, was a drastic revision of the founders' conception of Lancaster as a therapeutic family environment. Other legislative changes soon followed consolidating the move to classification by age. In 1870 the state passed a law by which seventeen-year-olds could legally be sent to Lancaster. And in 1871 a law was enacted providing that girls of sixteen who were considered incorrigible or badly placed originally could be transferred to Lancaster from other institutions by the court.

Reformers, still reluctant to reverse their earlier commitment to resist any grading scheme that would classify crime in age-specific terms, were confused by their increasingly difficult task—reforming older and seemingly more difficult girls. These legislative changes, which syphoned the younger girls away from Lancaster, must have provided some relief. The state had allowed reformers to continue to avoid overt policies of classification; at the same time, legislative measures effected those very policies. The result was that the girls sent to Lancaster would be older.

The diversion of youth from juvenile institutions led to a depopulation of both Lancaster and Westborough. However, this effort to redirect many youths from those institutions intentionally created for their care had two results: not only was the number of entrants reduced—a result Tufts considered a mark of success—but the schools were now populated by the hardest and most difficult, those considered least suitable for direct placement. The reform schools were left to deal with the most difficult cases. By 1879 there was a serious schism between the Board of State Charities, which felt that the policy of prevention by immediate placement resulted in "leniency toward young offenders" at the expense of "their good or the safety of the community," and the State Visiting Agent and some of the key reformers, who clung tenaciously to their antiinstitutionalism and their belief in immediate placement. This debate was only part of a general dissatisfaction, among not only its appointees but the general public, with the state welfare institutions under the board's jurisdiction.[33] Not by coincidence, the Lancaster trustees were also reassessing the internal program at this juncture. Dissatisfaction with the indenture system and the increased concern for efficiency were occupying their attention. Ultimately, discontent with state institutions, their programs and governance, resulted in the Reorganization Act, 1879. As a result of this act, the Board of State Charities and the state visiting agent were replaced by a more consolidated and bureaucratized agency—the State Board of Health, Lunacy and Charity. Gardiner Tufts was relieved of his duties as state visiting agent and was appointed first as superintendent of the State Primary School at Monson and later, 1885, as the first superintendent of the Massachusetts State Reformatory at Concord. Although neither governed the new agency, both Howe and Sanborn remained involved in commonwealth reform efforts; Sanborn was to assume leadership of the American Social Science Association. "The Reorganization Act of 1879 which created this new agency marks a critical point in the development of Massachusetts youth corrections policy. By this event the basic structural framework for institutional and non-institutional responses was in place. In 1820 there had been no formal public policy toward wayward youth. Sixty years later there were two well-developed approaches competing for dominance as a state policy."[34] Paternalistic welfare was rapidly being undermined by bureaucratic management.

Supposedly freed from its previous conflicts, the state continued to consolidate and bureaucratize its charities. However, by early 1879 increasing bureaucratization of the State Board of Charities further eroded the informal mechanisms that Tufts had sought to maintain at Monson. Also, bitter controversies arose between the board and Tufts over Monson's education and placement programs. The Primary School suffered the same fate as Lancaster; the legislature closed Monson in 1895. Between 1879 and 1905 two further administrative changes took place. In 1886 the State Board of Health, Lunacy and Charity was renamed the State Board of Lunacy and Charity; in 1898 this board was renamed the State Board of Charity. Neither of these reorganizations, however, had a critical impact on the actual policies of the reform schools; in particular, Lancaster did not change greatly after 1885, the year when the State Board of Health, Lunacy and Charity condoned the new definition of Lancaster as a midway place between the care of the young and a reformatory prison for the older. But no longer was the vision of the school one of innovation; rather, as we shall see, it became a formalized institution for custodial care and efficient vocational training.

6

The Waifs and the Wanton: The Girls of Lancaster in Its First Fifty Years

[It is] self-evident . . . [that] each unprincipled, impure girl left to grow up, and become a mother, is likely to increase her kind three to five fold [since] . . . original constitution is a much more important factor than either education or surrounding.

Louise Rockford Wardner, of the Illinois Industrial School for Girls, *Girls in Reformatories*, 1879

[Many criminal children] come into the world freighted down with evil propensities and vicious tendencies. They start out handicapped in the race of life.

Sarah Cooper, pioneer of kindergartens in California, *The Kindergarten as Child-Saving Work*, 1883

Amid the upheavals of the second half of the nineteenth century, the State Industrial School for Girls at Lancaster continued to accept dependent and deviant young females. But Lancaster changed in these years. Its students were "harder," and the earlier faith in their salvageability diminished. The function of the school remained intact—girls were to be sheltered, trained, and then sent out into the world prepared to be respectable women—and in large measure this goal was reached, despite obstacles that sometimes frustrated the efforts of the founders and officers; but society was undergoing tremendous transformations, and these transformations were to affect Lancaster. In particular, attitudes towards the entrants and their families changed radically.

In 1856 Bradford Peirce had described Maria F. sympathetically and optimistically, blaming her waywardness on bad environment and her parents' poverty, not her inherent character: "She is to be sincerely pitied as her childhood has been sadly diverted from the path of obedience and truth."[1] Seven years later, the trustees' report had this to say: "Many of them are children of parents who have lived in constant violation of some of the great laws of God; and by one of these wise and righteous laws, the sins of the fathers are visited upon the children."[2] Here is another portion of Peirce's initial testimony: "The commission of crime does not make a *criminal* in the ordinary acceptation [sic] of the word. . . . These children have sinned ignorantly, and they are still *children*. Visitors have expressed surprise to find such pleasant looking inmates in our institution; they have so long associated all the deformities of confirmed criminality with a criminal act, that they expect to find little desperadoes; but they are as human, as happy, as childlike as the members of any of our families. . . ."[3]

What had caused this change in attitude, this loss of optimism, in so few years? As the previous chapter argues, Lancaster was redefined in the post–Civil War years. It became a custodial and punitive institution whose function would be to take in "hardened" girls. This shift in function was paralleled by a shift in ideology, from environmentalism to hereditarianism. Deviance in a young girl was now regarded as the sign of a weak and depraved nature, a nature "subject to hereditary disease."[4] Such a girl was, of course, resistant to reform, more fit for custodial and punitive care than for redemption.

This shift in function and ideology was spurred by post–Civil War conditions. Increasing immigration, urbanization, and unemployment had put more children on the city streets.

Marcus Ames, superintendent in 1864, expressed the fears of the time in these words: "The number of idle, useless girls, in all our large cities, seems to be steadily increasing. They lounge or sleep through their morning, parade the streets during the afternoon, and assemble in frivolous companies of their own, and the other sex, to pass away the evenings."[5] In addition, Ames declared that the high schools in urban areas were corrupting more girls, even girls of "worthy and respectable families." Ames also decried an increase in intemperance. He was convinced that many of the girls had been ruined by the influence of their drunken parents and were poorly equipped for domestic labor. Ignorance of domestic skills meant ineligibility for employment in respectable homes from which they could derive their living and have shelter. And without such shelter they would make their homes on the streets.

Here are some more words, written in 1865, on the depravity of the kind of girl entering Lancaster: "Inheriting the most depraved tastes, born sometimes in the midst of filth, cradled in a heap of rags, breathing an atmosphere so thick with curses that they have become familiar to their ears, until the first uncertain lisping of her infant tongue draws the applause of those who listen, with pleased recognition, to the attempted oath . . . the will is bound captive by evil habits."[6] In brief, the Lancaster inmates were now regarded as "pests in the family" and "poisonously depraved."[7]

But there were some early hints of this shift in perception. In 1857, just one year after the school opened, they had been called "moral orphans on the by-ways and on the street . . . the wretched victims of neglect or coarse brutality."[8] The trustees' Second Annual Report began to question the viability of their scheme and their belief that all children were salvageable. They defended their changing attitudes as the logical result of their first year's experience. Although apologetic for their loss of evangelistic zeal, they explained away their creeping skepticism as an understandable outcome of a new experiment—after all, they said, "the whole course was an unexplored field" and Lancaster was in untested waters[9]—for which their studies of American and European precedents had been helpful but insufficient.

The records of Lancaster's entrants for the years from 1856 to 1905 give a concrete picture of these changes.[10] The records show that from 1856 to 1905 on the average 88.5 percent of the girls had never been in custodial care previous to Lancaster and 81.6 percent had never had a brush with the law. While these figures indicate that few Lancaster inmates could have been the hardened criminal so feared by the founders, still a small minority had experienced some sort of institutional life by the time they entered the state reform school. A very few belonged in both groups: those placed in custodial care and those with criminal records of some sort. Thus it is safe to assume that at least one-fifth had either been in a refuge of some sort or had appeared in court; probably more, up to one-quarter, had therefore experienced at least one instance of charitable or state intervention.

Of the roughly 11.4 percent who had been in custodial institutions, most had lived in refuges or almshouses; the rest had been in orphanages, workhouses, other state industrial schools, or asylums. The proportion varied from year to year, with 23.5 percent in 1875 to only 5.2 percent in 1885 having been in that position prior to admittance to Lancaster. More of the girls, 18.4 percent, had had some contact with the state's legal system. Most of this latter group had been in jail or a house of correction; several had been placed on probation by the court; a few had been at the State Primary School. The percentage of girls who had been in court also varied from year to year. The years with the lowest proportions were 1863 and 1880, with 8.7 percent and 8.8 percent, respectively. The year with the highest proportion, 1895, counted 34.8 percent in this category. As these numbers suggest, there was more than one net with which to catch young girls falling into ruin. But Lancaster, at least in the eyes of its staff and the court, was preferable to these other options such as jails or almshouses. For some of these girls, Lancaster undoubtedly presented an opportunity for schooling and training that did not exist at other institutions. For most it was, as hoped, their last contact with the state welfare or punitive system. But for some Lancaster would become simply an early experience in a long association with the state's institutions.[11]

The case of Melissa S., an orphan, provides an example of a Lancaster girl with a previous institutional history. At eight years of age Melissa had been sent to the Industrial School at Dorchester. In 1875 she was moved to Lancaster:

> The complainant, Miss Goodwin, is a manager of the Industrial School in Dorchester. They have labored hard to save [Melissa] from the present sentence. The complaint, after much deliberation, was made April 26th/75, when she was sentenced to the State Industrial School, but, at the suggestion of Miss Goodwin, the sentence was suspended, and [Melissa] placed again with her on probation, but as she continues to be disobedient to those with whom the school placed her, they refuse to retain her in their families, and now she is sent to this school.

As this demonstrates, Lancaster served as one further step in the attempt to tame and reform a young girl needing supervision. Another example underlines how Lancaster was sometimes used after other measures had failed, the case of Cathy C., thirteen years old, first on probation and then sent to Lancaster: "[Cathy] was complained of for larceny, and tried before Judge Forsaith some months ago, and was placed on probation. Since then she has committed a similar offense, before the one mentioned in this complaint." Two more girls may be used as evidence of Lancaster's place within the growing cluster of institutions for poor children. Sylvia D. had been in the "Rutland St. home—Boston—since then went to a place for three months, but returned of her own accord to the home again." After returning, she stole a shawl and was committed to the State Industrial School. And fifteen years later, in 1900, Helga D., having been in both the Little Wanderers' Home and the State Almshouse in Pittsfield, ended up in the State Industrial School since neither of the other two places suited her. Thus some of the students entering Lancaster had already been under state care or private charity for various periods of time ranging from a few months to many years.

Although it is a reasonable assumption that the families of Lancaster girls had also experienced some form of state care, the data collected from the records indicate that fewer of the parents and siblings of the Lancaster entrants had experienced institutional care than the Lancaster girls themselves. In fact, a study of the inmates' records indicates that the overwhelming majority of parents and siblings had not been in any institutions. The very few who had, approximately 3.1 percent of the fathers and 4.7 percent of the mothers, were most often in an almshouse or jail, with a few in workhouses, state hospitals, and asylums. Of the siblings, on the average at least 5.7 percent of the brothers and 6.1 percent of the sisters had been in an institution: slightly under half of the brothers had been sent to Westborough or another reformatory; the rest had been in jail, an orphanage, the Boy's Farm School, or the State Primary School. A few of the sisters who had lived in an institution had also been in jail, an orphanage, a workhouse, or a convent. Most significant is that more than half of this group of sisters had been in Lancaster. Evidently, once parents discovered the school, they made full use of the option, sometimes sending more than one daughter there.

Although a substantial minority of Lancaster's girls had been institutionalized previously, only a few of them had come to Lancaster directly from another institution. Most of the girls, however, came from a type of home environment. About 80 percent of them had, during the full fifty years under study, lived with families immediately before admittance. Therefore they had learned to conform to the duties and customs of household living, either within their own families or as household domestics. Their lives were in contrast to those of the girls who worked in the mills or lived on their own. Although the proportion of girls living at home or in placement varied somewhat over time, invariably a very large proportion had lived in a familial environment and probably had thereby made themselves acceptable candidates for Lancaster by having learned some of the habits considered necessary for women.

Nonetheless, although most entrants lived within families, relatively few of the girls, especially in the earlier years, came from families with two living natural parents. Many had experienced the death of at least one parent. For most of them throughout the first fifty years, death had joined with poverty to disrupt their lives. Between 1856 and 1876 approximately half the entrants had lost either father or mother; in addition, at least one out of eight was orphaned. Beginning with 1880, the number of girls without one or both parents decreased slightly; on the average 40 percent, as compared to the average of 50 percent for the first decades, had lost one parent, and fewer than one in ten were orphaned. These figures show that although four-

Table 6.1
Living backgrounds of Lancaster inmates (in percentages)

Year	Living with both natural parents	Living with one natural parent	Living with other relative	In service	Other, or in institution (e.g., orphanage)
1856	14.6	31.2	6.3	31.3	16.7
1863	15.4	27.7	23.1	15.4	18.4
1870	20.6	38.2	11.8	20.6	8.8
1875	17.9	37.3	9.0	19.4	16.4
1880	35.3	29.4	—	20.6	2.9
1885	38.6	33.4	5.3	7.0	15.8
1890	30.2	32.1	3.8	11.3	7.4
1895	33.8	29.3	12.3	10.8	13.8
1900	37.8	24.5	11.2	12.2	14.2
1905	37.8	36.5	9.5	4.1	12.2

Table 6.2
Lancaster inmates with at least one parent dead (in percentages)

Year	Motherless	Fatherless	Orphaned	Total
1856	30.9	16.5	17.5	64.9
1863	15.9	30.5	17.1	63.4
1870	33.3	19.4	11.1	66.7
1875	23.0	30.8	12.3	66.2
1880	29.4	11.8	5.9	47.1
1885	15.5	25.9	5.2	48.3
1890	17.6	25.5	9.8	52.9
1895	13.6	19.7	10.6	43.9
1900	21.0	21.0	8.0	50.0
1905	16.2	26.2	2.5	45.0

fifths came from some kind of family, during the first thirty years less than 35 percent on the average had two natural living parents; over the next quarter century only slightly over half the entrants came from such families. Thus throughout the full fifty years, at least 50 percent had experienced the devastation accompanying the loss of a parent (see tables 6.1 and 6.2).

For example, Julie O. came to Lancaster a virtual orphan. Julie's mother had died first, leaving Mr. O. alone and destitute with a young, dependent daughter to support. Unable to find work, Mr. O. had emigrated from England. The New World held few employment opportunities for him, and he wandered along the eastern seaboard in search of work. At last he went to sea, leaving his motherless child with "no one to protect and provide for her."

The poverty and job insecurity of Mr. O. was typical of most of the fathers of girls entering Lancaster. Less than one-third of the fathers earned steady incomes; 70 percent of their daughters who entered Lancaster between 1856 and 1905 had experienced little financial stability in early childhood. On the average, only 65 percent of them had living fathers, most of them menial laborers or unemployed. Often the record keepers did not bother to record fathers' employment at all. Many of them were likely unemployed or had deserted their families; I estimate that this was the case for 30 to 50 percent of the girls with living fathers. That is, at least 22 to 33 percent of the whole sample was from impoverished families. Relatively few girls came from families with the resources to take care of every one of its members. Another 35 percent were fatherless, which often meant their families had no sources of income. Although a few mothers were

Table 6.3
Ethnic backgrounds of Lancaster inmates (in percentages)

Year	American	Irish	English speaking (English, Canadian, etc.)	Black American	Non-English speaking (e.g., Russian, Italian)
1856	40	26	19	11	4
1863	66	24	2	7	—
1870	85	—	9	6	—
1875	75	6	11	4	3
1880	73	3	21	3	—
1885	73	2	19	2	4
1890	81	4	11	2	2
1895	67	2	19	11	1
1900	63	3	18	11	5
1905	67	—	12	9	12

able to compensate this loss with low-level employment as laundresses, domestic servants, milliners, or seamstresses, most of this group lived in abject poverty. For these girls and their siblings, the future offered no relief.[12]

In the opening year about half (51 percent) of the entrants were native-born. During the next fifty years the proportion of American-born inmates became greater, eventually accounting for at least three-quarters of the group. After 1856, when 49 percent were foreign-born, these immigrant girls ranged from only 9 percent in 1870 to 26 percent in 1863 and 1900. Among this group of foreigners placed in Lancaster, almost all were English speaking. With the exception of 1905, the last year under study, when half the immigrant girls did not speak English (12 percent of the whole group), the proportion of non-English-speaking entrants averaged only 2 percent a year, ranging from 0 to 5 percent. During the fifty years studied, 6 percent of the inmates were Black Americans. Although this figure is disproportionately high when compared to the number of blacks in the state at that time, the black population was steadily growing as black families migrated from the South. They, like the Irish, were poor and dislocated, and there is no evidence that they were selected for Lancaster any differently than the other girls (see tables 6.3 and 6.4).

However, what is more significant than the girls' birthplaces is the ethnic backgrounds of their parents. A much higher number of parents than of children were foreign-born. Never during the first fifty years

Table 6.4
First languages and birthplaces of Lancaster inmates (in percentages)

Year	English speaking, American-born	English speaking, foreign-born	Non-English speaking, foreign-born
1856	51	45	4
1863	74	26	0
1870	91	9	0
1875	78	19	3
1880	76	24	0
1885	75	21	4
1890	83	15	2
1895	78	21	1
1900	74	21	5
1905	76	12	12

was a majority of either the fathers or mothers American by birth. In contrast to the relatively low percentages for the girls (from 9 to 26 percent), for their parents the percentage born outside the United States ranged from a low of 51 percent (of mothers in 1885) to a high of 82 percent (of fathers in 1856), averaging two-thirds. These figures suggest a certain continuity, as well as some change over time; as the nineteenth century drew to a close, as might be expected more entrants came from non-English-speaking families. Always present, girls with parents who could not understand English became more numerous after Lancaster's first quarter century, so that by 1905 over a third belonged in this group (see table 6.5).

Nonetheless, as in the first year, in later years most of the parents were either Yankee American or Irish. The difference in numbers between the two groups was slight and varied according to immigration patterns. As previously noted, Lancaster seemed to house an almost equal number of Irish Catholic and Protestant American girls. What is important is that most parents spoke English. Also, since the majority of the inmates were increasingly American-born, we can assume that, as in the opening year, assimilation played a role in their being consigned to a state institution. Their parents had been in the country long enough to internalize American social norms, to speak the language of the probate court, and ultimately to know how to use the system to find shelter for their daughters (see table 6.6).

Another descriptive variable, parental character, tells us more about social theories of intemperance than it tells about the girls. Each case record described the parents, and by 1870 space was provided on

Table 6.5
Ethnic backgrounds of parents of Lancaster inmates (in percentages)[a]

Year	American		Irish		English speaking (English, Canadian, etc.)		Black American		Non-English speaking (e.g., Russian, Italian)	
	M	F	M	F	M	F	M	F	M	F
1856	13	13	54	55	15	16	8	5	11	11
1863	21	21	62	58	10	8	7	8	—	4
1870	31	30	47	39	12	24	3	6	6	—
1875	32	29	28	35	13	15	6	6	14	15
1880	40	40	33	33	18	18	3	3	6	6
1885	33	31	32	23	19	28	16	2	—	16
1890	27	27	31	36	13	6	2	2	27	29
1895	25	28	29	27	21	19	10	10	15	16
1900	19	20	19	21	21	17	12	12	28	30
1905	18	19	19	14	17	19	6	10	37	38

a. M = mother; F = father.

Table 6.6
First languages and birthplaces of parents of Lancaster inmates (in percentages)[a]

	English speaking, American-born		English speaking, foreign-born		Non-English speaking, foreign-born	
Year	M	F	M	F	M	F
1856	21	18	69	71	10	11
1863	28	29	72	66	0	3
1870	34	36	60	64	6	0
1875	38	35	48	50	14	15
1880	43	43	51	51	6	6
1885	49	33	44	51	7	16
1890	29	29	44	42	27	29
1895	35	38	50	46	15	16
1900	31	32	41	38	28	30
1905	25	29	36	33	37	38

a. M = mother; F = father.

forms for recording parental "character." In most cases, this meant "temperate" or "intemperate." Occasionally other words, such as "good," "immoral," and "honest," appeared in that space.[13] In the full descriptions under "Remarks" more information along these lines was provided; the most common entry was a reference to the sexual improprieties of the girls' homes. The point of such comments was to excuse the girls from culpability, for although they were considered partly to blame for being "willful," "stubborn," or "keeping low company," they were also partly excused if their parents were "poor and miserable," "very intemperate," "pernicious influences," "undoubtedly severe in their discipline and profane in their language," or "lewd, profane and incompetent." Frequently judgments of the character of the homes, as opposed to the parents, were inserted into the record; these ranged from "excellent," "ordinary," and "perhaps worthy," to "miserable, evil and very low," and simply "very bad, indeed."

Not every entrant's case sheet recorded parental character, as many of the girls were orphaned, half-orphaned, or of "unknown" parentage; also, especially in the earliest records, this subject was simply passed over. When it was included, the fathers were described most often as intemperate. Sometimes there were observations on their work habits and morality: for example, "worthy," "industrious," "hard-working and poor," and "keeps low company"; nonetheless, seldom were they described without some mention of their drinking habits, which seemed to matter more than any other aspect of their lives and personalities.

Although only a few mothers' character assessments are given in the case records, most of those center again on drink. And even more than intemperate fathers, intemperate mothers were subject to harsh words. Considering it was generally thought then that mothers transmit viciousness to children through breastfeeding—"an intemperate mother nurses her babies with alcoholized milk"—it is not surprising that even though there were fewer instances of intemperance reported among mothers than among fathers, the power of contamination was considered stronger and, therefore, more horrifying in the mother. Intemperate women were considered to be acting in defiance of their prescribed familial roles as moral guardians and therefore as agents of social havoc.

The morality of the mothers also mattered greatly to the school. A description of the character of the mother or stepmother appears more often than that of the father in the earliest entries. Many of these women were, like their husbands, "worthy, industrious citizens," struggling to raise their families. On the whole, they were temperate, poor, and respectable—even the Lancaster records recognized them as moral. Yet a mother with good character who kept an "ordinary" home, while more deserving of praise, was given less attention than the woman who "receives men at all hours," "has been known to entertain different men on different nights," "stays out late many evenings," "sometimes does not return to the home for several days," or "fills the house with bad company" and "persons of questionable morals." For while a father "known to have a bad character" exerted an evil influence over his daughter, a mother who "runs around" and "associates with lewd persons" was even worse. Obviously a "disorderly home" whose offspring were "scantily clad," "neglected" and "sorely lacking moral instruction and example" could be blamed only upon the mother. The daughter of a bad mother was to be pitied; the mother was to be censured and condemned.

But a completely "disreputable home" could taint a girl irreversibly. This sentiment, voiced in the school's records during its first decade, was to become more common under the impact of social Darwinism. Intemperate parents were singled out for causing irreversible depravity among children: "A given dose excites the animal nature to powerful and ungovernable activity, and utterly paralyzes reason, conscience and the will. But a smaller dose does the same thing, only in a less degree. It is morally certain that the frequent or the habitual overthrow of the conscience and will, or the habitual *weakening* of them, soon establishes a morbid condition, with morbid appetites and tendencies are surely transmitted to the offpsring."[14]

Table 6.7
Complainants against Lancaster inmates (in percentages)

Year	Family	Good citizen	State officer	Official from other institution, employer (placement), or guardian
1856	40.9	6.1	31.8	21.2
1863	70.3	—	16.2	13.5
1870	50.0	5.6	38.9	5.6
1875	28.8	16.9	54.2	—
1880	77.8	5.6	11.1	5.6
1885	74.1	7.4	14.8	3.7
1890	74.1	—	25.9	—
1895	60.0	—	24.0	16.0
1900	64.7	—	20.6	14.7
1905	73.5	—	20.6	5.9

But, given their poverty and wretched lives, is it any wonder that some parents sought solace in alcohol? Historical research shows that alcohol consumption in the nineteenth century in the United States was generally quite high by modern standards. Alcoholism afflicted countless families, from all classes. However, it was especially widespread in the laboring class; intemperance was quite often linked to poverty and foreignness.[15]

As noted in chapter 5, during the first year it was the girls' own families who had filed the majority of complaints against the entrants to Lancaster. The same holds for the next fifty years as well. This was not unique to Lancaster. Most boys at Westborough were also sent there by their relatives, the most common complaint being "stubbornness."[16] Parents learned early to play along with the state so that their children might obtain some financial and emotional support. After the first year, with the exception of 1875, more than half of the girls were sent to Lancaster on complaints made by their families, which almost always meant their parents. In 1875, 28.8 percent of the complainants were family members: in 1870, 50 percent; and in the other years, between 60 percent and 77.8 percent. It did not matter whether the girl was Irish or Protestant American; desperation, bred by poverty, unemployment, death, or physical uprooting, and the fact that there was but one option available forced Irish families and Protestant American families into the same course of action (see table 6.7).

Parents usually charged their daughters with stubbornness, although occasionally parents complained of their daughters' willful disobedience, idleness, vagrance, and disorderly behavior. The charge of stubbornness was leveled aginst a girl who attended dances, one who frequented a known house of prostitution, one who left home, and one disconcerted by the death of a father. The inference is that parents sent their daughters to Lancaster not because they were stubborn, but out of desperation, as a last recourse. Some parents' complaints specify difficult behavior. In this case, the girls' parents, obviously frightened by their daughters' waywardness, suspected, probably correctly, that the city streets were a temptation that would lead their girls to ruin:

Case 309—She is complained of for stubbornness and disobedience. For two years past, she has been in the habit of leaving home and returning at all hours of the night, and for the last six months, has been absent most of the time, sleeping in alleys and entries, wandering around the streets and saloons with bad boys, and has been in bad company generally. 1863

Case 294—[For] leading an idle, vagrant and vicious life, as was fully proven by the Parents, and the Officer who took her from a wretched Dance Hall corner of Richmond and North Streets, Boston. 1863

Case 864—[She] has been in the habit of visiting the low dance halls of Boston, absenting herself from home for several days and nights at a time. Recently she was absent eight days and nights in succession. She appears to have lost all reverence for her father and to have been the associate of the vicious and abandoned. 1875

Case 888—She is inclined to lewdness: has absented herself from home late evenings, and recently was away three days. She seeks the company of boys, and her father and Mr. Cook, the Chaplain of the Boston Jail, in their testimony, furnished the evidence of this special tendency to lewdness.

The evidence showed constant objection to yield to the wishes and instruction of her father and home government. 1875

Case 892—The mother goes out washing, and after J— left school she made the acquaintance of a bad girl in the neighborhood while her mother was at her work, who led her astray. She has absented herself from home from one to ten days, and refuses to abandon her associates and entirely disregards the directions and wishes of her mother. 1875

Case 1540—This girl ran away from home and came to Boston with M—H—, an I.S. girl, and lived on or near Beach St. a man named R—D— paying the girl's board and he occupying a room in the house. She says she came with M— because she was a friend of hers, and she wanted to accommodate her. [She] claims she has committed no immoral act and does not appear hardened. 1890

In a single-parent or parentless home, it was hoped that Lancaster would oversee daughters in the way no longer possible at home.

Case 307—Her Father is dead, her Mother is a neat and industrious woman of considerable refinement and tender feeling, supporting herself by vestmaking. She says she is unable to control the temper of her little girl. This seems to be her only fault, she has no vicious tendencies, is truthful and has always attended Sabbath School. 1863

Case 885—B—'s parents do not live together. The mother is an easy, shiftless kind of a person, and B— is beyond her control and seems determined to have her own way. She has been away to Boston three times of late, and remained over night, and frequents places of bad repute. One time she was gone a week, and was then found at the Albany Depot, in company with a man forty years of age, waiting for the 3 P.M. train for New York where she was going with him. She refused to go home. Swears and fights her sister. Is very resolute, determined and high-tempered. "Will need watching or she will escape." 1875

Since for many parents one purpose of the public school was to oversee children, a daughter's failure to attend school prompted her parents to turn to Lancaster as the alternative institutional solution:

Case 299—She has been in the Catholic School for a time, and latterly with her Mother, who enters complaint against her for stubbornness and truancy, as being unwilling to work out, and so wilful as it [sic] beyond her control. 1863

Case 305—She is complained of for truancy from school, for being out late at night—even four nights in succession. The week previous to her coming here, she was out in company of two wild girls in the Camp at Readville. 1863

The officers and trustees were fully aware of this complicity. In fact, the trustees' report of 1862 used this dumping of responsibility onto the shoulders of the state as an excuse for some of their own failures. They pointed the finger of accusation at the parents: "If any portion of the inmates fail to become reformed, the failure is too often attributed to a defect in the system, or its improper management; but in making up a verdict, it should be borne in mind that the subjects turned over to us have nearly all been pronounced *ungovernable, unmanageable* by their parents and their friends at home. This being the fact, can it reasonably be expected that *all these* shall be thoroughly purified and turned out models of excellence and propriety?"[17]

Although the majority of the complaints originated with the family, state commitment also brought many girls to Lancaster. The percentage of girls committed due to state complaints fluctuated in the first thirty years, but it always remained second to the family's, except in 1875, when it was responsible for bringing 54.2 percent of the girls into the school. For 1880, however, the state's role in committing girls through the court was a meager 11.1 percent. The percentage of state interventions remained at a low level, roughly 20 to 25 percent, from 1893 through 1905.

During Lancaster's first thirty years, well-meaning neighbors and other do-gooders were instrumental in placing approximately 7 percent of the girls. This held true, however, only until 1886, at which time civic involvement was assumed by the various jurisdictional agents, such as school officials and philanthropic managers.

It appears that some extrafamilial complainants, including policemen, neighbors, teachers, ministers, and officers of the state, intervened with the intent to save girls by separating them from their parents: "Among the girls who have proved most satisfactory have been several who have been carefully watched by private societies or guardians, and who, on proving unmanageable and in danger were committed . . . at the critical moment, before their lives had become tainted by actual vice."[18] The message from the reports seems to be that committing a potentially depraved girl to Lancaster was looked on as a charitable and responsible act. This is also the likeliest interpretation of instances of almshouses or the Shakers committing one of their charges to Lancaster.

That the majority of the complainants were family members undermines two popular assumptions: first, that reform schools represented a malevolent plot of the state to take poor girls away from their families by legislative sanction; and second, that Irish Catholic parents bitterly opposed the admittance of their children to Protestant state institutions. Dickensian images of the heartless State hauling off weeping, protesting children from their humble, helpless parents stir our emotions but are historically inaccurate. And while Catholic parents at the outset did exhibit great hostility to Protestant institutions, especially those for the young, which they recognized as attempts to undermine their own religious or ethnic identities, nevertheless they brought their girls to Lancaster.[19]

The probate court could order a girl to Lancaster. There were laws regulating criminal behavior of minors as there were for adults. There were also status offenses specifically applicable to children. Two statutes allowed for sentencing to Lancaster for crimes against morality. According to Public Statutes Chapter 89, Section 25, a girl charged with "leading an idle, vagrant or vicious life" could be so sentenced. Similarly, Chapter 207, Section 29, allowed "stubborn" children to be labeled guilty juvenile offenders, the sentence for which was reform school. Of course, crimes falling into the adult category, for example, larceny and assault, were also grounds for sending a child to reform school.[20] The judge's discretion was critical in cases of the last type; all depended on whether, in the judge's view, jail or reform school was the soundest solution.

As we have seen, most of the girls brought into probate court, whether by parents or officials, were charged with crimes against morality, that is, behavorial crimes. Consistently, from the first year until the turn of the century, over three-quarters of Lancaster's entrants were so charged. With a few exceptions, the rest of the girls were charged with stealing—usually a small sum of money or an item of clothing—that is, property crimes. The proportion of property crimes to behavorial crimes remained more or less constant over the fifty years studied, approximately one to four. The lowest percentage of girls entering for property crimes was 13.8 percent, recorded in 1905, with the next lowest being 14.7 percent, in 1895. The highest percentage was 24 percent, in 1900, with 22.2 percent and 22.1 percent in 1870 and 1875, respectively. During, and only during, the first two decades of Lancaster, a very small number, about 2 percent, of the girls had been charged with assault or other crimes involving a victim, usually a parent or guardian. But being so few in number, crimes of violence do not affect overall observations, which will concentrate therefore on property and behavorial crimes.

Stubbornness was by far the most frequent complaint brought against the girls from 1856 to 1905. From 39.7 percent (1875) to 61.1 percent (1870), the average being 55 percent, of the inmates were so charged during this period. As indicated, this was a catchall, the formula by which most young and dependent girls were sent away. But not all stubborn daughters were alike. Some were simply deprived, children for whom relief was sought. Others were ungoverned, in danger of falling into the criminal class, children who (roughly in descending order of frequency) stayed out nights, kept "bad men company" (both of which activities often meant or implied having sexual relations with men), refused to obey parents, frequented places likely to lead into criminal behavior (for example, liquor halls and houses of prostitution), ran away from home, lied and stole, consorted with "bad" and "low" women, or ran away from placement.

The next five largest categories of behavorial crime, according to the average percentage of the whole group over time charged with that particular offense, were idleness and viciousness, including disorderliness, 10.6 percent; wantonness, lewdness and lasciviousness, 4.6 percent; vagrancy, 3.6 percent; fornication, 2.6 percent; and drunkenness and disorderliness, 1.1 percent. Other charges grouped together as morality transgressions, each contributing less than 1 percent to the total over time, were deceitful actions, disturbing the peace, truancy, and running away from home (see table 6.8).

Reading the descriptions of these "crimes" tells us more about what was considered proper for nineteenth-century girls than about the actual charges brought against Lancaster's entrants. To determine the real reasons why girls were sentenced to Lancaster, it will be necessary to analyze more closely the charges by which they were sentenced. Such an analysis rests on the observation that the girls so charged were of five types: those who committed property crimes; those who lacked a home; those in want of moral guardianship; those who indulged in immoral, that is, sexual, activity; and those in need of protection from physical abuse.

For girls of the first type, that is, girls charged with property crimes, the crimes were almost always petty larceny. The charges were usually filed by the police or another state agency rather than by parents and stemmed from instances of proven criminal behavior. Most of the larceny, however, consisted of stealing things of little value: "a shawl belonging to Mrs. D—," "the sum of $3.00 taken from a counter in the store of a Chinaman," "a dress or other articles of clothing from a boarding house." Invariably the girl's criminality stemmed from a minor offense; crimes of greater magnitude were punished more severely than by a sentence to a reform school—for instance, by commital to Sherborn Prison.[21] Minor thefts of clothes or small sums of money entitled a girl to a second chance; such thieves were appropriate candidates for the Lancaster program, whereas larceny on a greater scale signaled an irreversible criminal tendency, and therefore unsuitability for rehabilitation by the school.

What about the great majority of girls who had not been judged guilty of property crimes? The charges by which they were brought to probate court divide them into the following four types: those lacking a home; those in need of moral guardianship; those who were immoral; those in need of physical protection. It is important to reiterate that this conclusion comes from analyzing the case record, not from cataloguing the official complaints. In fact, it is one of the major findings of this study that a close examination of the case records

Table 6.8
Girls admitted to Lancaster by categories of complaints (in percentages)

Year	Assault and battery	Larceny	Property damage	Stubborn	Idle and vicious, disorderly behavior	Wanton, lewd, and lascivious	Vagrancy	Fornication	Drunkenness	Miscellaneous: truancy, beggary, deceit, runaway
1856	2.0	19.2	—	22.2	21.2	10.1	9.1	—	1.0	15.1
1863	2.5	20.3	—	46.8	12.7	1.3	2.5	—	1.3	12.7
1870	—	22.3	—	61.1	11.1	2.8	2.8	—	—	—
1875	1.5	20.6	1.5	39.7	25.0	1.5	7.4	2.9	—	—
1880	—	20.6	—	58.8	8.8	8.8	2.9	—	—	—
1885	—	15.8	—	57.9	5.3	8.8	8.8	1.8	1.8	—
1890	—	18.5	1.9	59.3	1.9	9.3	1.9	5.6	1.9	—
1895	—	17.6	—	48.5	19.1	1.5	4.4	4.4	2.9	1.5
1900	—	24.0	—	61.0	4.0	2.0	1.0	4.0	1.0	3.0
1905	—	13.8	—	60.9	6.9	5.7	1.1	4.6	1.1	5.7

shows that frequently a reported charge was neither the immediate nor factual cause of committal. Thus three girls committed on identical charges, such as "disobedience" or "stubbornness," may have been committed for three different reasons. This is explained by the laws governing placement at the school. Only certain charges allowed a girl to be committed; parents and the state used those charges even when evidence indicated that other reasons lay behind the useful official complaint. For instance, "stubbornness" appeared often in the records of a girl whose real fault was wantonness. A parent was unlikely to declare publicly that a daughter was wanton but very likely to assert that she was stubborn. Also, Lancaster itself was not inclined to accept thoroughly bad, that is, lewd, girls.

For girls of the second type, that is, girls for whom the only alternative to the family situation was confinement in a state institution, although the charge brought against them was never "in need of a home," the school records indicate that this was often precisely the case. Given the desperation and difficulties of most of the girls' families, such a finding is not surprising. For an early example, consider the case of an orphan in 1863 who had been "without any parental influence for many years." Having been shuffled around to "a good number of places," including the Shakers, but never staying long at any, it is no surprise that she "seemed eager to come to the school." Two 1875 entrants may also be used as examples. One entry form from February of that year reads: "The mother of C— died last Dec. and since that time she has been disobedient and unmanageable. She has left several times without permission, going to Boston; has no home to speak of. . . . She is very impertinent, but is intelligent and has kind feelings." Obviously upset by her mother's death, this girl was committed by her father, a laborer of "good" character who did not know what else to do with her. A few months later another girl came to the reform school, also without an alternative. Having been "taken from school last January by her mother under the claim her services were needed at home," this entrant had been found wandering the streets alone. The record labeled her as "leading a vagrant and vicious life," but her story is that of a poor girl doing "extremely well in school" until her family pulled her out and left her begging for food on the streets. Like many girls, her real crime was homelessness. A final example from 1890 shows clearly that certain entrants probably found greater stability at Lancaster than they ever had with their families: "This girl's father is a drunkard her mother a bad low woman who does not live with her husband: girl has had no home since she was eleven years old: has been working at the almsh. [sic] for $1.00 per week: was disobedient: her parents cannot be found."

Girls of the third type had homes, but because their homes lacked moral guidance, they were deemed in immediate danger of falling. For instance, Jane Ellen F. had a home but was brought to the school in 1863 because "she was so getting beyond control that it was only a question of time, relative to her ruin." In other words, she had not yet committed a misdemeanor, but the fear based on her misbehavior that she might soon fall led to her sentence to the state reform school. Another case also testifies to the role of moral guardian played by the school. A foundling was sent to it on charges of "stubbornness and disobedience" brought by both her adopted mother and a court official. Her record acknowledges openly that the school was not to punish but to prevent wrongdoing:

> Has been brought up by [her adopted parents] tenderly as an only child, and very dearly loved by them, and until within a few months past, was to them all they could wish, except she was not always truthful. . . . still she has been a great favorite with them.
>
> They recently discovered that she has lied to them and learned facts which lead them to believe she is in danger and that the only way to save her is to remove her for a time, at least, from temptation.

Girls of the fourth type were thought to need more than moral guidance. They needed isolation from the streets and their companions because they had already sinned, that is, were "unchaste." A fairly large number of girls were brought to the state reform school for having consorted with men. Unlike the third type of girls, who were merely in danger of forsaking virtue, girls of this type had already succumbed to temptation; they needed to be prevented from further transgressions. Nonetheless, only a few girls were formally charged with fornication or lewd and lascivious behavior. A larger number were sentenced on lesser charges, most often stubbornness, even though "loose habits and morals" were the real reasons for the complaint. An early example is the case of Dominique S., sent to the school for larceny in 1875. Her record substantiates the original complaint but gives evidence of the underlying reasons: "This girl stole a pair of shoes from C— D— and has frequented houses of ill fame in Boston." Clearly the latter comment gave the real cause for her incarceration, not the former. Ten years later, Mary T. entered for stubbornness under similar circumstances. In this case, the record acknowledges the falsity of the charge: "After leaving school [Mary] worked for a month in Porter's Shoe Shop in Lynn—then going with bad company without her Father's knowledge—she was enticed into lewdness and for about three months this has been going on when the Fa. was informed and he at once complained of her. When on the seventh of January she was brought before the court and placed on probation for two years and then not doing any better she was committed to this school—but on the charge of *Stubbornness.*"

Evidence from the general remarks of the individual cases indicates a rather high incidence of this type of case, particularly in the last quarter of the nineteenth century. Certainly more "lewd and lascivious" girls—which may be interpreted in the twentieth century as sexually active girls—came than the official records would indicate. The following four cases from 1885 (cases 1289, 864, 2328, and 1290) document this point. All four girls entered this year on the complaint of "stubbornness," two by parents, one by a stepmother and an officer, and one by neighbors. The girls were of American, Irish, English, and French parentage, between 13 and 15 years of age.

Case 1289—Last summer this girl worked in a place on Waltham St. but left and did housework for her Mo. but of late has kept bad company and admits having had criminal intercourse with several men. 1865

Case 864—This girl has been working in Lancaster's shop of Lynn till Mch 1st when she was persuaded to go into a house of ill fame on Lowell St. Boston and remained there till her arrest. 1875

Case 2328—Has been in a house of ill fame on Prospect St. Boston for quite a while—is evidently a hard girl and her appearance is against her. 1900

Case 1290—She was complained of by the neighbors who charged her with the crime of cohabiting with different men in a barn—she admitted the charge—and said it had been occurring for a long time. 1885

This pattern continued, as more girls accepted by the school gave evidence of "moral failings" more serious than those of the written complaint. In 1890 Ellen V. entered Lancaster, having appeared before the court "on a charge of stubbornness, but this is not her worst fault. She was arrested in bed with two other young girls and a young man. . . ." Similarly, Jean R. found herself at Lancaster in March of 1895 for being an "Idle and Disorderly Person." What had she done to earn that label? "This girl was arrested in a shop with three men. She visits fruit and other shops kept by Italians, also houses of ill fame, is immoral, out all night, is disorderly on the street, keeps disreputable company, drinks, etc."

The above charges of idleness and disorderliness covered up the deeper sin of visiting various shops, probably for immoral purposes. Ellen, Jean, and others like them did not fit neatly into the reformist vision of pliable, tender girls imperiled by the evil temptations of the city. Rather, these girls had, it seemed, embraced immorality. Such examples must have caused consternation among their wardens. It was one thing to protect a child from contamination; it was quite another thing to shelter one already turned wanton. In the 1884 Annual Report the superintendent lamented the rise in immoral behavior—while making clear it was understood that Lancaster's role went far beyond dealing with stubborn girls:

> The old complaint of "stubbornness" is still a frequent one, and covers a "multitude of sins" of which stubbornness is the very least. . . . By far the larger number of girls are really sent to the school for most serious offences against morality. It cannot be doubted that the graver offences to which allusion has been made are increasing, and that the school as a check to an immoral career, and an opportunity for training and influence which may permanently change the life and character is now more than ever needed.[22]

For the fifth type of Lancaster girl, the need was for physical protection, for shelter from physical abuse, especially by relatives. One 1863 entrant, whose "mother says the girl is beyond control," was the victim of incest by her stepfather, who by this time was in the House of Correction. The record reads, "[We] are pained to know that the Father has held as intimate relations with her, as with her Mother." Another entrant, a thirteen-year-old who arrived in 1875, was undoubtedly also a victim of sexual abuse. Charged with fornication, Eileen C. had been living with a younger sister in a one-room tenement also occupied by an older sister, her older sister's husband, and their baby. The brother-in-law was Eileen's "partner in guilt." Beneath the chaste language of these and other records lie untold stories of forced incest and abuse. Susan K., another example from 1885, was charged with larceny. The record gives the barest outline of a truly pitiful story. This twelve-year-old had taken "from the house of her aunt in Dalton a small waggon [sic] to draw her clothes in when she ran away." Upon further reading, one can readily understand why the young child attempted to run away. Sentenced ostensibly for this supposed theft of her aunt's property, she had "been terribly abused by her mother and compelled to submit to lewd men on numerous occasions." Similarly, another 1885 entrant, whose "father is now in the House of Correction for abusing her," was charged with stubbornness and placed at the school. A girl committed five years later on the same complaint provides one more example of how part of Lancaster's role as it evolved was to protect daughters from their violent parents. In this case "the mother drinks and abuses the girl. About a year ago the girl was enticed by her father into a disreputable house. Both parents were very severe with her and, she states, used her for lewd purposes."

In summary, the recorded complaints tell us not only about the Lancaster girls but about the use and misuse of the courts to obtain their entry into Lancaster. They tell us that there were five general reasons, often unrelated to the formal complaints, for sentencing girls to Lancaster: to punish petty larceny; to supply a home; to effect moral salvation; to prevent further "lewd" acts; and to provide protection from physical abuse. In every case the need to alleviate some form of deprivation was apparent. The desperation and the wretched poverty of most of the families whose daughters ended up at the school shines through the descriptions of both the girls and the acts of which they were accused. Most of the girls were sent to reform school ultimately because of poverty and its consequences. Thus nearly all of the girls accused of larceny, as well as the girls sent to Lancaster for any of the four charges that shared the label "morality offense," had experienced hardship prior to arrival at the school. Sometimes there was more than one reason for a sentence, as this example of a daughter of temperate religious parents indicates: "Is not an immoral girl, is not considered under the average in intellect. The home is poor. The mother and girl have been stealing together. The mother has been sentenced for 3 months. The father is unbalanced." Another case underscores the multiplicity of causes that combined to sentence a girl—not only to condemn her but to protect her. Ellen L. had stolen money, was in want of a proper home environment, was well on her way to ruin, and furthermore was the victim of abuse:

> She was committed to us on complaint of Mary E. Haley, for having stolen goods from her, to the value of $25.00. The girl pleads guilty, but says she did it at the command of her mother, who took the money as soon as it was stolen and the mother is now in Jail for the offence. Her Parents are miserably intemperate, quarrelling and abusing each other. [Ellen] says she has often been beaten by her father when he was intoxicated, for trying to help her mother against him. The girl although so young, has been seen herself to be intoxicated.

The charges against the girls varied, but, as all of the above case records document, the actual motives for confinement varied even more. On the whole, the girls in the school between 1856 and 1905 were sent there for one or a combination of the five reasons given. As is also clear from the data, both families and the state were sincere in their endeavor to save the girls. Admittance was perceived as a chance for betterment and beneficial training. Not suprisingly, then, did parents or other relatives send girls to the school in hopes that they would receive a good home. The aunt of Julie S., for instance, asked that the child be readmitted to the school after her discharge, since "she needs a good home where she will receive instruction and be controlled." The aunt's application "was refused, under the law"; unfortunately, it was then, as it is now, the case that the need and demand for refuge such as that offered by the state reform school were greater than that provided.

School officers were aware that parents regarded Lancaster as a guardian as well as a reform institution, and all interested parties—state, school, and parents—were willing to fuse status offenses and specifically criminal acts under such general rubrics as stubbornness in order to make it possible for girls to enter Lancaster.

Lancaster's original purpose had been to act as a surrogate home for young girls whose only crimes were behavorial and petty criminal offenses. But, as we have seen, some of the charges were cover-ups for somewhat more adult activities, and it was not long before innocent children were rare among the residents at the state reform school. Concurrently, the average age of the Lancaster girls went up. Indeed, although the age of admission to Lancaster had been legally established at its founding at between 7 and 16, from the very beginning only a few Lancaster girls were under 12, and most of them were pubescent. The largest group by far was composed of those between 14 and 15. The mean age of the entrants rose steadily over the period studied: 12 years, 9 months in 1856; 13 years, 9 months by 1870; 14 years, 9 months by 1890; and 15 years, 8 months in 1905. A further breakdown into age groups shows even more clearly that the school increasingly accepted older girls. In the youngest group, a noticeable drop in numbers started after the very first year, when 14.6 percent of the girls were between 7 and 10. Not a single 7-year-old was recorded in the period under study after that year, and not one 8-year-old after 1870. Even 9-year-olds were absent after 1875. In 1880 a mere 5.9 percent of the entrants were 10. After that year, only a few so young passed through Lancaster's gates; these girls were the few 10- and 11-year-olds no longer sent to Monson State Primary School, which closed in 1895. Similarly, girls aged 11 to 13, who had accounted for two-fifths of the first several years' classes, also started dropping out of the picture after 1863. Their representation among

Table 6.9
Entrance ages of girls sent to Lancaster, by age groups (in percentages)

	Age group				
Year	7–10	11–13	14–15	16–17	Mean age
1856	14.6	39.2	42.3	4.1	12.8
1863	12.3	39.2	48.7	—	12.9
1870	5.6	22.3	72.2	—	13.8
1875	4.4	26.5	44.1	25.0	14.1
1880	5.9	17.6	53	23.5	14.3
1885	—	24.1	55.2	20.6	14.4
1890	—	13.2	56.6	30.2	14.9
1895	2.9	24.9	39.7	32.4	14.4
1900	1.0	26.0	53	20.0	14.3
1905	—	16.2	59.2	24.5	15.8

the entrants fluctuated for the duration of the period between a low of 13.2 percent in 1890 and a high of 26.5 percent in 1875. Fourteen- and 15-year-olds always formed a large part of each year's class, on the average making up a little more than half of the entrants. Their relative size did increase somewhat over time from the low of 42.3 percent.

This remarkable change occurred in a comparatively short time span. Although a few 16-year-olds had been accepted the first year, none entered in 1863 or 1870. It is critically important, however, to our research that starting with 1875 this group no longer constituted a tiny minority; it had become a noticeably large part of the Lancaster community. From that year on until 1905, 20 to 32.4 percent of entrants were 16- and 17-year-olds, thus comprising a substantial proportion of the school population. From the first year, when girls 14 and over made up less than half of the school population, their numbers steadily increased, so that by 1905, 83.7 percent of the entering girls belonged in that age group. The rapid rise in the number of older girls unbalanced the proportion of older to younger. The school that had started as a surrogate family for defenseless girls evolved rather quickly into an alternative reformatory for unmanageable young women (see table 6.9).

The age mix hoped for reminiscent of that in private families had not prevailed for very long. This steady increase in age confused the officers of the school. And, as we shall see, it had a tremendous impact on its actual program. Along with this age increase came a different kind of girl; in the view of those who reported, she was harder, less dependent, and more depraved. The founders of the school had counted on a different class of girls. They had not counted on legislative interference at the instigation of the Board of State Charities. Instead of poor, dependent waifs who moved them to tenderness, the school's officers were receiving girls who were older, tougher, less appealing. Proportionately fewer young girls were arriving to soften the older girls and reinforce the family atmosphere. But more striking to the officers was the absence of appealing, affectionate, prepubescent girls to pull at their heartstrings. The officers at Lancaster resented this age change as an interference with their experiment, and they regarded the 1870 acts, discussed earlier, and the opening of other institutions as the major causes of Lancaster's problems. They blamed state intervention, not their program; in the face of increasing difficulties, they clung to the idea of the family-style reform school as the solution for social problems for girls.

Nevertheless, girls attending Lancaster from 1856 to 1905 for the most part could be counted by the school's officers as successes. After leaving the school, the overwhelming majority, 75.4 percent, went to live in a family grouping—with parents (35 percent), with spouses (17.4 percent), or in placement (23 percent)—rather than on the streets or in other institutions. Obviously, the administrators of the school could be proud of this record, since such a large number achieved what had been the initial goal: life with a family. (It should be noted, however, that a girl's return to her own home did not necessarily signify the school's success—especially if conditions at home had not changed.) A few of the girls, 5 percent, ended up on their own. Most of them worked at menial jobs. The remaining inmates, 19.6 percent of the total, were either institutionalized in jails, asylums, or in hospitals; or died.[23]

This pattern remained constant for the first forty years of the school. However, two critical changes in this trend occurred after 1890. First, there was a marked decrease in the number of girls returning to their parental families, particularly among the oldest girls, of whom only 16.4 percent returned to live with their parents. Second, there was a noticeable increase in the transfer of girls from Lancaster to other institutions. Whereas only 5.3 percent of the 1895 group were transferred, 13 percent of the 1900 group and 18.2 percent of the 1905 group were. Most of them were sent to the Sherborn Reformatory or the Home for the Feeble-Minded (see table 6.10).

The pattern emerging from these first follow-ups held true in later studies by the administrators at the school; that is, most girls remained living within a family context, although the conjugal family usually

Table 6.10
Living situations of inmates immediately following indenture (in percentages)

Year	No mention	Return to family	Marriage	Placement in service	Living with friends or on own	Living in institution (Lancaster or other)
1856	4.7	25.6	33.7	10.5	18.6	7.0
1863	1.3	59.7	2.6	18.2	11.7	6.5
1870	5.9	50	14.7	17.6	2.9	8.8
1875	7.8	28.1	12.5	25	9.4	17.2
1880	6.7	33.3	20	33.3	—	6.7
1885	2.6	41	15.4	12.8	—	28.2
1890	—	36.6	24.4	12.2	4.9	22.0
1895	6	29.8	14	42.1	8.8	5.3
1900	—	34.5	19	21.4	3.6	15.5
1905	—	16.4	12.7	41.8	—	29.1

replaced the parental. Of the three-quarters discussed, by the time of the last follow-up most were living with husbands in homes of their own. A small number of girls still lived and worked alone, and a substantial minority had been confined in institutions elsewhere. On the whole, there was little to indicate that many were living dissolute lives; those most susceptible were probably out of temptation's way, by virtue of their incarceration in other institutions.

The legislature had upset the careful organization of the school by allowing older and hardened girls to enter. Furthermore, parents in the commonwealth added to Lancaster's burden of functions by manipulating the system of entrance procedure; by claiming that their daughters were uncontrollable, they obtained for them a free, safe, secure home. These unanticipated interferences forced the school to change direction and change the program to fit the needs as they emerged. The problems that had led to the establishment of the school could not be wholly solved through the efforts of a single institution. Lancaster took its place in the array of state machinery set up to counteract or alleviate the pressures brought into the commonwealth by industrialization, urbanization, and growth.

Did Lancaster redirect the girls? Would they have fallen into ruin without it? Or would they have led "respectable" lives in any case? In other words, was Lancaster a success? It is hard to say. What can be said is that whatever successes were claimed for the Lancaster of 1905 were being claimed for an institution fundamentally different from the Lancaster of 1856.

7

The Twilight of a Dream

It has been stated in a former report that there would be injustice in consigning to prison, without a trial at Lancaster, many girls who seem so initiated in vice as to be almost hopeless cases. The same opinion is maintained now, and that, useless as it often seems to expect the reform of such at Lancaster, there must be no hopelessness with those who work for them.

Annual Report, State Industrial School for Girls, 1884

It is the policy of the Trustees to place the girls in country homes, as best suited to them when they first leave the school, offering less excitement and less temptation than the larger towns and cities, and the theory is undoubtedly correct; but in fact there are few places so small as to be free of objectionable companions, and some of the most lamentable cases of return to wrong-doing have been in country villages, where worthless, idle young men, too apt to infest such communities, have been all too ready to lead the girls into forbidden paths. Nor are the cases unknown where the girls have been misled by members of the very family in which they lived, and who were pledged to protect them, and, in the words of the circular they receive with them, "to exercise a kind parental oversight and watchful care over them, with judicious and proper restraint."

Annual Report, State Industrial School for Girls, 1884

In these reports the Trustees of the Massachusetts School for the Feeble-Minded in their report of 1885, have frequently called attention to the necessity for making provision for the protection of adult female idiots. The danger of their becoming the victims of the lust of profligate men is too apparent to require more than mere mention. Not only should the imbecile woman be protected for her own sake, but we must guard against the curse of her offspring. Idiocy and imbecility depend to a large degree upon hereditary and pre-natal causes.

Annual Report, State Industrial School for Girls, 1887

Systematic classification of inmates at Lancaster by age and by crime, a firmly entrenched policy by 1885, formally completed the winnowing out process begun by legislative acts and institution building in the early 1870s and marked a reversal of the mid-century reformist vision. Despite these changes, however, neither reformers nor the state came to regard Lancaster as unnecessary. In fact, many social architects now considered it more coherent, and therefore more manageable, than before. By legislative alteration of its structure and program, Lancaster had been assured a place in the network of the Commonwealth's institutions for the poor and dependent. Indeed, the legislative and administrative changes imposed on Lancaster were part of a more general national move toward consolidation, rationalization, and systematization in the postwar era. A review of the process by which Lancaster came to be absorbed in a new institutional bureaucracy will complete this portrait of the first half-century of the State Industrial School for Girls.

Lancaster's initial program, based on the optimistic assumption that all girls could be trained and rehabilitated to live as happy and respectable women, was three fold: religious instruction, domestic training, and common schooling—all to take place in a family-style environment. Lancaster's early administration took great pride in the educational achievements of its students: "Some of our girls can hardly be excelled in reading in any of our common schools; the same is true of their spelling and penmanship. . . . a visitor listening to their general exercises in mental arithmetic, could scarcely keep pace with them. . . ."[1] Even as late as the twelfth Annual Report, the trustees continued to express pride in their program and quoted the accolades heaped upon Lancaster by the commissioners of the Prison Association of New York to the New York State legislature in 1867: "If we might venture among so many excellent institutions to single out any that seem to us to possess an excellence superior to others, we could not hesitate to name the Reform Schools of Massachusetts; and of those we should feel as little hesitation in pronouncing first among its peers, the Industrial Girls at Lancaster."[2]

Further, Lancaster's trustees continued to adhere, at least publicly, to their commitment to family-style reform. And to the extent that Lancaster served as a model for other reform efforts throughout the nation, the trustees had additional reason to claim success.[3] It was this self-congratulatory spirit that prompted the trustees to oppose at first the Howe-Sanborn report; in fact, as late as 1867, the trustees in their outline of the purpose of and program at Lancaster report that "the graded system is not attempted, girls of all ages and degrees of moral and intellectual culture being associated in each house."[4]

Lancaster's early administration also took pride in its domestic training program. But here it acknowledged difficulties, particularly with the system of indenture, which was geared to producing domestic servants. Since there was, at least in theory, a demand for servants,[5] this development was unexpected and resulted in an effort in 1861 to reassess the school's training program. In 1868 the curriculum was changed to widen the variety of housekeeping skills taught and to upgrade them, in the hope, as the trustees put it, that "[the girls would] readily find safe and respectable homes, liberal wages and kind friends." In the thirteenth Annual Report, 1868, the trustees insisted that the new curriculum would retain the best of the original program and also enrich the life prospects of their inmates: "This plan offers no interruption to their obtaining a good common school education, but on the contrary will give them greater cause for perseverance, greater trust and confidence in their own ability and power, and although their future position may be humble, still it will be respectable and may become one of confidence, trust and affection."[6]

Although domesticity had always been, at bottom, the primary objective of Lancaster's program, the increased stress on domestic training was now explicitly stated and justified as that aspect most relevant to the attainment of true womanhood. The details of this report read as a general social prescription for the happy lives of women: "Almost every woman is destined to have a leading or subordinate part in the management of a family. Preparation for the ready and intelligent performance of household duties, the lowest as well as the highest, is therefore, of the first importance. Now, as perfect cleanliness is essential to health of body and of mind and to cheerfulness, all the arts of washing and scouring should be early learnt and practised, so as to form and fix the habit of doing them well, thoroughly, rapidly, and willingly."[7] The next report, 1869, lists in detail the chores most essential for the fulfillment of the girl's natural role leading to her contentment: "These arts should include not only the washing of tables and dishes, but the scouring of floors, stairs, windows and walls, and of clothes, and especially of bed-clothes, and bedsteads. These duties occur every day in every family. They should, therefore, be done methodically, and the habit of method and order should be insisted upon amongst the most important attainments."[8]

These sentiments express explicitly just how strongly a girl's salvation was linked to her assimilation of prescribed female virtues. In spite of changes in the outside world and an expanded jobs market for

Table 7.1
Major occupations in which women were found: 1850

Occupation	Number	Percentage of total listed
Domestic service	330,000	58.3
Clothing	62,000	11.0
Cotton textiles	59,000	10.4
Teaching	55,000	9.7
Shoes	33,000	5.8
Wool	19,000	3.4
Hats	8,000	1.4
Total	566,000	100

Source: Stanley Lebergott, *Manpower in Economic Growth: The American Record since 1800*. New York: McGraw-Hill, 1964, p. 520. Copyright 1964 by McGraw-Hill Book Company. Reprinted with permission.

women, the reformation of potentially wanton young girls continued in a most conservative vein. Regardless of a commitment to complete reformation, it was still believed that poor and wayward girls were best rehabilitated by remaining in positions of maximum public scrutiny and within a supervised domestic context. The same reformers who praised the "old-fashioned" way also inadvertently voiced their skepticism that any woman could retain her respectability while living and working on her own. As these excerpts suggest, training a student to be a domestic fulfilled several goals at once. She would learn how to run a household; she would gain experience while at the school—thereby keeping costs down and contributing to its functioning; she would assume a role considered proper for females although working; and, furthermore, she would acquire salable skills within a fairly limited job market (see tables 7.1 and 7.2).

The trustees and administrators obviously knew that employment in occupations other than service, such as teaching, clerking, and factory work, was increasingly available to women. But they had reasons for their focus. First, there was a market for Lancaster girls in service. Since most of them were English speaking and native-born—and were already trained in domestic chores—they were considered lucky finds in an age when Eastern and Southern European immigrants were unwelcome in native middle-class homes. At this time there was a "servant problem," as contemporary novels, magazines, and diaries of ladies indicate. David M. Katzman's study of domestic service, *Seven Days a Week*, documents this perpetual employer lament about the lack of desirable servants. He quotes a *Good Housekeeping Magazine* article entitled "Our Hetty" written by a middle-class matron: "Thor-

Table 7.2
Female servants and laundresses per 1,000 families

	1880		1900		1920	
	Servants	Laundresses	Servants	Laundresses	Servants	Laundresses
Boston	219	20	167	25	79	8
Rest of Massachusetts	109		104	12	46	4
Buffalo	145	12	118	15	47	8
New York City[a]	188	29	141	22	66	8
Rest of New York	113		87	11	43	8
Detroit	147	14	115	17	35	6
Rest of Michigan	74		70	6	28	6
Denver	109	18	101	20	50	8
Rest of Colorado	34		42	11	23	7
Baltimore	212	65	159	74	91	48
Rest of Maryland	152		115	20	60	27
Atlanta	331	233	214	238	136	113
Rest of Georgia	85		67	60	53	54
New Orleans	206	80	157	101	121	86
Rest of Louisiana	65		59	34	56	32

Source: Compilation of data from the 10th, 12th, and 14th national censuses (1880, 1900, and 1920, respectively). (See David Katzman, *Seven Days a Week: Women and Domestic Service in Industrializing America*, p. 286.)
a. As of 1880, Brooklyn is included in New York City.

oughly competent girls for general housework are not to be had for love or money in some places. Girls rush into stores and shops as salesladies and go half-starved, half-clothed, and half-housed, and wear themselves out in soul and body rather than degrade themselves by going out as servants."[9] Second, domestic service, unlike other female occupations, provided the home environment thought essential for continuing Lancaster's work of redemption: "We think work of this kind better and safer for them than a trade, because housework in a private family is the only life that affords for them sufficient protection after they leave the school. Allowing a girl to board, and work in a shop or factory, gives a freedom which they would too often abuse."[10]

However, not all householders would tolerate the special problems brought into their homes by the Lancaster girls or undergo the demanding complications of indenture. The job market was thus reduced and placement became difficult. Marcus Ames, Lancaster's superintendent from 1861 to 1875, neglected to investigate the true reasons for fewer families looking to take girls into their homes. He did not examine the current employment criteria, but nostalgically looked back to the earlier part of the century as the "good old days" when girls had been readily accommodated into the homes of the privileged.

Carol S. Lasser has found in her research on Salem Female Charities that as early as 1837 the relations between female domestics and sponsors had changed "to resemble that of employer and employee." Because of this change in social relations, the Salem Female Charitable Society had abandoned its placement program.[11] Ames, rather than confront these changes in social structure, continued to long for a return to this charitable impulse that, he believed, was shared by Lancaster's founders and the outside Christian world:

> Ought not Christian and benevolent families to inquire whether it be right for them to lavish labor and expenditure upon themselves alone, when many are around them destitute, whom a little effort and self-denial might bless and save? We would think more of the Gospel's influences might be exerted in this direction: One great embarrassment in our labors here is the difficulty of finding suitable families who will patiently bear with the faults of our girls, and, in a loving spirit, continue the efforts at reform here commenced, but not fully established. . . .[12]

Continuing in this religious tone, Ames appealed for the help of families not only to take girls in but also to participate in the effort to reform them. Benevolent concern would win out, he felt, so that even if a girl did not prove to be a good servant, her benefactors would, in a loving spirit, help in the larger mission of her reformation.

Common schooling, originally seen as an essential feature of Lancaster's program, became less important as the push for domestic training increased. Lancaster's directors had ceased to believe that education beyond a minimum was critical for rehabilitation. Thus they trimmed the common schooling curriculum and became increasingly committed to vocational training as the most effective way to reform wayward girls. And so the role of the school became, more and more, supplying servants to the rich, and as girls outside Lancaster increasingly looked for other work, Lancaster continued to train them to be servants. By 1869, education at Lancaster had come largely to mean vocational (specifically, domestic) training. The zeal for common schooling for all was pushed aside, and in its stead the education of Lancaster girls became synonymous with domestic training.

The new educational standards for inmates were basic literacy only and the ability to do "simple reckoning." A new appraoch to the value of mathematical skills typified the overall change in attitude toward the needs of poor women—perhaps all women: "Most of the arithmetic taught in the common schools we regard as useless to every woman, and the acquisition a waste of time."

Learning orderliness was emphasized over learning the 3 Rs: "Order and method may be best taught by doing everything methodically, at set hours, and in exact and definite order, and by keeping everything in its place. Exact method, faithfully pursued through all the years of childhood, will form habits which will naturally extend themselves to the character, to all the thoughts as well as acts."[13]

By 1875 the indenture system—a necessary component of Lancaster's domestic-training and reformation programs—was in even more serious danger. At least 15 percent of the girls were requiring more than three placements. A few required as many as five or even six. In later years both the percentage and the number of placements required increased (see table 7.3).

The 1877 Annual Report blamed the families with whom the girls were placed for this rise; these families, the report stated, did not provide appropriate shelter for the girls and frequently returned them to the school on the claim that they were unsuitable workers. The truth of the matter, however, is that families often failed to live up to the founders' fervent hope that they would continue the school's work, that they would assume parental responsibility for the state's charges, thereby saving wayward girls—and only secondarily benefiting from these girls' cheap labor. Needless to say, these families rarely

Table 7.3
Lancaster inmates indentured (in percentages)

	Number of indentures				
Year	0	1–2	3–4	5–6	7 or more
1856	37.8	60.2	3.0	—	—
1863	42.7	52.4	4.8	—	—
1870	11.1	77.7	11.1	—	—
1875	20.6	63.2	7.4	8.8	—
1880	20.6	35.3	29.4	11.8	—
1885	7.1	32.2	39.3	12.5	12.4
1890	3.7	37.1	24.1	22.3	13.0
1895	4.4	45.6	14.7	16.2	19.1
1900	6.1	30.3	26.2	18.1	20.1
1905	11.6	51.1	23.2	11.6	3.5

acted as parents. The Lancaster girl's place in the household was only that of an indentured servant; she was in no way part of a loving family circle. Thus the girls were, once again, deprived of that solid family life for which Lancaster claimed to make restitution, and which the girls still required: "The restraints of routine are removed; they are excited by their surroundings; are indiscreetly trusted, fail to meet the requirements, and are returned to the school as unsuitable, if not altogether unworthy. It is difficult to impress upon those seeking assistance in domestic service the moral obligation resting upon them, when taking a Lancaster school-girl, to watch over her, to shield her from temptation and to help her in the paths of virtue."[14]

The indenture experiences of Isabella B. were not atypical. In 1875 at age thirteen she came to Lancaster as a result of a complaint by her stepmother that she was stubborn and disobedient. Nevertheless, she was soon discharged to her stepmother. Seven months later, the stepmother, complaining of failing health, returned Isabella to Lancaster. Isabella then remained at Lancaster for almost two years, after which time she was placed out. Within two years, Isabella was placed with five different families. She was reported as contented and happy with her first three placements. However, the families thought her "not very capable or efficient."[15]

As the difficulties faced by Lancaster's indenture program continued, even intensified, the trustees were forced to recognize that their system for the rehabilitation of girls was faltering. Certainly the trustees were aware of this by the 1870s. Their Annual Report of 1875 blames it on the financial panic of 1873: "During last winter several girls were kept in the institution who were ready for other homes and services. The families applying for them belonging to the class of families in which it is most desirable to place such girls, felt the financial pressure and lack of employment."[16] Partly in response to this economic downturn and partly through the desire to give girls unsuited for domestic service some alternatives, Lancaster made its program more comprehensive. Vocational training was added to Lancaster's curriculum, which caused further degradation of its educational program. The trustees justified this by social science "evidence" that the poor, the deviant, and the female had smaller brains and limited mental ability. Superintendent Marcus Ames, with sentiments similar to those of Eliza Farnham at Sing Sing earlier, opposed this new direction. He resigned, and most of the matrons and assistants resigned with him.

But the change in policy continued. By 1877 the trustees were recommending that a new house be built solely for the provision of vocational training facilities in order to prepare residents for "some form of labor, which, while immediately benefitting them, would afford another means of livelihood after leaving the school, and which might besides prove remunerative in some degree by the State." This was especially important for some of the older girls, who had been in Lancaster too long and had not been successfully placed. The type of labor envisioned by the trustees was "either mechanical, manufacturing of horticultural or a combination of these." By 1884 the program at Lancaster was diverging significantly from its original intent. The 1884 Annual Report assessed this change quite negatively: Girls were being placed as soon as they were judged ready rather than when they had reached sixteen. The average length of confinement was therefore short and the training minimal. Girls who resisted training were being dispatched to Sherborn Reformatory, and those deemed incapable were being farmed out as dull-witted or incorrigible. The new policy undermined the whole idea of family style as Lancaster became less a residence and more a holding station for expedient detention and quick job training and placement. In effect, Lancaster now functioned as a quasi-employment agency and rarely as an institution for rehabilitation.

The trustees' policy was deliberately to keep school life hard, to reject any conveniences or pleasures that might provide ease and well-being, for the girls must never lose sight of the burdens of their responsibilities. It was considered critical that a reform institution hold high the virtues of hard work: "Then it is believed that work is a reforming influence—work which will tire the body and employ the brain. Work so engrossing as to occupy the thoughts, drive out, or rather to displace, longings for the past, and anticipation of a future like that past."[17] This new emphasis on vocational training was justified as the solution to the problem of disappointing placement procedures:

> If the families who avail themselves of the opportunity offered by the wards of the State to get cheap service were, in reality, the places of reform Dr. Howe so vividly pictured in his ideal system, that ideal would have become a reality; but, as it is, we must take human nature as we find it and not as we would have it; and we can no more expect the larger part of persons employing these girls to do missionary service in their behalf, than we can expect the girls themselves, bred in an atmosphere of lawlessness, ignorance and impurity—all of which comes to them as an inheritance—at once to be obedient, docile and pure.[18]

Because many of the girls would be at Lancaster for only a short while before placement, the trustees despaired on thoroughly training them in the available time and feared that Lancaster would become an institution merely for custody. They had to speed up their training to meet the timing restrictions so girls could earn a living upon leaving. Within this new context, any who defied quick training were to be sent to Sherborn and jailed.

The trustees recognized that Lancaster was now primarily a school for quick vocational training. The original program had become a historic whim. Multiple placements in a relatively short time period were the lot of many; moving from one family to another to yet another within a single year characterized an ever growing number of Lancaster girls. Such constant displacement was a far cry from finding a surrogate family exuding Christian love and warmth.

The decline in the period of training and the increasing number of indentures were rationalized as side benefits of the new program: "Even if she is returned to the school and placed again, several times, she is likely to form more self reliant habits than by a continuous stay in an institution. If her conduct while on probation is such as to make close restraint necessary for her safe keeping, or such as to show that she does not intend to lead a decent life, the commissioners for prisons will be petitioned for her transfer to Sherborn Prison."[19] The trustees justified the practice of transferring "resistant" girls to prison by arguing that this both protected their schoolmates and gave them a second chance to become acceptable members of society: "The law permitting the Prison Commissioners to transfer, at the request of the Trustees, from the school to the prison, is a potent safeguard against the abuse of the milder system of the school. . . . One girl almost helplessly and defiantly immoral, was transferred in 1883 from the Industrial School to the prison, and was, after two years' service, received again at the school, where she remains, subdued, obedient in spirit as well as in act, and hopeful of the better life awaiting her outside."[20]

Superintendent Brackett completed her report in 1889 by straightforwardly labeling Lancaster's new role. No longer was it a reform school, shelter, and home; it was rather a training school: "As soon as a girl who is teachable becomes in any way helpful, she is sent to a place to earn money for herself, while some new girl takes her place in the school, to be taught and sent out in the same manner; thus making the school not a place of detention, but a training school for those who are capable of becoming self-supporting."[21]

The trustees' report, which followed, pointed to great success. Lancaster was now, according to this report, eminently suited for its purpose, job training, and its girls, so specifically and carefully trained, readily found employment. The probate court acknowledged this success by sending more girls to Lancaster. As a result, a large pool of employable girls at Lancaster came into being, from which the superintendent could fill placements selectively. And selective placement made Lancaster that much more attractive as a job agency.

The officers and trustees now gave themselves over completely to training programs. Only girls considered trainable were now admitted; incorrigible girls were sent to prison, and after 1890, the "dull-witted" to the Massachusetts Home for the Feeble-Minded. Lancaster had solved its problems—by dropping reform and education in favor of jobs; it had become a British-style vocational school, which its founders had judged unacceptable.

Lancaster's change in program coincided with a major shift of emphasis in the outlook of public educators, which was prompted by the late-nineteenth-century demand for formal industrial education. Indeed, the reform schools became the model for the public schools. Public educators were at first reluctant to downplay common schooling, which they regarded as necessary to realizing American democracy. In fact, the Fay Commission report of 1856 had rejected vocationalism as un-American. For American children, however—and especially for poor and immigrant American children—more responsive educational programs became imperative. By the turn of the century reform schools were looked on as being a blueprint for the education of the lower classes, and especially for the newly freed blacks, in keeping with the demands of the new industrial world. David Snedden's *Administration and Educational Work of American Juvenile Reform Schools*, published in 1907, expressed the opinion that "the public schools will eventually find it to their advantage to adopt the same system" as the reform schools.[22]

It must be pointed out that differentiated curricula is not necessarily vocational training. Such curricula had come into use shortly after public education had been established in the United States. The Boston School Committee, from the opening of its schools, had instituted special courses of study by social class and gender. In 1864 the Annual Report of the Boston School Committee said of the differential training given to poor and foreign girls, "Among the matters of general interest which merit our attention, we may say that in the Bowditch School, which is attended by pupils of foreign parentage mostly, special attention has been given to sewing." In the same year one of the quarterly reports directly linked coursework in sewing to the needs of the poor, and in 1874 the superintendent of the Winthrop School claimed "that the thorough education of . . . girls in sewing and the cutting and making of garments . . . will have a marked effect upon the domestic economy and happiness of the rising generation."[23] Still, it was not until the 1880s that industrial training for poor and immigrant youth was formally established in the public school system. For similar reasons public schools also introduced kindergartens into their programs. The rationale for these education programs echoed that of the reform schools. Further parallels are to be found in the institutions of learning for Black Americans established at this time, of which the Tuskegee Institute in Alabama, founded by Booker T. Washington in 1881, was prototypical.[24]

The reasons educators put forward in support of vocational training for poor youth in the public schools were almost identical to those given by Lancaster's officials; both held that training in "manual skills" would elevate the lower classes and blacks. Both educators and reformers—heartily supported by the industrialists for their own ends—were well aware that the times demanded industrial education as a means of preparing students—especially immigrants and the poor—to fulfill the needs of industry.

By 1890, however, the schools did not have adequate resources or capabilities for preparing students to fill the needs of expansionist industrial activity. Therefore vocational training shifted perspective and broadened itself. The emphasis became job oriented.[25] At this point the traditional American belief in equality through education underwent a great change. The aim of education became not equality but the assurance of socially appropriate economic opportunity.[26]

As Lancaster shifted from the mission of reforming young girls to the routine of preparing them for the job market, it increasingly adopted "good-management" categorization procedures. Age, crime, family background—categories once thought antithetical to the evangelical ideal of saving children—now began to define its mode of operation. This development was hastened and reinforced by state intervention. In particular, Sections 8 and 10, Chapter 359, of the Acts of 1870, which in essence gave the visiting agent of the Board of State Charities the power to decide which girls were to be admitted to Lancaster, led to a selection criterion based in large part on age—the younger were to be sent into homes, and the older to reform school. As older girls were more physically mature and possibly more sexually experienced, a correlation was established between age and criminality. This reinforced the trend toward separating younger from older girls—to save a young girl, one first had to remove her from such evil presences as older girls—which only strengthened classification by age as an admission criterion.

To appreciate fully the impact on Lancaster of this development, it will be useful to sample again the school's original optimism, its belief that wayward girls could be lovingly guided to respectable adulthood only in a family environment, a natural mix of children of all ages:

> The proper discharge of household duties and the suitable initiation of every pupil into the proper discharge of each, would seem to require a combination of persons of various degrees of strength and skill in the same house, working together for a common end; for there can be no question that one of the leading objects of the institution is to be continued effort to introduce every pupil as fully and as completely as possible into what, in a well ordered family, are common domestic duties and occupations, and in this way to awaken a love of such employments as are best calculated to sustain and cherish a healthy and kindly social sphere, and to call out their intellectual powers in a way to give them activity and strength.[27]

Doubts about the ameliorative effects of family-style grouping of the children had crept into the trustees' Annual Report as early as 1857, however. A year's experience had failed to prove conclusively that the girls necessarily enhanced the lives of the other girls in a family setting, that the younger, "innocent" girls softened the natures of their older, frequently "depraved" sisters, or that the older girls automatically assumed mothering roles. In his Second Annual Report, Bradford Peirce had asked for two additional houses. They were needed, he felt, in order to accommodate the flood of applicants to the school that had arisen. Although his recommendations came to naught, the rationale behind his words reflects a degree of disappointment in results and foreshadows gloomy policies to come: "This would enable us to separate those of a tender age from the older girls and to conduct, with a somewhat modified discipline, a department which might be considered preventative, anticipating temptation, and guarding the inmates from the peril of personal contact with the young offenders whose reformation is attempted in the other homes."[28] Not willing to go all the way in policy change, Peirce suggested a monitorial system that would be a compromise in the educational program without conceding ideological change. By the monitorial method, begun by the British educator Joseph Lancaster, the older girls could still work with the younger ones, not as standard procedure, however, but as a privilege based on merit and behavior; as Peirce's report put it, "The labor and care incident to the training of these young girls can be, with the best results, largely shared by the older inmates of the school who have secured and justified the confidence of the officers."[29] Doubts were even raised that the girls were as innocent and savable as had been believed: "The school has much less work of this prevention to perform, and much more of the labor of reformation than was anticipated in its establishment. The community will learn with pain, that actual crime trenches upon an earlier age than is generally supposed, and that the reason why more juvenile offenders, especially girls, are not brought before the courts is not because their offenses are not discovered, but from sympathy for their tender age, and the knowledge of the certain ruin of jail, their early crimes are overlooked."[30]

In the Third Annual Report, 1858, Peirce again raised the issue of classification by age, the experience of another year having intensified his doubts that the family-style environment was the best way to save wayward girls: "The conviction grows stronger in our minds of the safety and even expediency of having older girls together in the same family, rather than to have them classified by age. It is rarely that the older girls simply corrupt the younger, but is the decidedly and persistently *bad* girls, whether old or young that spreads a dreadful leaven in the company."[31] Nevertheless, Peirce and the trustees continued to believe that mixture by age was necessary to simulate a family-style environment: "We have found one of the most impressive appeals to the older girls to be based upon the effect of their example and words upon the children. In a number of instances they have chosen one of the younger girls to watch over, and it is quite affecting to notice the sensitive anxiety with which they mark the conduct and reprove the least semblance of wrong. Among this class (the older girls) are some of great promise, and there are several that we should not hesitate to employ as teachers and assistants in the kitchen."[32] Despite his doubts and ambivalences, Peirce concluded that Lancaster's family atmosphere could reform its charges by noting that

> it has been our experience that very few children who have been committed for larceny or vagrancy, by public officers, [have an] advantage over those who are sent for defects of character. Nearly all are neglected, uncultivated subjects of bad habits; but still children susceptible to improvement. Each one becomes a special study and an object of personal solicitude; and it is the rare exception, and not the general rule, that any heart fails to respond to persistent kindness. The little truants, street merchants and thieves of Boston and the large cities are fully incorrigible as any class we have.[33]

Peirce's Fourth Annual Report, 1859, reflected further wavering of conviction. He remained faithful to the Lancaster philosophy, but modified it to the extent of suggesting that classification, while undesirable within the school proper, be the basis on which the probate judge sentenced. According to this suggestion, different kinds of girls should be sentenced to different kinds of institutions, and if a girl sentenced to Lancaster proved beyond the school's powers to reform, she should be relocated:

> If all the persistent, evil disposed girls be gathered into a family together, understood to be the pariahs of the institution, their very home, a badge of dishonor to them what prospect can there be of their ultimate reformation? If a girl cannot be controlled or touched in her sensibilities after such a trial as the peril of her ruin will demand at our hands, and secure from our awakened interest, the only classification in her case is *out of the institution*. The insane hospital, some singularly devoted family, or a house of correction, will offer the proper alternative.[34]

From the sixties on, the oft repeated discussion of classification signified beyond doubt that the officers of Lancaster were faltering in their beliefs and were no longer comfortable with their original line of thought. Various reports and recommendations reflect Peirce's ambivalences. In 1865 the Howe-Sanborn report articulated explicitly the dilemma of squaring the belief in the redemption of all children with the dismaying reality that some children were not being reformed. The trustees' Twelfth Annual Report, 1868, quotes the superintendent's decision to accept some form of classification: "I am more favorably inclined than ever before to such a classification as would be afforded by having one house devoted to the reception of the worst girls we are obliged to receive, together with those who are returned to us having fallen into vice or crime, and after a period of detention therein, under a closer restrained more rigid discipline than is desirable for the majority of our girls, be permitted to enter our other houses on an equality with them."[35] (But the trustees piously tempered this with a pronouncement that "faith and hope in the good to be found even in the 'hardest and worst cases' gives strength for continued effort."[36])

By the early 1870s a combination of legislative changes, discussed earlier, and a growing set of institutional options by which the state could care for and confine the dependent and deviant finally brought overt classification. The State Primary School at Monson opened in 1866 for the expressed purpose of housing destitute and deprived young children. Until 1872 this primary school was an adjunct to the Monson Almshouse. In that year, however, it became an independent entity, whose function was to serve as a primary school for destitute and deprived younger girls, while Lancaster was to assume the responsibility of a reform school for older girls. (There is a certain irony in this. Lancaster's problems were solved by an admissions policy that separated the redeemable (the younger) from the irredeemable (the older)—it took the older and sent the younger to Monson. But by 1895 Monson itself was facing in severe form Lancaster's problem: Caring for both the redeemable (young) and the irredeemable (also young)! Indeed, the 1895 report by Monson's trustees pinpoints this problem—which now could not be solved by an age categorization—as the cause for the school's shutdown: "For many years the conviction had been growing in their minds that an institution which gathered together in one establishment children of such various histories and tendencies as were sheltered in the Primary School was in itself an evil. . . ."[37])

The 1873 report of Lancaster's trustees accepted this new scheme of classification reluctantly, regarding it as unwarranted and ill-advised state interference: "If *only those* deemed incorrigible are sent, vice will have the ascendancy—'good will be overcome by evil.' It would be an attempt to reform by placing the fallen sinner in company no better than her own. The classification would be unnatural, rendering reform more difficult."[38] It was felt that as a consequence of this intervention the state had succeeded in destroying the original mission of the school.

The legislative reports of this time describing Lancaster's new entrants make dismal reading. They are filled with complaints of the girls' increasing incorrigibility and the perceived need for more specific facilities for punishment. For us, these reports not only establish that the natures of the entrants were perceived as hardened but illustrate the waning of reform zeal that had prevailed less than two decades earlier and show that Lancaster's role in the network of state institutions had shifted from reformatory to dumping bin.

In 1877 another legislative initiative sentenced hardened girls, those considered less capable of being trained at Lancaster, directly to Sherborn Reformatory for Women, Chapter 208, Section 3, of the Acts of 1877 allowed the Lancaster trustees also to transfer girls deemed unsuitable for Lancaster to Sherborn. This policy worked at first, but soon became inadequate to handle Lancaster's entrants, who were of an increasingly hard character. It was decided by the trustees that these later entrants required something between a prison and an industrial school, a new department, to be set up as part of Lancaster. This decision to establish at Lancaster a separate punitive confinement is indicative of the change Lancaster underwent from its first days as a social experiment intended to restrain with "cords of love" to an institution intended to restrain by punitive treatment in houses of detention. The school officials justified this decision with the claim that "isolation or separate confinement, as the case may require, is conceded to be one of the most effective methods of bringing to a sense of duty the insubordinate."[39] The trustees and officers also formulated new policies to deal with the "incorrigibles"—transfer to Bridgewater and Tewksbury Prison or Sherborn Reformatory. Acting Superintendent Frank B. Fay proposed this one year later as a precaution against their ruinous influence on the rest of the girls: "Girls of a certain character, who have been long in the school and give no evidence of reform, are a constant source of disturbance. It seemed to me that we ought to look at the 'greatest good of the greatest number' even at the risk of injury to the one sent out."[40]

In keeping with the resigned tone of the report and acknowledging that Lancaster now housed a tougher and older group, Fay ended his report with a discussion of "Hereditary Taint." His words chillingly revealed the perceived irreversible hardness of the inmates, their supposed criminality, and the little hope held for their redemption: "If the hereditary taint from which our girls suffer were more physical only, we should never tire in our efforts to relieve the sufferer."[41] By the 1880s it was clear that Lancaster's officers and trustees considered Lancaster a punitive institution. In 1883 the State Board of Health, Lunacy and Charity discussed the school as principally a custodial place used almost solely for detention. The trustees precisely defined Lancaster's new role in 1885: "The Industrial School occupies a position more important than many it has held since its establishment. It is now a middle place between the care of that Board [Health, Lunacy and Charity] and a Reformatory Prison."[42]

Lancaster's evolution from rehabilitative shelter to a place of punitive detention was now complete. Lancaster was to be a "middle place": "Direct from the courts, without this preliminary training, this living in the air of wholesomeness and truth, they could not be retained one week in respectable homes. Nor would any of the class now admitted to the Primary School at Monson without injury to the inmates of that school, or with the same changes for their own reformation as they have at Lancaster."[43]

It is interesting to note here that although the tone of such reports implied and the accusations of the officers stated that the entrants were hardened girls, the inmates continued to enter under the same criminal charges as they had in 1856. The trustees and superintendents reported girls to be harder, but complaints of "stubbornness" served as an umbrella to mask crimes such as streetwalking and running away. As chapter 6 documented, in the 1860s officials were aware that many of the girls' parents had manipulated the sentencing procedures of probate court so that they could procure some state aid in their efforts to rear or rid themselves of their daughters. These officials now accused the commonwealth of manipulating justice by charging some depraved girls with petty larceny so as to make it legally possible to sentence them to the reform school, an act of leniency to the girls but of harm to Lancaster:

> The old complaint of "stubbornness" is still a frequent one and covers a "multitude of sins" of which stubbornness is the very least. For this offence, "pure and simple," but seven have been committed during the year, though this has been an ostensible cause in many cases. For larceny, not connected with other vices, only one, while during some years those complained for this offence have been a quarter of the whole number.
>
> By far the larger number of girls are really sent to the school for the most serious offences against morality. It cannot be doubted that the graver offences to which allusion has been made are increasing, and that the school as a check to an immoral career, and an opportunity for training and influence which may permanently change the life and character, is now more than ever needed.[44]

The hereditarian argument, first voiced by Samuel Gridley Howe in 1865, was in the ascendant now at Lancaster, as a system of classification: "The inmates are lodged in four separate family houses, each with its own staff of officers. This division allows a careful classification within the school, a classification depending upon the character and previous history of the girls, and not upon age or conduct within the institution. As there is no promotion from house to house, a perfect isolation is thus secured of those who might otherwise contaminate the more innocent."[45]

Although conclusive evidence of the scope of the classification scheme at the school is difficult to determine, a trend over time may be perceived in the assignment of incoming girls to the various houses. Certain houses appear to have been at least partially reserved for certain types of entrants. Entrants could not be sorted completely since their assignments depended largely on where available spaces happened to be; nevertheless, their placements were not totally random. Studying the assignments by crime and chastity suggests the use of some classification system. Starting with the 1880s, houses one and four were assigned to entering girls who had committed crimes against morality, rather than property, and who were unchaste. When house eight was built in the early 1890s, it, too, received an above average number of unchaste girls. Conversely, house two received a more even distribution of girls charged with morality and property crimes. House three, destroyed by fire earlier and rebuilt in the 1890s, and house six, built in 1894, both received a disproportionately high number of the relatively few "chaste" girls. These data indicate that an active implementation of classification over and above legislative dictates was in effect by 1880. These trends continued for the next twenty years. By 1905 each house was receiving its own type of entrant assigned to it, according to the nature of crime committed and chastity considerations.[46] It is very likely that after entrance even further classification took place as girls were sorted, measured, and perhaps reassigned in accordance with a more rigid set of criteria. For instance, many Lancaster girls were reassigned to Mary Lamb Cottage because they were judged to be feeble-minded or incorrigible. Girls were now cases to be treated rather than souls to be redeemed. The treatment, unfortunately, was not to be very helpful. Michel Foucault in *Discipline and Punish* discusses the case as "an individual as he may be described, judged, measured, compared with others, in his very individuality; and it is also the individual who has to be trained or corrected, classified, normalized, excluded, etc." Although on first reading Foucault's description seems to suggest that this process is scientifically correct and modern, the process of sifting, sorting, and labeling defies the reformist ideology, which espouses the reformability of all. The introduction of handling the needy as cases seems to be scientifically correct and modern but, in fact, objectifies the individual and subjects him or her to observation and evaluation by a person with greater power: "The chronicle of a man, the account of his life formed part of the rituals of power. The disciplinary methods reversed this relation, lowered the threshold of describable individuality and made of this description a means of control and a method of domination."[47] In a sense this new, "modern" hereditarianism was a return to the gloomy conclusions of Calvinist predestinationism.

The same process by which the operating procedure at Lancaster came to be dominated by an elaborate system of classification was in effect throughout the commonwealth's entire institutional network. The Massachusetts School for the Feeble-Minded, Waltham, opened a custodial wing in 1890. In that same year the State Board of Insanity passed acts that enabled transfers to be made from Lancaster to either a hospital for the insane or this custodial wing: "The state board of insanity may, on the request of the trustees of the Lyman and Industrial Schools, transfer from either of said schools to the Hospital Cottage for Children at the Mass. School for the Feeble-Minded any inmate whose condition would be benefited by such transfer, upon the certificate of a physician that such person is a suitable subject for treatment at either of the last-named institutions."[48] Thus was put in place a sophisticated system of classification: The simple went to the Home for the Feeble-Minded; younger girls, into Monson—and later directly into domestic service; incorrigible girls, to Sherborn; and the rest, to Lancaster.

Records at both the Massachusetts School for the Feeble-Minded and Lancaster indicate that this systematization and consolidation of state charities often brought about maltreatment. For example, many girls who were known not to be feeble-minded were nonetheless sentenced to the Massachusetts School for the Feeble-Minded. In 1909 Dr. Walter Fernald, a high-ranking official at that institution and in the forefront of the Eugenics Movement, diagnosed some of the most difficult girls at Lancaster as "moral imbeciles" and later "defective delinquents" and recommended their transfer to his school. This gave relief to Lancaster, but did untold tragic harm to many of the girls so judged. By 1910 this operation was in full swing and Dr. Fernald reported that "since the last meeting, I have been again to Lancaster, cooperating with officers at Lancaster State Industrial School in the examination of defective girls."[49]

According to Dr. Fernald, one strong indicator of feeble-mindedness in young girls was sexual activity: "Imbeciles of both sexes show active sexual propensities and perversions at an early age. This tendency to promiscuous sexual relations is almost always present."[50] For some of the girls, their sexual proclivities were sufficient cause for their transfer to the Massachusetts School for the Feeble-Minded. One such case, Hattie F., was transferred from Lancaster in 1900. Brought to the school for stubbornness, she was "known to have been unchaste," but was "not considered under the average in intellect." She was also reported as able to read and write. There is no indication in her record that she is in any way mentally damaged. Yet after "evil companions led her away" she was transferred to the Massachusetts Home for the Feeble-Minded.[51]

In 1908 Dr. Fernald addressed the American Medico-Psychological Association in a paper entitled "The Imbecile with Criminal Instincts," in which he argued that socially unacceptable behavior is a form of mental deficiency and used Lancaster girls Beulah S. and Mary R. to illustrate his point.[52] Beulah S., a one-time Lancaster inmate, had been deserted by her parents as an infant and left to the mercy of the state. At age fourteen she mothered an illegitimate child and afterward was sent to Lancaster for theft and incorrigibility. Her poor record while at Lancaster prompted her transfer to the Massachusetts School for the Feeble-Minded. When she was twenty-six, Dr. Fernald described her as having "keen sexual propensities," and although she "reads well . . . and has (g)ood command of the language," as having the mental capacity of "a child of 11 or 12." Accordingly, Fernald labeled her "moral imbecile" and consigned her to the custodial department of the institute.

Mary R. entered Lancaster reportedly as unchaste and "diseased." Her Lancaster records report her as "of average intellect." Her mother, who worked in a mill, was accused of an incestuous relationship with Mary's older brother. Given the hereditarian argument that sinfulness begets sinfulness, the Lancaster officials did not express great surprise that Mary, after five placements in four years, had an illegitimate child. Although Mary was reportedly a good mother, the baby was sent away from its mother and placed in the Infants Asylum. Soon after, Mary R. was returned to Lancaster and then transferred to the Massachusetts Home for the Feeble-Minded.[53]

Susannah D. fared no better than her two Lancaster sisters. Her Lancaster record is one of the few that expressed doubt about her intellectual capacity. However, although "considered under the average in intellect," the record attributed her "cross and ugly" behavior to stubbornness "inherited from her mother's side of the house" rather than to any intellectual deficiency. Susannah D. was later transferred to the Massachusetts Home for the Feeble-Minded, whose records characterize her as a "sexual pervert."[54] In spite of the questions her two sets of records raised regarding her mental capacity, Dr. Walter

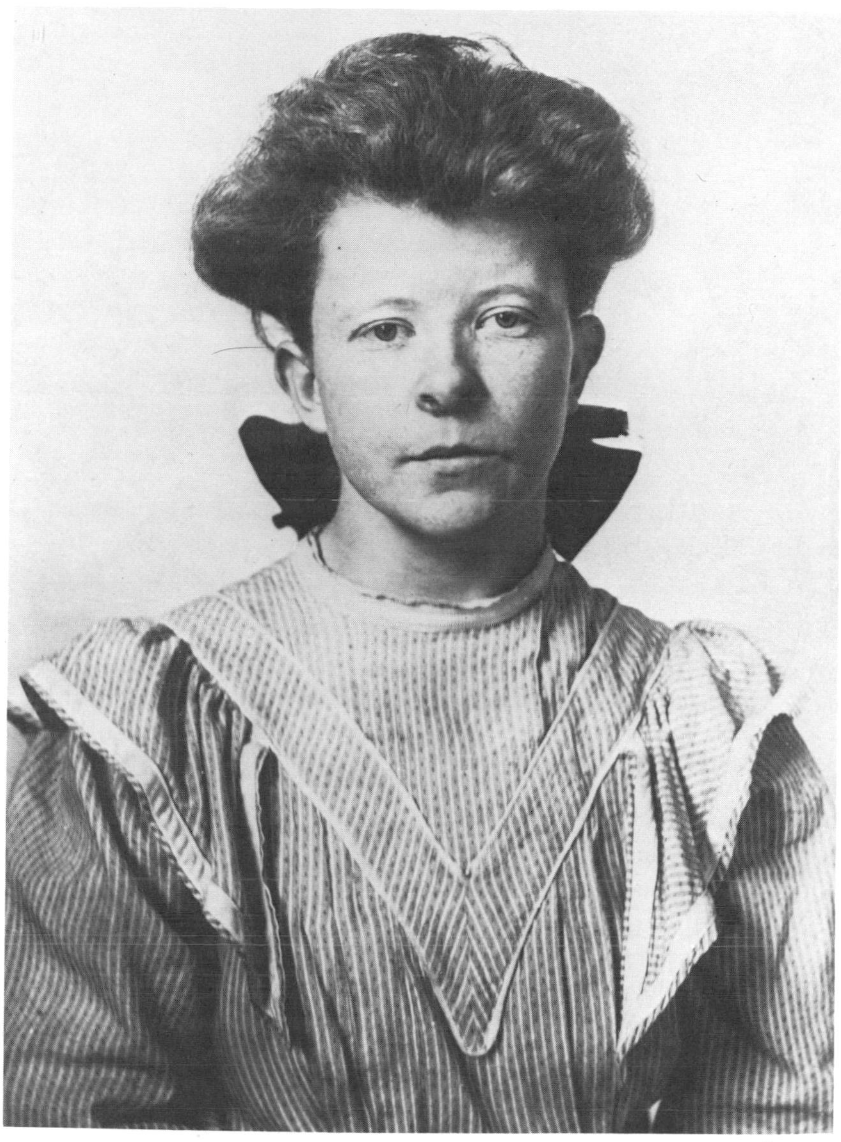

A 1909 photograph of a former Lancaster inmate transferred to the Massachusetts School for the Feeble-Minded.

A 1909 photograph of vocational training class at the Massachusetts School for the Feeble-Minded. Some of those shown are former inmates of Lancaster.

Fernald included her in his paper as a case study to illustrate that lack of sexual control was a sure sign of moral imbecility, requiring, as happened to many other Lancaster girls, incarceration in the custodial wing of the school for the feeble-minded.

Many of the girls who were transferred from Lancaster to other institutions fared no better than those sent to the Home for the Feeble-Minded. They, too, were labeled by the various state officials as needing either punishment or custody in reformatories, jails, state hospitals, or almshouses. Upon entrance to Lancaster they began a life of state institutionalization. Thus Selma D. entered Lancaster as a "stubborn" twelve-year-old. Within six years she had been returned to Lancaster from placement, subsequently shuffled from the school to Tewksbury State Hospital, then to Sherborn Reformatory, and finally to the Massachusetts Home for the Feeble-Minded.[55]

One consequence of this proliferation of institutions was that it ensnared some girls in the state's institutional web. A few girls may have benefited by a transfer from one institution to another; but for many others it was a drawn-out nightmare, a lengthy involvement with the state's apparatus of judgment, reevaluation, placement, and custodial care.

The Lancaster trustees, like their mid-century coreformists, had dreamed a beautiful dream that benevolence would conquer deviance. But there had arisen a new belief in "scientific" truths, particularly those pretending to explain the nature and cure of deviance, and these became the steering forces in reform. The educational program at Lancaster changed over time as it squared with the labor market and accommodated older and harder entrants. The trustees and administration at Lancaster were part of an increasingly formalized network of state charities. By 1880 the school's function was defined by trustees and administrators alike as offering training specifically for poor but employable girls. Those deemed incapable of domestic training (that is, proper female socialization) were classified as best benefiting from custodial care as either feebleminded, insane, or morally incorrigible. Thus Lancaster was left free to provide training for those most suited for and likely to find a place in the labor force.

Belief in scientific techniques, systematization, and efficiency justified reformers' classification of dependents for treatment. Through classifying, transferring, and training, reformers effected a new mode of pseudoscientific thinking and treated their charges accordingly. There was little sentiment for those girls who were older, and often wanton. The original dream of mid-century that all girls could be saved had become by the 1880s a whim relegated to historical memory.

8

Conclusions and Speculations

Heaven is not reached at a single bound.
[Poem popular at State Industrial School for Girls, Lancaster]

By the end of 1905 the State Industrial School for Girls, Lancaster, had admitted 2,833 girls, of whom more than 75 percent left the school and lived poor but respectable lives. Most of these three-quarters lived as the reformers hoped. That is, they lived with families, either natural, conjugal, or in placement. Of this group almost all worked in their own homes or as domestics in the homes of others, roles for which they had been trained. The rest were institutionalized elsewhere or died before they were twenty-five. Only a very few were reported as living dissolute lives.

How can the history of the first fifty years of this experiment, heralded as a landmark of reform, promising to help alleviate social problems by saving wayward girls, be evaluated and understood? Assessing the success of any institution involves a close examination of espoused goals and actual effects on both clients and society. Certainly, studying society's changes in attitudes toward the girls and the program persuades the reader that the school soon fell from a period of reformist vision and loving care to one of harsh judgment, rudimentary job training, and punitive custody. Understandably, therefore, the story of Lancaster is one of dashed hopes. However, it is difficult to leave the story of Lancaster solely at this level. The overwhelmingly sad tales of the lives of poor women in general give pause. Given the wretched options available to poor girls during the last half of the nineteenth century, we must question whether Lancaster helped, hindered, or simply provided a brief pause on the road to adulthood.

Examining this comprehensive portrait of the school, including its backgrounds, inmates, and program, leads the reader to question the extent to which changes in clientele resulted in modification to the institution itself. Did the school change because the type of entrant changed or, conversely, did the school succumb to external pressures and change due to historical events—in particular, the legislation regulating age of entrants? It is most plausible that external circumstances, internal pressures at the school, and actual changes in clientele interacted, so that all three influenced the unfolding of the history of Lancaster and its girls.

Tying together trends and events in the last half of nineteenth-century America enriches our understanding of the times in which this story takes place and highlights the appropriateness of studying an institution such as Lancaster. More than simply one reform school, the State Industrial School for Girls captures and helps illustrate the hopes and fears of earnest reformers. Comprehending the whole tale involves examining a richly colored tapestry woven from many interconnected threads: reform thought, expectations for respectable womanhood, popular reaction to a turbulent century, the consequent development of a school for re-form, and the devolution into a state facility for incarceration. Lancaster both reflected and influenced opinions on criminality, juvenile delinquency, and reform treatment. Most important, it also illustrated general opinion about nineteenth-century female respectability and the training considered appropriate and necessary to forming it.

Uncovering and analyzing who the entrants were and what happened to them in and after Lancaster gives a partial answer about the effects of the school on the lives of many of its inmates. We cannot, however, assess the degree to which the school really did mediate in the future lives of the girls or to what extent it merely sheltered them and later placed them in jobs. Did many of the girls leave Lancaster and live as they would have regardless of the treatment they received in the institution? If so, the major contribution of Lancaster was to provide care and custody, not reformation. Or was the training and supervision at the school critical for many who might, indeed, have fallen into dissolute lives without state intervention during their adolescent years? It seems most reasonable to accept Lancaster as playing several roles depending on the actual inmate, and society's demands. Lancaster may have provided no more than shelter for poor and difficult girls; it may have been little more than a way station for them. It may have offered some comfort to some parents "skidding" from the lower class to the underclass. This is likely, as the girls at Lancaster seem to have come from families like the ones Stephan Thernstrom describes in *Poverty and Progress*, families "unable to rise out of the most depressed impoverished segment of the manual laboring class." Perhaps Lancaster prevented this fall for their daughters and returned them to society as still poor, but respectable, women.

Lancaster obviously served girls differently. The following letter, written by a former inmate of Lancaster close to the turn of the century, illustrates the positive role Lancaster played in providing family life and love to a young girl like Jane B.[1] Her letter suggests that religious training, education, friendship, and surrogate-family care gave her a richer life than she could have received elsewhere. It is sad to realize that in fact the tone of her letter is similar to that of the letters written by girls in preparatory schools and academies:

Supt. of Girls Industrial School, July, 19 . . .

Dear Madam,

I am one of the old girls of that institution and have often thought I would write and ask if some girl could copy the poem "Heaven is not reached at a single bound." This was the first line and it was such a beautiful poem I would like my children to commit it to memory. I just bought a set of books, ten in the set and only a portion of this poem was in the poem book, so if I could get it from the girls I should be very grateful to you both. I was [Jane B.]. I am twenty-nine years of age now and have a lovely home and four fine healthy children and I can say honestly without the training I received from that school I should never have been able to keep a home as it should be kept and I very often think of the school especially when I am sewing for my family, there is always plenty to be done I can assure you as three of my children are girls the oldest nearly nine years of age. Their names are Olive, Doris and Hazel, the boy's is Merrick.

I would like to know if Auntie Corry is still there. I suppose not, I loved her better than any one also Auntie Hawley. I wish I knew if any of the officers are there now that were there in my time. I was fond of them all. Did Miss Warren marry Mr. Swift that lived across from Good Rest? I should love dearly to know. I suppose the girls have all gone and made homes like myself or found other pleasant occupations, I never have regreted being there only I did long many times to have my freedom but I see now where it was for my own good, *every*one remarks what good children I have and they are and I do all I can to make them so, I shudder to think, of the failure I would have made had I not gone to that school and I never was locked in my room only for an occasional recreation.

I have been in the hospital and been very sick at times and have heart trouble beside and I am trying to keep out of having another operation and the doctors have advised me to walk out in the fresh air but not to tire my self so I have decided to get subscriptions for the different papers. I know the school used to have a goodly supply of them so I am asking you to renew or begin to take a subscription for some of them, which will be a great favor. . . . If you could help me in this you would be doing me a great favor. . . .

Hoping to hear from you soon.
I am Sincerely Yours,

Jane B.'s letter indicates that for her Lancaster was a positive experience; but we can never be certain what her life would have been had she never lived at the school.

Alice P.'s records also read as a "success" story.[2] She experienced many indentures, stole some small items while in placement, was returned to the school, and was placed out again. In spite of this rocky record, however, the final account of her life reads as an unexpected triumph for Lancaster: "Mr. D— reports [Alice] to be married in . . . to . . . who is mechanic earning $3.50 a day, and who is a very decent young man of 25 yrs. (sic). He is too good for [Alice], but she seems to be fond of him, and he is attached to her. She will be married as soon as [Alice] becomes of age. [Alice] was married on . . . and they are living in. . . ."

For many other girls, however, their post-Lancaster experiences were much more mixed. For example, Sarah S., after several placements, ran away from her job as a domestic servant with a family and returned to live with her mother. Soon after, she married. However, the next entry on her report states that she "left her husband . . . on account of ill usage, as she says. Is taking care of her fathers [sic] family. Her mother and the infant being dead she manages the family well. Helping her father take care of the family." The earlier account of her life was catastrophic, yet she was reported on two later occasions as "doing well." This judgment was due to her gainful employment in a mill, where she is reported as "steady in her work and neat—and faithful in her care of the family."

Heartbreaking in our eyes as these reports are, they describe nineteenth-century successes, that is, wayward girls who become respectable women, living domestic lives. The records of Sally R., Ida G., and Esther S. are even more gloomy: Sally R., for example, after several placements, returned to Lancaster. In spite of her training at the school, she left and eventually was found in a house of "ill fame." From there, she was again returned to the school, and then transferred to Sherborn Reformatory. The trustees took pity on Sally and requested that she return from Sherborn to Lancaster and then be placed out again. The modern reader might view Sally's story as pathetic; but the reformers viewed it as a partial success, since, after spending time at Sherborn, she was released, and the final entry reads "A very nice letter [was] received from Sally expressing her gratitude for what the School has done for her. Says she is leading an honest, upright life and no one can say a word against her. Her home is in. . . . Her husband's name is. . . . She says she is poor and that her married life has not been a happy one. She has five children but only three are living." Again, Sally expressed feelings of warmth and gratitude toward the school. Her life was unhappy, one of hardship and misery, but she was no longer living a morally dissolute life. How would the founders have interpreted this report?

Like Sally, another "graduate" 's story is also one of questionable success. After two unsuccessful placements, Ida G. was sent to Tewksbury Hospital, where she gave birth to a daughter. Soon after, her illegitimate child died and Ida was transferred from the hospital to the state almshouse. She escaped from the almshouse almost immediately. But, the report concludes, rather than living a life on the streets, she eventually married.

Yet another "graduate," Esther S., had given birth to a child at fifteen years of age and had then been sent to the school in 1895 as a result of her father's complaint that she was stubborn. Lancaster trained and placed Esther in service. The record for Esther describes her as "always pleasant and willing" and indicated the pride the administration took in their ability to keep her in good placements and away from her sister, whom they saw as an unsettling influence. In fact, the last entry in her report recounts that she was awarded the Fay prize for successfully living up to the expectations of the school by her diligence and uprightness.

In the eyes of the Lancaster officials, the sine qua non for success was marriage—not happiness. Certainly, most Lancaster graduates who married, and especially those who both married and worked outside the home, lived economically poor and hard-working lives. Some also suffered abuse as married women; violence had been a factor in the incarceration of a few inmates, so it is likely that a few faced similar situations even after attaining the goal of marriage. However, the alternatives to family life and/or employment for most nineteenth-century women, particularly the poor, were grim indeed. In this light, it may have been that most Lancaster girls fared at least as well as their equally poor sisters who had not been incarcerated at a reform school. In fact, for some the job training and placement may have given them a slight edge in future employment and eligibility for marriage.

Some of the girls fared poorly and did not become the respectable women Lancaster had hoped to create. A typical case of such a failure is that of Charlotte F., who arrived at the school with a friend in 1880. According to the records, Charlotte, then 15 years old, was found in a house of ill fame and had "been away from home quite a while." She was subsequently placed out and married within a year. The 1883 Lancaster record reports that the superintendent "found [Charlotte F.] in a house of ill fame . . . and was returned to the school." From the school she was sent to jail.

Mathilda M., like Charlotte F., continued to live as if the training at Lancaster had had little or no impact on her. In 1886 she was brought to the school by an officer for being idle and vagrant. She was then living with a man to whom she was not married "but passed as his wife." According to the court file, she had no other home to which to go. Two years after Mathilda was brought to Lancaster, she was indentured and was reported by the woman with whom she was placed as "not doing very well." The report states that she stayed out many nights and was "not be trusted alone even to attend church." In fact, "several times when she was supposed to be in church she has been . . . in very bad company." Although she was reported as "doing better," less than a year later she gave birth to an illegitimate child, and by the time she was eighteen she had been sent to Tewksbury Almshouse. The rest of her record is a somber tale of several short placements in domestic service and returns to various state almshouses; very likely she then went on to a permanent life of poverty, perhaps prostitution.

The outcomes of those transferred to other institutions are even more difficult to assess. For many, like Hattie F. and Beulah S. (see chapter 7), transfer from Lancaster to the Massachusetts Home for the Feeble-Minded resulted in their being relabeled moral imbeciles. The act of transference within the system and reclassification caught such girls in the web of institutional life, perhaps for the rest of their lives. Although some girls must have benefited from custodial care and more appropriate reclassification, it is sobering to think of the many for whom the outcome was stigmatization and unending custodial ensnarement.

Lancaster is central to our understanding of nineteenth-century penal reform and its changes. Lancaster's founders had hoped to create an institution for the reformation of poor and potentially wayward girls. These founders, like the other mid-century reformers, truly believed that family-style institutions, cottages housing small groups of dependents supervised by surrogate parents, would save all wayward children by giving them the environment in which to reform and flourish. A critical feature of this environment, they held, was the separation of younger children from older and harder criminals so that the younger could be saved from corrupting influences. In the largest sense, Lancaster was the reformers' solution to the urban crisis. The ideas of Lancaster's founders grew from a strong faith in the inherent innocence of children. But in the first half-century of Lancaster's existence, this faith crumbled. Scientific explanations for deviance and classification according to types of deviance, theretofore considered applicable only to the treatment of adults, came to be accepted as relevant also to the treatment of youthful offenders. In the end, Lancaster was hardly different from a prison.

By studying Lancaster we gain social and historical insight into the period's notions of gender and class. At that time the nature of women was presumed to be domestic. Lancaster was designed to address this stereotype. Therefore it offered what was "natural" for the reformation of poor girls, that is, a program of domestication. The theories of the causes of wayward behavior were to change, from environmentalism, which blamed poverty and slum life, to hereditarianism, which blamed vicious parents, especially mothers, so that the definition of "natural" changed from a state of externally induced conditions to internal character weaknesses. Lancaster's job, however, continued to be the domestication of girls so that they would be better able to fulfill their "natural" roles.

In keeping with nineteenth-century attitudes, it was especially important that women be respectable, morally upright, and industrious, since as wives and mothers they were expected to ensure social order. Although Lancaster's program moved from common schooling to domestic training as the key to reformation, it could still claim success because most of the Lancaster girls went on to lead lives of domestic respectability; as long as the Lancaster girls did not end up in jail or on the streets, they were counted as "successes."

Most of the Lancaster girls came from domestic situations, were trained in a family-style institution to be domestic, morally upright, and hard working, were placed out into families, and then ended up in families of their own—either parental or conjugal and frequently both. It appears, then, that at some level Lancaster selected girls who were predisposed to fare well in the school's program. In the eyes of the state, most of them did. Few rose above their station. They remained poor, but honest. Few resorted to prostitution—the major worry of the founders of the school. The social planners, however unconsciously, perpetuated the class structure that was a major factor in the poverty of the girls' families. Yet, given the options then available to the poor—

and these were practically nonexistent—Lancaster was at least an alternative.

At bottom, Lancaster is of course the story of a reform institution for poor girls. We now need similar portraits of other institutions to begin to compare the reform treatments of both genders and also to gain understanding of earlier efforts to alter the lives of those labeled deviant. By so doing, we shall be able to better our own efforts. Beyond this, by telling us about the nineteenth-century history, in America and Europe, of education and reform and welfare institutions, Lancaster becomes the occasion to study the impact on personal lives of social and economic forces. And finally, the story of Lancaster is a sobering tale of the decline of reform hopes into social control. There is sufficient evidence that the institutional attempt to counter the unchecked forces of economic and technological change was not by itself sufficient. However, the story is not simply a gloomy revisionist parable of a wicked elite imposing its will on passive masses. Instead, it is an account of mixed feelings, mixed intentions, and mixed results. By its own lights, in large part the school worked. But its lights were very dim indeed.

Notes

Prologue

1. Bradford Peirce, handwritten case report, Case Record Book, 1856, pp. 1–2. The material on Maria is taken from pages 1 and 2.

2. Bradford, K. Peirce, Second Annual Report, Public Document 16, 1857, p. 26.

3. For a more detailed description of this development see Michel Foucault, *The Birth of the Clinic* and *Discipline and Punish*; Gerald N. Grob, *The State and the Mentally Ill* and *Mental Institutions in America*; David W. Lewis, *From Newgate to Dannemora*; Barbara Gutman Rosenkrantz, *Public Health and the State*; and David J. Rothman, *The Discovery of the Asylum.*

Chapter 1

1. The books listed in this note detail colonial community life and aspects of governance. In all, the mechanisms for self-regulation and the importance of the family to community well-being are stressed as critical aspects of community life. See Kenneth A. Lockridge, *A New England Town: The First Hundred Years*; Edmund S. Morgan, *The Puritan Family*; David Rothman, *The Discovery of the Asylum: Social Order and Disorder in the New Republic*; and Michael Zuckerman, *Peaceable Kingdoms: New England Towns in the Eighteenth Century* and "William Byrd's Family," in *Perspectives in American History*, vol. 12, 1979, pp. 253–311.

2. David J. Rothman, ibid., pp. 4, 5.

3. The Americans based their colonial laws on the British Poor Law. Therefore, Laws of Transfer and Removal—those English laws that vested in local governments the authority to ship dependents back to their former and supposedly legal places of residence to receive welfare aid—were adopted in the American colonies. Likewise, strangers who threatened to become dependent were "warned out"; that is, they were made formally aware, in no uncertain terms, that they were unwelcome in the community, as they threatened to become public burdens. They could not expect public aid or remain destitute within the town or village. They had to return to their "places of residence" for tending. Americans, like the British, were concerned with aiding the dependent. Yet they harbored a profound suspicion of, and were uncomfortable with, the unworthy.

4. Information on the size of the population of the United States, as well as immigration statistics and breakdown by ethnic group, and figures on the urbanization process during the nineteenth century were gathered from *Bureau of the Census, Historical*

Statistics of the United States. A more complete picture of the changing demographics of the United States in the 1800s may be obtained from appropriate charts therein.

5. The preponderance of immigration from Ireland, England, Northern Europe, and Germany continued into the 1880s. In the post–Civil War period, the newcomers increasingly were non-English-speaking Southern Europeans and Slavs. This change undoubtedly affected Americans' views of the immigrant. Earlier immigrants, originally regarded as unacceptably different and threatening, became less so as new, more frightening and despised groups entered the country. For instance, the Irish, previously ostracized and feared, gained a measure of acceptance and respectability as freed blacks and Russian Jews became highly visible.

6. Charles Eliot Norton, quoted in Barbara Miller Solomon, *Ancestors and Immigrants*, p. 11.

7. On the American response to immigration, see Barbara M. Solomon, ibid., and Oscar Handlin's excellent works, especially *Boston's Immigrants* and *The Uprooted*.

8. From "Address of the Board of Managers of the American Protestant Association, with the Constitution and Organization of the Association," quoted by Ray Allen Billington in "The Origins of Nativism in the United States, 1800–1844," PhD dissertation, Harvard University, Cambridge, MA, 1933. Billington's work appeared in book form in 1935.

9. Quoted in Billington, ibid., p. 267.

10. See Billington, ibid., pp. 168–187, 200–210.

11. For further discussion, see Stephan Thernstrom, "Urbanization, Migration and Social Mobility in Late Nineteenth Century America," in Raymond A. Mohl and Neil Betten, eds., *Urban America in Historical Perspective*, pp. 193–207, and *Poverty and Progress: Social Mobility in a Nineteenth Century City*, pp. 1–165.

12. Figures on the urbanization of the United States may be found in *Historical Statistics of the United States*, pp. 8–12.

13. Figures on age distribution may be obtained from the *Historical Statistics of the United States*, p. 29.

14. On other educational endeavors, see Michael B. Katz, *The People of Hamilton, Canada West*, and Michael B. Katz, Michael J. Doucet, and Mark T. Stern, *The Social Organization of Early Industrial Capitalism*.

15. *Historical Statistics of the United States*, pp. 22–29.

16. Bradford K. Peirce, *A Half-Century of Juvenile Delinquents*. Peirce used Charles Dickens's *American Notes* to illustrate the impact the slums of New York made on the visitor and on human well-being. Although Dickens's trip was in 1842, historians had described the Five Points as a slum area by 1820. See especially Carroll Smith-Rosenberg, *Religion and the Rise of the American City*. Smith-Rosenberg describes the Five Points and details the mission movements instigated by the Evangelicals in an attempt to alleviate suffering as well as to impose some control on this chaos; see especially pp. 225–244 for a detailed description of the Five Points House of Industry.

17. The two important reports quoted were the Quincy Report, or the *Report of the Committee on the consideration of the Pauper Laws of this Commonwealth* (Boston, 1821), and the *Report of the Commissioners appointed by an Order of the House of Representatives, Feb. 29, 1832, on the Subject of the Pauper System of the Commonwealth of Massachusetts* (Boston, 1835).

18. Although outdoor relief came to be considered as irresponsible—a way of encouraging pauperism—in fact, its practice continuued to be far more prevalent than institutionalization.

19. For further evidence of the change in Massachusetts law regarding paupers, see Jonathan Leavitt, Esq., *A Summary of the Laws of Massachusetts Relative to the Settlement, Support, Employment and Removal of Paupers* (1810). For a discussion of the process of the development of institutional responses to urban problems, see David J. Rothman, *The Discovery of the Asylum*, and Michael B. Katz, "Origins of the Institutional State," *Marxist Perspectives* 1:4 (1978).

20. Pauper statistics may be found in *Abstract of Returns of the Overseers of the Poor in Massachusetts for the year end November 1, 1846* prepared by John G. Palfrey, secretary of the commonwealth. The quotation from *The Crisis* may be found in Billington, "The Origins of Nativism," pp. 525–526.

21. All population and institutional statistics for the commonwealth, 1860, in this and the following paragraphs come from the *Census of Massachusetts, 1860.* Prison statistics for 1846 may be found in *Abstract of Returns of the Keepers of Jail and Overseers of the Houses of Correction* (Boston, 1846) for the year ending November 1, 1846, prepared for the use of the legislature by the secretary of the commonwealth.

22. See Douglas Jones, "The Strolling Poor: Transiency in Eighteenth Century Massachusetts," *Journal of Social History* 8:28–54 (1975).

23. Winthrop S. Hudson, *Religion in America*, vol. 2, pp. 113–198. On religious influence and activities in America, see Hudson, *Religion*. Clifton E. Olmstead, *History of Religion in the United States*; and Carroll Smith-Rosenberg, *Religion and the Rise of the American City*, pp. 40–96. Tract societies distributed religious tracts and other propaganda in an effort to expose the irreligious or ignorant to Christianity. The major goal was, of course, conversion.

24. Edward Jarvis, *Insanity and Idiocy in Massachusetts: Report of the Commission on Lunacy*, 1855, p. 52.

25. Charles A. Cummings on Herbert Spencer's *Social Statics or the Conditions Essential to Human Happiness Specified and the First of Them Developed* in *North American Review* 86:81 (1858).

26. For a more in-depth discussion, see Michael B. Katz, "The Origins of the Institutional State."

27. Stephen Simpson, quoted in Lawrence Cremin, *American Education: The National Experience 1783–1976*, p. 132.

28. Christopher Lasch, *Haven in a Heartless World: The Family Besieged.*

29. Horace Mann, First Annual Report, Boston School Committee, 1837.

30. The following historians discuss the concern with classifying the dependent and/or deviant as a crucial step in rehabilitative treatment: Gerald N. Grob, *The State and the Mentally Ill*; David W. Lewis, *From Newgate to Dannemora*; Robert M. Mennel, *Thorns and Thistles*; and Rothman, ibid.

Chapter 2

1. Gide Beaumont and A. de Tocqueville, *On the Penitentiary System in the United States and Its Application in France; With An Appendix On Penal Cultures, and Also, Statistical Notes* (Philadelphia, 1833), Francis Leiber, translator, conclusions.

2. David W. Lewis, *From Newgate to Dannemora—The Rise of the Penitentiary in New York, 1816–1848*, chapter 1; the quotation is on p. 29.

3. For a more complete account see E. C. Wines, *The State of Prisons and Child-Saving Institutions in the Civilized World.*

4. Lewis, *From Newgate to Dannemora*, p. 37.

5. Quoted by Lewis, ibid., p. 38.

6. See Lewis, ibid., and Wines, *The State of Prisons.* Among those reformers who advocated the Walnut Street prison style and strict solitary were key Massachusetts reformers: Samuel Gridley Howe, Horace Mann, and Charles Sumner. In 1845 they insisted, contrary to the opinion of Louis Dwight, then head of the Prisons Discipline Society, that the use of isolation continued the best method of reformation in spite of its alleged failures. What now seems ironic and cruel seemed to them humanitarian. They insisted that the use of total isolation gave the depraved inmate the greatest chance to reform and also made the necessity of harsh punishment less likely.

7. The congregate style originated there and was to become the model for penitentiaries throughout New York State, though with tremendous variations.

8. See Lewis, *From Newqate to Dannemora*, p. 93. Lewis presents the marching procedure as part of a routine intended to humiliate the convict and, therefore, to encourage his repentance. Marching was associated with pride and dignity; the shuffle, with which the march alternated, was a mark of degradation. This walking routine was carefully supervised and convicts were severely punished if they violated it by talking.

9. This quotation and the one following are from Lewis, ibid., p. 286.

10. In the middle decades of the nineteenth century in America, sentimental attitudes toward women gave rise to many social reforms. See Lewis, ibid., pp. 156–174; Douglas E. Branch, *The Sentimental Years—1836–1860: A Social History*, particularly chapters 7 and 8.

11. Lewis, ibid., p. 46.

12. John D. Davis, *Phrenology, Fad and Science: A 19th Century American Crusade.*

13. For a detailed description of Eliza Farnham and her life, her programs, efforts and eventual disappointments at Sing Sing, see Lewis, *From Newgate to Dannemora*, pp. 235–250.

14. "Gray on Prison Discipline, Boston Public Schools, *North American Review* 66:145–146 (1848).

15. In 1877 Elmira Reformatory opened in New York; it represented a major innovative effort to segregate youthful and first offenders and rehabilitate them by removing them from the more hardened criminals. In 1880 the State of Massachusetts opened Sherborn Reformatory for women; it was for young women too old and/or too hardened for the State Industrial School for Girls, Lancaster, and too young for the corruptible environment of jail. In 1885 Concord Reformatory, Concord, Massachusetts, opened. The irony underlying the reformatory movement was that it was seen as a great reform innovation, yet it managed to accomplish precisely what early Victorian reformers had resisted—classification of youth. Older and seemingly harder youth could now be transferred to reformatories. Yet only two decades earlier these schools had deliberately mixed age groups in an effort to make their schools more like a natural family and less like a prison.

16. Smith-Rosenberg, *Religion and the Rise of the American City*, pp. 125–159, details the correlation between evangelism, fear of and concern for poor children, and

religion in this chapter. See also Carl F. Kaestle, *The Evolution of an Urban School System*, pp. 120–126, 180–184.

17. De Beaumont and de Tocqueville, *On the Penitentiary System of the United States* (1833).

18. For further details on the House of Refuge and *parens patriae*, see Robert S. Pickett, *House of Refuge: Origins of Juvenile Reform in New York State, 1815–1857*, pp. 57–79, and Steven Schlossman, *Love and the American Delinquent*, chapter 1. Schlossman has ably argued that the acceptance in the nineteenth century of *parens patriae* as states' rights over children reestablishes the colonial community concept, since by its means the state could act as the community and ensure the protection of the dependent. As Schlossman has helpfully explained, *parens patriae* was really an outgrowth of a principle of equity law, which was gradually incorporated into American legal theory.

19. Pickett, ibid., Schlossman, ibid., and Smith-Rosenberg, *Religion and the Rise of the American City*. These three historians detail the influences behind the founding of the refuge as well as its significance in the evangelical enthusiasm of the times. Indeterminate sentencing was the legal act by which the state assumed responsibility for protecting a child until his or her adulthood. The termination of a sentence, therefore, was based on age and whim, not the original offense of the child. In reality, most children were released long before reaching their majorities.

20. Mennel, *Thorns and Thistles*; for a detailed description of the apprenticeships sponsored by the Refuge as part of its program, see, in particular, pp. 20–23.

21. For a detailed discussion and thoughtful analysis of these administrative arguments, see Kenneth R. Geiser, Jr., "Reform School Reform: The Nature of Change in a Social Policy Biography," PhD dissertation, MIT, 1977. On the philosophical influences on Wells, among whom was Johann Pestalozzi, see Mennel, ibid., pp. 24–27.

22. For a description of Tuckerman and the Boston Farm School, see Geiser, ibid., pp. 39–41. See also Jo Manton, *Mary Carpenter*, pp. 48–52, which describes the influence of Tuckerman on Mary Carpenter.

23. Geiser, ibid., pp. 41–53; Michael B. Katz, *The Irony of School Reform*, pp. 164–170; Branch, *The Sentimental Years*, chapter 7.

24. For details of the funding, see Geiser, ibid., and Katz, ibid.

25. On the goals of Westborough, see Public Document 23 (Commissioner's Report on Westborough), 1847, especially pp. 44–47.

26. See, in particular, Geiser, "Reform School Reform," pp. 40–48, and Katz, *The Irony of School Reform*, pp. 197–198.

27. See Branch, *The Sentimental Years*, and Kathryn Kish Sklar, *Catharine Beecher*. On crusades against prostitution, see Paul Boyer, *Urban Masses and Moral Order in America, 1820–1920*, p. 18. For further discussion of these issues, see Virginia Penny, *Think and Act: A Series of Articles Pertaining to Men and Women, Work and Wages* (Philadelphia, 1869).

28. On prison statistics see chapter 1 and W. David Lewis, *From Newgate to Dannemora*; this topic will also be discussed in greater depth in chapter 4. The literature on female criminality and its links with poverty and sexuality is scant. At Lancaster, however, these links are obvious and may be an indication of just how strictly society controlled females, especially young ones. Estelle B. Freedman's study of women's prison reform in America, *Their Sister's Keepers: Women's Prison Reform in America,*

1830–1930, contains information on women criminals and provides critical insight into the questions raised by her work, including female criminality and the responses to it. Information on Boston's courts may be found in Barbara Hobson's "Sex in the Marketplace: Prostitution in an American Victorian City, Boston, 1820–1880," PhD dissertation, Boston University, 1981.

29. Statistics and information on crimes committed by females were obtained from Middlesex County Superior Court Criminal Dockets, 1850–1905; Middlesex County Archives, Cambridge, Massachusetts; Suffolk County Superior Court Dockets, 1840–1860, Suffolk County Archives, Boston, Massachusetts.

30. On the imagery of, and expectation for, women in antebellum America, see Barbara Welter, "The Cult of True Womanhood," *American Quarterly* 18:151–174 (1966).

Chapter 3

1. Commissioner's Report, Massachusetts House Document 43, 1854.

2. Information on the commissioners is scanty, but may be found in various Who's Whos of the nineteenth century. The quote about Fay came from *Biographical Dictionary of American Congress: Who Was Who in American Politics*, p. 225; see also *Appleton's Cyclopedia of American Biography*, James Grant Wilson and John Fiske, eds., vol. 2 (New York, 1887).

3. The act that established the commission and outlined its task was a Massachusetts Legislature Resolves of April 12, 1854; quotations are from this legislation.

4. For discussion of the debate, see Bruce McPherson, *Between Two Worlds: Victorian Ambiguities about Progress*.

5. Information on the commissioners' many activities be found in their report to the legislature, the act that established the commission (see note 3), especially pp. 8, 29–30.

6. The full questionnaire and most of the responses were printed in the appendix to the full report. The responses given here are all from this appendix, pp. 29–34.

7. The notion of discernment is based on British common law, which considers children to act without discernment when they are too young to be able to distinguish between right and wrong. For a comprehensive discussion of the use and abuse of the doctrine *parens patriae*, see Steven Schlossman, *Love and the American Delinquent*, pp. 13–14.

8. See note 6.

9. The first quotation is from the appendix, p. 34; the second from the Commissioners' Report, p. 6. The following quotations from respondents to the questionnaire are from the appendix also.

10. See David W. Lewis, *From Newgate to Dannemora*, p. 28, and Crane Brinton, *The Shaping of Modern Thought*.

11. On Eddy, see Blanche D. Coll, *Perspectives in Public Welfare—A History*, p. 5; Lewis, ibid., p. 5; Robert Pickett, *House of Refuge*, pp. 23–26, 31–37; and Carroll Smith-Rosenberg, *Religion and the Rise of the City*, p. 50.

12. On Griscom, see Pickett, ibid., pp. 4, 10, 106–109; Smith-Rosenberg, ibid.; and Steven L. Schlossmann, *Love and the American Delinquent*, p. 22.

13. Lewis, *From Newgate to Dannemora*, p. 17. The description is quoted by Michel Foucault, in *Discipline and Punish*, p. 201.

14. R. Richard Wohl, "The 'Country Boy' Myth and Its Place in American Urban Culture: The Nineteenth Century Contribution," *Perspectives in American History* 11:112 (1969).

15. Stanley K. Schultz, *The Culture Factory*, pp. 47–49.

16. William O. Shanahan, *German Protestants Face the Social Question*, pp. ix, 59.

17. Mennel, *Thorns and Thistles*, pp. 74–83; Shanahan, ibid., pp. 74–83; Wohl, "The 'Country Boy' Myth", pp. 112–113. Wichern headed the new Protestant movement, the Inner Mission, which was dedicated to philanthropic work. His work at Rauhe Haus was in keeping with the meliorism of this movement.

18. Norbert Muller, "La Colonie Agricole Penitentiaire De Mettray, 1839–1939," unpublished memoir, Université de Tours, 1976, pp. 1–5.

19. In *La Peine de Mort*, Hugo expressed, through his account of condemned prisoner Claude Gueux, his commitment to humane social reform to alleviate the suffering of the poor and his abhorrence of the penal system. The constant torment of Jean Valjean in *Les Miserables* was also meant to impress Hugo's audience with the horrors resulting from the class struggle in France and to illustrate the link between abject poverty, which Hugo attributed in large part to the dislocation caused by modernity, and supposed criminality.

20. Bradford Peirce, *A Half Century with Juvenile Delinquents*, p. 178.

21. It is interesting to note that de Metz used the military march as a method to instill pride and self-respect in his boys; Sing Sing broke the military march with a shuffle to discourage this feeling in the inmates.

22. De Metz, *Rapport*, pp. 1–43, and "Statuts Constitutifs" in *Société Paternelle* (Paris, 1832), pp. 1–12. See also the anonymous *A Propos des Etrenus*, pp. 1–41. Much of this description is based on personal observation and my reading of various documents at the school Mettray, itself, in the summer of 1976.

23. See the works cited in note 22. Descriptions of Mettray are also found in various unpublished reports from Colonie de Agricole and in reports of the Royal Philanthropic Society (London) and especially in a letter written to William Gladstone, treasurer of the Royal Philanthropic Society, by Sydney Turner, president and chaplain of the Royal Philanthropic, and Thomas Paynter, police magistrate, 1846.

24. Interestingly, a private school for wealthy boys considered difficult and unruly by their parents was created at Mettray in 1858. They were kept separate from the *colons*, but like them were expected to benefit from Mettray's rural setting and strict military atmosphere.

25. Smith-Rosenberg, *Religion and the Rise of the American City*, pp. 34–69. Of special interest is Daniel Defoe's *Moll Flanders*, which makes clear the hardships, including Newgate, endured by women who, like Moll, were from the underclass.

26. For example, Charles Dickens and Lord Shaftesbury, author of *The Dens of London: Forty Years' Mission Work among the Outcast Poor of London* (London, 1844). See also the *Second Shaftesbury Lecture*; Jo Manton, *Mary Carpenter and the Children of the Streets*; and Massachusetts House Document 20, 1855, pp. 63–71.

27. On the goals of the society, see the anonymous "The Philanthropic Society, 1788–1840," an unpublished thesis delivered to Redhill; Officer's Report to Royal Philanthropic Society, 1829–1848; and Officer's Report to the Royal Philanthropic Society, Redhill, Surrey, 1848–1900. The quotation is taken from Sydney Turner, *Account of the Philanthropic Society*, 1848, p. 5.

28. Charles Dickens's *Oliver Twist* makes clear the idea that city environment was itself a threat, and considering the conditions of nineteenth-century cities, this was quite sensible. Fagin's band of "ruffians" was not a fiction on Dickens's part; in fact, it was a surrogate family, and the closest thing to a family many city boys ever knew. For additional contemporary expressions of nostalgia for the pastoral, see Cooke Taylor, "Notes of a Tour in the Manufacturing Districts of Lancashire, 1842," pp. 11–14, quoted in Steven Marcus, *Engels, Manchester and the Working Class*, and Mrs. Gaskell's novel *Mary Barton*, which juxtaposes the rural and the urban environments to show the salubriousness of the former.

29. Commissioner's Report, House Document 20, 1855, pp. 66–68.

30. Robert Mennel, *Thorns and Thistles*, pp. 37–49; Schlossman, *Love and the American Delinquent*, pp. 42–48; and Wohl, " 'The Country Boy Myth.' "

Chapter 4

1. Massachusetts House Document 43, January 1855, "An Act," p. 6.

2. Ibid., pp. 15, 53.

3. In 1863 Peirce left Lancaster to become the superintendent at the New York House of Refuge. He remained there until 1889. After leaving the New York House of Refuge he became editor of the *Zion's Herald Methodist Weekly*. Between 1863 and 1869 Peirce wrote four books, the titles of which indicate his interests and give us a good picture of him: *Life in the Woods: The Adventures of Audubon* (1863); *Trials of an Inventor: Life and Discoveries of Charles Goodyear* (1866); *The Word of God Opened* (1868); and *A Half Century with Juvenile Delinquents* (1869).

4. This quotation is from Catherine Beecher, given in Willystine Goodsell, *Pioneers of Women's Education in the U.S.*, as is the quotation following (pp. 127 and 147, respectively). Beecher's words had great impact on leading intellectuals of the day; see the review by S. E. Sewall in *The North American Review* 30:327–340 (1830). Peirce's words are from his 1858–1859 Annual Report on Lancaster to the Massachusetts Legislature, Public Document 24, 1858–1859.

5. Boston School Committee, Annual Report, 1867.

6. Massachusetts 13th Annual Report, 1868, p. 2.

7. The quotations on Lancaster's goals are from the 1858–1859 Annual Report, pp. 22–25.

8. These statistics, taken from US census figures, do not include all people. For example, subsistence farmers were not included. Regarding women in particular, census takers would not be inclined to ask women who claimed no occupation whether they had some other sort of employment, such as part-time or seasonal work. Also, the type of work some women did to help support their families, for example, taking in boarders, was often not the main source of family income and therefore would not be considered as employment. There were other reasons for taking the census results with a grain of salt: some women did not regard home-style industries as worthy of mention; husbands might not mention their wives' help in family businesses; some women might not want to admit to working. All this suggests that the official figures on female employment are understated.

9. This and the next two quotations are from Peirce's First Annual Report, Massachusetts House Document 20, 1856. The first quotation appears on p. 35; the next two quotations are from pp. 31–32.

10. Michael Katz, *The Irony of School Reform*; Jo Manton, *Mary Carpenter and the Children of the Streets*; Robert Mennell, *Thorns and Thistles: Juvenile Delinquents in the United States, 1825–1940*; Robert Pickett, *House of Refuge*; Steven Schlossman, *Love and the American Delinquent*; and Carroll Smith-Rosenberg, *Religion and the Rise of the American City*.

11. Oscar Handlin, *Boston's Immigrants*; Maldwyn A. Jones, *American Immigration*; and US Department of Commerce, Bureau of the Census, *Historical Statistics of the United States: Colonial Times to 1970*, pp. 87–121. On Catholics and Protestant institutions, also see Daniel Calhoun, ed., *The Education of Americans: A Documentary History*, pp. 158–171, and Carl F. Kaestle, *The Evolution of an Urban School System: New York City, 1750–1850*, pp. 148–158.

12. To calculate these occupational rankings, I used the scale of occupational rankings devised by Mai-Liis Gering and Michael B. Katz, "A Guide to the Study of Family and Class in Ontario's Past," which appeared as a draft copy in 1973 and was published by Michael B. Katz in *The People of Canada West—Family and Class in a Mid-Nineteenth Century City* as appendix 2, pp. 343–348. I was also guided by the Five Cities Project (Theodore Hershberg, Philadelphia, PA; Michael Katz, Hamilton, Ontario; Stuart Blumin, Kingston, NY; Laurence Glasco, Buffalo, NY; and Clyde Griffin, Poughkeepsie, NY), "Occupation and Ethnicity in Five Nineteenth Century Cities: A Collaborative Inquiry," rough draft, 1973.

13. Peter R. Knights, "Population Turnover, Resistance, and Residential Mobility in Boston, 1830–1860," and Leo F. Schnore and Peter R. Knights, "Residence and Social Structure: Boston in the Ante-Bellum Period," both in Stephan Thernstrom and Richard Sennett, eds., *Poverty and Progress, Social Mobility in a Nineteenth Century City*.

14. This calculation defines a move as change of residence to another town; for those whose families had wandered within town, who had been placed with families, or had been in a series of institutions, the moves would be unmeasured but even more common.

15. Case studies are drawn from Lancaster's records of the individual entrants—the circumstances of their placement at the school and their subsequent activities. The cases in this chapter are taken from Bradford Peirce's hand written Record Book 1, cases 6, 12, 2, 5, 33, and 71.

16. See Steven Schlossman, *Love and the American Delinquent*, pp. 59–62. When discussing children's crimes it is essential to understand the position of children in nineteenth-century America. Parents had absolute rights over children, including their earnings and property. Most stubborn children were regarded as "uncontrollable" and subject to punishment.

17. Case studies 5, 33, and 71 were the sources of information on Abigail, Maria, and Margaret.

18. I have tried to code the indenture years by arranging the data in the following categories: successful indenture: unsuccessful indenture: attendance at other institutions; no indenture; decision made for the girl to be given a "special" chance (that is, something better than indenture).

19. To answer this I examined the living situation and the employment of each girl twice in order to record changes over time. This is particularly important as there is, in most cases, more than one recorded follow-through. In addition, I arranged the data on living situation into the following six categories: with own relatives or complainant; in placement; dead or in other institutions; remaining in or having

returned to Lancaster beyond discharge; married; on own. Similarly, I arranged the data on employment or other activities into these categories: no employment due to institutionalization; no employment due to death; employment at "respectable" but menial work; work in a job that indicated mobility; a life of "dissolution."

Chapter 5

1. For more information on references, see Ronald G. Walters, *American Reformers 1815–1860*. Also see Harold Schwartz, *Samuel Gridley Howe*, a comprehensive picture of the various aspects of Howe's life; Jonathan Messerli, *Horace Mann*, p. 301; Michael B. Katz, *The Irony of Early School Reform*; and Robert M. Mennel, *Thorns and Thistles.* The Howe-Sanborn report was the Second Annual Report of the Massachusetts Board of State Charities, Public Document 19, 1865. Direct quotes in the text from this section are from pp. xxii–xxxviii, and xlv–lviii.

2. Second Annual Report of the Massachusetts Board of State Charities, p. xxiii.

3. Ibid., p. xxiv.

4. Ibid., p. xxv.

5. Ibid., p. xxiv. Jarvis's work, like other "scientific" research of the time, reflected contemporary racist attitudes. See Edward Jarvis, *Insanity and Idiocy in Massachusetts—Report of the Commission on Lunacy, 1855*, with a critical introduction by Gerald N. Grob.

6. Second Annual Report, p. xxiv.

7. This quotation, and the one following, are from the Second Annual Report, p. xlv.

8. Robert Weibe's *The Search for Order—1877–1920* provides a thorough and insightful discussion of post-Civil War America. See also Samuel P. Hays, *The Response to Industrialism 1885–1914*; Robert H. Bremner, *American Philanthropy*; Melvyn Dubofsky, *Industrialism and the American Worker, 1865–1920* (an excellent discussion of labor during this period); and Eric F. Goldman, *Rendezvous with Destiny*. Walter Hugins, ed., *The Reform Impulse, 1825–1850*, is useful for background.

9. Temperance in some form has always had its advocates in America. From colonial days right through to the passage of the twenty-first amendment rescinding prohibition, there have been movements to regulate alcohol consumption through legislation. See Ian R. Tyrrell, *Sobering Up: From Temperance to Prohibition in Antebellum America, 1800–1860*; Robert L. Hampel, *Temperance and Prohibition in Massachusetts, 1813–1852*; and Jack S. Blocker, Jr., *Retreat from Reform: The Prohibition Movement in the United States.*

10. Hampel, *Temperance and Prohibition*, chapter 4. See also Tyrrell, *Sobering Up*, pp. 5–9, 319.

11. Quoted in Tyrrell, *Sobering Up*, p. 152.

12. Data on demographic trends in Massachusetts come primarily from two sources: *Commonwealth Census Reports, 1860, 1877, 1880*, and *Historical Statistics of the United States*, p. 29. Figures on the United States come from *Historical Statistics of the United States*, pp. 8–12, 20–22, 54. On the fertility of American women, see *Statistical History of the United States*, pp. 23–24, and *Statistical Abstract, 1962*, p. 54. Also see Daniel Scott Smith, "Family Limitation, Sexual Control, and Domestic Feminism in Victorian America," in Nancy Cott and Elizabeth Pleck, eds., *A Heritage of Her Own.*

13. See note 12. Massachusetts was a national leader in industrial and urban growth throughout the nineteenth century.

14. Reverend Josiah Strong, *Our Country: Its Possible Future and Its Present Crisis* (New York: Baker and Taylor, 1885). See also Solomon, *Ancestors and Immigrants* on immigration restriction.

15. Trustees, Second Annual Report, 1857, Public Document 16, pp. 11, 14.

16. Trustees, Eighth Annual Report, 1863, Public Document 24, pp. 5–8.

17. Ibid., p. 15.

18. Pressure increased as demand accelerated for more places to accommodate needy girls. The Lancaster officers tried to cope with this need by enlarging House Number Five.

19. Superintendent's First Annual Report, 1856, Public Document 21, p. 13.

20. See Dubofsky, *Industrialism and the American Worker*; Samuel P. Hays, *The Response to Industrialism, 1855–1914*.

21. Quoted in Paul Boyer, *Urban Masses and Moral Order in America, 1820–1920*, p. 126.

22. Austin Phelps's introduction to Strong, *Our Country: Its Possible Future*, Introduction.

23. See Richard Hofstadter, *Social Darwinism in America*; Stephen J. Gould, *The Panda's Thumb* and *The Mismeasure of Man*; Jeffrey M. Blum, *Pseudoscience and Mental Ability—The Origins and Fallacies of the IQ Controversy*, especially pp. 25–42; and James M. Lawler, *IQ, Heritability, and Racism*, especially pp. 39–42.

24. Quoted in Hofstadter, *Social Darwinism*, p. 27.

25. Ibid., p. 42.

26. Sumner, Spencer, and other social Darwinists used "scientific" principles to prove the inferiority of various groups of humans. Viewed as subspecies, these groups, especially blacks, were believed innately unworthy.

27. Superintendent, Eleventh Annual Report, 1866, p. 18.

28. Debate on these questions has recently reintensified, with sociobiology playing the role now that social Darwinism played earlier. Any historical treatment of these debates becomes easily confused because different historical periods assume different principles and definitions. I am grateful to Barry L. Bull for helping me to clarify some of the questions and to sort out historical definitions.

29. Elizabeth Evans, quoted in Carl Degler, *At Odds: Woman and the Family in America from the Revolution to the Present*, p. 280. Both Degler and Linda Gordon, *Woman's Body, Woman's Right, Birth Control in America*, discuss social purity; see, especially, Degler, pp. 279–297, and Gordon, pp. 116–135.

30. Dubofsky, *Industrialism and the American Worker*, p. 30. See also *The Search for Order*.

31. On American education at this time, see David B. Tyack, *The One Best System: A History of American Urban Education*; Michael B. Katz, *Class, Bureaucracy and Schools*; Stanley K. Schultz, *The Culture Factory, Boston Public Schools, 1789–1860*; Lawrence A. Cremin, *The Transformation of the School: Progressivism in American Education, 1876–1957*.

32. Second Annual Report of Board of State Charities, p. xlvi.

33. Kenneth R. Geiser, Jr., "Reform School Reform: The Nature of Change in a Social Policy Biography, "PhD dissertation, MIT, Cambridge, MA, 1977.

34. Ibid., pp. 52–53. Geiser's thesis goes on to examine the implications of the various administrative reorganizations from 1865 to 1972.

Chapter 6

1. Bradford K. Peirce, handwritten case report, State Industrial School for Girls, Case Record Book, 1856, p. 2.

2. Trustees' Eighth Annual Report, State Industrial School for Girls, Public Document 24, 1863, p. 5.

3. First Annual Report, State Industrial School for Girls, 1856, p. 34.

4. Trustees' Annual Report, State Industrial School for Girls, 1863, p. 5.

5. Annual Report of the Superintendent, State Industrial School for Girls, 1864, p. 8.

6. Massachusetts Second Annual Report of the Board of State Charities, p. 3.

7. Tenth Annual Report, State Industrial School for Girls, 1866, p. 3.

8. First Annual Report, State Industrial School for Girls, 1856, p. 35.

9. Second Annual Report, Public Document 16, 1856, p. 11.

10. The case histories of the girls at the State Industrial School for Girls, Lancaster, for the period 1856–1905 are the source of the quantitative information presented in this chapter. Portions of certain case records are presented in order to fill out the statistical portrait with qualitative information. The particular examples were chosen to illustrate trends documented by the numbers. Care was taken to ensure that representative samples were used in the text. The examples come from extrants of every type of background—Yankee, Irish, "colored," "Russian Jew," French Canadian, and so forth. One striking finding is the similarities among these girls. For the purposes of this chapter, for each case the entire record was read, including correspondence and newspaper articles that were occasionally attached. Case numbers quoted or discussed in the text for this and later chapters are the following: 1863, cases 289–312, 324, 325, 343, 355; 1870, cases 748–752, 777–783; 1875, cases 862–867, 875, 884–892; 1880, cases 1059–1064, and 1073–1080; 1885, cases 1274, 1279–1289, 1293–1302, 1315; 1890, cases 1535–1545, 1550, 1578–1587; 1895, cases 1847–1852, 1858–1865, 1885–1887, 1894, 1907; 1900, cases 2285–2292, 2313, 2322–2328, 2356, 2358, 2368, 2375.

11. The development of other institutions within the state is more fully discussed in the next chapter. Some of Lancaster's girls became trapped in the web and went on from Lancaster to prison, the state home for the feebleminded, or a state almshouse. A few undoubtedly needed such care; for others, however, there was no alternative.

12. To calculate these occupational rankings, I used the scale of occupational rankings devised by Gering, Mai-Liis, and Katz and drew also on the Five Cities Project; see note 12, chapter 4. See also Peter R. Knights, "Population Turnover, Resistance, and Residential Mobility in Boston, 1830–1860," and Leo F. Schnore and Peter R. Knights, "Residence and Social Structure: Boston in the Ante-Bellum Period," in Stephan Thernstrom and Richard Sennett, eds., *Poverty and Progress: Social Mobility in a Nineteenth Century City.*

13. Indeed, the topic most frequently occurring in the records is the parents' temperance.

14. Second Annual Report of Board of State Charities, p. xxv.

15. See Robert Hampel, *Temperance and Prohibition in Massachusetts, 1813–1852.*

16. Michael Katz, *Irony.*

17. Annual Report, State Industrial School for Girls, 1862, p. 18.

18. Annual Report, State Industrial School for Girls, 1892, p. 22.

19. In a few cases, where the religion was not specified, I assumed that Irish and Irish-American girls were Catholic. On the Catholic response to public education, see Daniel Calhoun, ed., *The Educating of Americans: A Documentary History*, especially 158–171, and Carl F. Kaestle, *The Evolution of an Urban School System: New York City, 1750–1850*, pp. 148–158.

20. Status offenses, which were not explicitly criminal, were precisely the grounds upon which many girls were sent to Lancaster.

21. Annual Report, State Industrial School for Girls, 1884, p. 15.

22. Ibid.

23. Included in this 19.6 percent of girls in institutions were a few who remained at Lancaster beyond 21; it was uncommon, but not out of the question, for some of the girls in the study to return to the school or remain there.

Chapter 7

1. Massachusetts, 10th Annual Report, Public Document 21, 1865, p. 12.

2. Massachusetts, 12th Annual Report, 1867, p. 7.

3. On Lancaster's role as model for various American reform efforts, see Robert M. Mennel, "The Family System of Common Farmers: The Origins of Ohio's Reform Farm 1840–1858," *Ohio History* 89:125–156 (Spring 1980), and "The Family System of Common Farmers: The Study of Ohio's Reform Farm, 1858–1884, *Ohio History* 89:280–322 (Spring 1980), and also, Steven Schlossman, *Love and the American Delinquent*.

4. 11th Annual Report, 1867, p. 2.

5. On the demand for servants at this time, see David M. Katzman, *Seven Days a Week*; Michael B. Katz, Michael J. Doucet, and Mark J. Stern, *The Social Organization of Early Industrial Capitalism*; and Carol S. Lasser, "Mistress, Maid and Market: The Transformation of Domestic Service in New England, 1790–1870," PhD Dissertation, Harvard University, Cambridge, MA, 1981.

6. Massachusetts, 13th Annual Report, to the Board of State Charities, Public Document 20, 1868, p. 2.

7. Ibid.

8. Massachusetts, 14th Annual Report, to the Board of State Charities, Public Document 20, 1869, p. 1.

9. David Katzman, *Seven Days a Week*.

10. Massachusetts, 14th Annual Report, to the Board of State Charities, Public Document 20, 1869, p. 1.

11. Carol S. Lasser, *A 'Pleasingly Oppressive' Burden: The Transformation of Domestic Service and Female Charity in Salem, 1800–1840*.

12. Massachusetts, 10th Annual Report, 1865, p. 14.

13. Massachusetts, 14th Annual Report, to the Board of State Charities, Public Document 20, 1869, p. 1.

14. Massachusetts, 22nd Annual Report, Public Document 20, 1877, p. 12.

15. For a discussion of the cases presented in this chapter, see note 10 in chapter 6.

16. Massachusetts, 20th Annual Report, Public Document 20, 1875, p. 1.

17. Massachusetts, 29th Annual Report, to State Board of Health, Lunacy and Charity, Public Document 18, 1885, p. 44.

18. Ibid.

19. Massachusetts, 32nd Annual Report, to State Board of Health, Lunacy and Charity, Public Document 18, 1887, p. 13.

20. Massachusetts, 29th Annual Report, to State Board of Health, Lunacy and Charity, Public Document 18, 1885, p. 19.

21. Massachusetts, 34th Annual Report, to State Board of Lunacy and Charity, Public Document 18, 1888, p. 12.

22. P. 159.

23. Boston School Committee Reports, 1864, 1874.

24. I wish to thank Linda M. Perkins for helping clarify the role Tuskegee Institute played in educating black youth in the 1880s. For further discussion on the education of black girls in the North, see Linda M. Perkins, "Fanny Jackson Coppin and the Institute for Colored Youth: A Model of Nineteenth Century Black Female Educational and Community Leadership, 1837–1902," PhD Dissertation, University of Illinois, Urbana, 1975.

25. See Barbara Brenzel and Walter McCann, "Education, Technical," in *Encyclopedia of Sociology*, and for a more detailed account, Marvin Lazerson, *The Origins of the Urban Public School* and Marvin Lazerson and W. Norton Grubb, eds., *American Education and Vocationalism.*

26. For a detailed discussion of this phenomenon, see David Tyack, *The One Best System.*

27. Massachusetts House Documents, 1855, p. 15.

28. Massachusetts, 2nd Annual Report, House Document 16, 1857, p. 10.

29. Ibid.

30. Ibid., p. 10.

31. Massachusetts, 3rd Annual Report, House Document 24, 1858, p. 29.

32. Ibid.

33. Ibid.

34. Massachusetts, 4th Annual Report, House Document 24, 1859, p. 28.

35. Massachusetts, 12th Annual Report, Public Document 23, 1863, p. 7.

36. Ibid.

37. Commonwealth of Massachusetts, Trustees Report Primary School, 1895, p. 9.

38. Massachusetts, 18th Annual Report, to State Board of Health, Lunacy and Charity, Public Document 20, 1873, p. 6.

39. Massachusetts, 22nd Annual Report, to State Board of Health, Lunacy and Charity, Public Document 20, 1877, p. 7.

40. Massachusetts, 23rd Annual Report, to State Board of Health, Lunacy and Charity, Public Document 20, 1878, p. 24.

41. Ibid., p. 15.

42. Massachusetts, 28th Annual Report, to State Board of Health, Lunacy and Charity, 1885, p. 16.

43. Ibid., p. 19.

44. Massachusetts, 29th Annual Report to the State Board of Health, Lunacy and Charity, Public Document 18, 1884, p. 15.

45. Massachusetts, 32nd Annual Report to the State Board of Lunacy and Charity, Public Document 18, 1887, p. 14.

46. The data on classification by house was obtained through an analysis of assignment by age and crime. The findings cited in the text were derived from cross tabulating relevant variables to uncover any trends.

47. Michel Foucault, *Discipline and Punish,* p. 191.

48. Massachusetts Board of Insanity, Public Document 28, 1899, p. 60.

49. Unpublished record of Dr. Walter E. Fernald, the Walter E. Fernald State School, 1910.

50. An unpublished record of Dr. Walter E. Fernald, the Walter E. Fernald State School, 1908.

51. State Industrial School for Girls, case record 2336, 1900.

52. A rough copy of this paper is filed as 25–47 in the collected papers of Dr. Walter E. Fernald, the Walter E. Fernald State School, 1908.

53. Ibid., pp. 1, 11, 13, 14.

54. Unpublished records of the State Industrial School for Girls (case 2210) and "The Imbecile with Criminal Instincts," Walter E. Fernald State School, 1908 (case 1901). These two case records for Susannah D. have been cross checked.

55. State Industrial School for Girls, record 2222, 1899, and "The Imbecile with Criminal Instincts," Walter E. Fernald State School, 1908.

Chapter 8

1. The letter from Jane B. was attached to her case record at the State Industrial School for Girls. Her case and others used in this chapter are included in the list of cases given in note 10, chapter 6.

2. Here I use the term "success" as the trustees and administrators of Lancaster would. That is, the girls were living with families and not financially destitute. I consider these criteria very minimal and wonder whether the officers felt differently than they publicly admitted.

Bibliography

Abstract of Returns of the Keepers of Jails and Overseers of the Houses of Correction for the year ending Nov. 1, 1846. Prepared for the use of the Legislature by the Secretary of the Commonwealth. Boston: Dutton and Wentworth, State Printers, 1846.

Adam, Hargrave L. *Woman and Crime*. Clifford's Inn, London: T. Werner Laurie, 1915.

Anonymous. *A Propos des Etrenus*. Paris: n.p., 1863.

———. *Notice Sur les Colonies Agricoles D'Hambourg et de Mettray*. Handwritten official account, no date given.

———. "Second Shaftesbury Lecture to Shaftesbury Society" (pamphlet), 1918.

Aries, Phillipe. *Centuries of Childhood—A Social History of Family Life*. New York: Vintage Press, 1962.

Arnold, Matthew. *Culture and Anarchy*. Cambridge: Cambridge University Press, 1960.

Axinn, June, and Levin, Herman. *Social Welfare: A History of the American Response to Need*. New York: Dodd, Mead, 1975.

Bailyn, Bernard. *Education and the Forming of American Society*. Chapel Hill: University of North Carolina Press, 1960.

Bainton, Roland H. *The Reformation of the Sixteenth Century*. Boston: Beacon Press, 1960.

Bannister, Robert C. *Social Darwinism: Science and Myth in Anglo-American Social Thought*. Philadelphia: Temple University Press, 1979.

Beecher, Catharine E. *Woman Suffrage and Woman's Profession*. New York: George Maclean, 1872.

Bender, Thomas. *Toward an Urban Vision*. Lexington: University Press of Kentucky, 1975.

Best, Geoffrey. *Mid-Victorian Britain, 1851–1875*. New York: Schocken Books, 1972.

Bezucha, Robert J. *Modern European Social History*. Lexington, MA: D. C. Heath, 1972.

Billington, Ray Allen. "The Origins of Nativism in the United States, 1800–1844." PhD Dissertation, Harvard University, 1933.

Blackwell, Elizabeth. *Essays in Medical Sociology*. New York: Arno Press and The New York Times, 1972.

Bledstein, Burton. *The Culture of Professionalism in the Middle Class and the Development of Higher Education in America*. New York: W. W. Norton, 1976.

Blocker, Jack S., Jr. *Retreat from Reform: The Prohibition Movement in the United States 1890–1913*. Westport, Ct: Greenwood Press, 1976.

Blodgett, Geoffrey. *The Gentle Reformers: Massachusetts Democrats in the Cleveland Era*. Cambridge, MA: Harvard University Press, 1966.

Blum, Jeffrey M. *Pseudoscience and Mental Ability—The Origins and Fallacies of the IQ Controversy*. New York and London: Monthly Review Press, 1978.

Boies, Henry M. *Prisoners and Paupers: A Study of Criminals and the Public Burden of Pauperism in the United States; the Causes and Remedies*. New York: G. P. Putnam & Sons, 1893.

Bolton, Sarah K. *Social Studies in England*. Boston: D. Lothrop and Company, 1888.

Boorstin, Daniel J. *The Americans—the Colonial Experience*. New York: Vintage Press, 1958.

———. *The Americans—the National Experience*. New York: Vintage Press, 1965.

Boston Children's Friend Society. *Fifteenth Annual Report of the Boston Children's Friend Society*. Boston: I. R. Betts, 1848.

Bowles, Samuel, and Gintis, Herbert. *Schooling in Capitalist America*. New York: Basic Books, 1970.

Boyer, Paul. *Urban Masses and Moral Order in America, 1820–1920*. Cambridge, MA: Harvard University Press, 1978.

———, and Nissenbaum, Stephen. *Salem Possessed: The Social Origins of Witchcraft*. Cambridge, MA: Harvard University Press, 1974.

Branch, Douglas E. *The Sentimental Years, 1836–1860*. New York: Hill and Wang, 1965.

Braverman, Harry. *Labor and Monopoly Capital—The Degradation of Work in the Twentieth Century*. New York: Monthly Review Press, 1974.

Bremner, Robert H. *American Philanthropy*. Chicago: University of Chicago Press, 1960.

———(ed.). *Children and Youth in America—A Documentary History*, Vols. 1, 2, and 3. Cambridge, MA: Harvard University Press, 1970.

Brenzel, Barbara M. "The Girls at Lancaster: A Social Portrait of a Nineteenth Century Reform School for Girls," *Feminist Studies* 13 (Winter/Spring 1976).

———. "Nineteenth Century Reform Schools: Prevention, Punishment or Rehabilitation." Paper presented at American Historical Association, December 1976.

———. "Domestication as Reform: The Socialization of Wayward Girls," *Harvard Educational Review 50(2) (Spring 1980).*

Brinton, Crane. *The Shaping of Modern Thought*. Englewood Cliffs, NJ: Prentice-Hall, 1950.

Bronowski J., and Mazlish, Bruce. *The Western Intellectual tradition*. New York: Harper and Row, 1960.

Brundage, James A. "Prostitution in the Medieval Canon Law," *Signs: Journal of Women in Culture and Society* 1(4) (Summer 1976).

Bullough, Vern L. *The Subordinate Sex: A History of Attitudes toward Women*. Baltimore: Penguin Books, 1974.

Calhoun, Daniel. *The Intelligence of a People*. Princeton: Princeton University Press, 1973.

———(ed.). *The Educating of Americans—A Documentary History*. Boston: Houghton Mifflin, 1969.

Callahan, Raymond E. *Education and the Cult of Efficiency*. Chicago: University of Chicago Press, 1962.

Cantagrel, F. *Mettray et Ostwald—Etude Sur les Deux Colonies Agricoles*. Paris: Librarie de l'Ecole Societaire, 1842.

Carlyle, Thomas. *Past and Present*. London: J. M. Dent, 1966.

Cary, John, and Weinberg, Julius. *The Social Fabric: American Life from 1607 to the Civil War*. Boston: Little, Brown, 1975.

———. *The Social Fabric: American Life from the Civil War to the Present*. Boston: Little, Brown, 1975.

Chesney, Kellow. *The Victorian Underworld*. Harmondsworth, Middlesex: Penguin Books, 1970.

Chevalier, Louis. *Laboring Classes and Dangerous Classes in Paris during the First Half of the 19th Century*. New York: Schlossman, 1973.

Church, Robert L. *Education in the United States*. New York: The Free Press, 1976.

Cohen, David K. "Loss as a Theme in Social Policy," *Harvard Educational Review* 46 (1976).

Coll, Blanche D. *Perspectives in Public Welfare—A History*. Washington, DC: US Government Printing Office, 1969.

Conway, Moncure Daniel. *Emerson at Home and Abroad*. New York: Haskel House, 1968.

Cott, Nancy F. *Root of Bitterness: Documents of the Social History of American Women*. New York: E. P. Dutton, 1972.

———. "Young Women in the Second Great Awakening in New England," *Feminist Studies* 3(1/2) (Fall 1975).

———. *Bonds of True Womanhood*. New Haven: Yale University Press, 1977.

Cremin, Lawrence A. *The Transformation of the School: Progressivism in American Education, 1876–1957*. New York: Vintage Books, 1964.

———. *American Education: The Colonial Experience 1607–1783*. New York: Harper and Row, 1970.

———. *American Education: The National Experience, 1783–1876*. New York: Harper and Row, 1980.

———Cross, Barbara M. *The Educated Woman in America: Selected Writings of Catharine Beecher, Margaret Fuller, and M. Carey Thomas*. New York: Teachers College Press, 1965.

Davis, Allan F. *Spearheads of Reform: The Social Settlement and The Progressive Movement*. New York: Oxford University Press, 1967.

———. *American Heroine: The Life and Legend of Jane Addams*. New York: Oxford University Press, 1973.

Davis, John D. *Phrenology: Fad and Science*. New Haven: Yale University Press, 1955.

Davis, Natalie A. " 'Women's History' in Transition," *Feminist Studies* (Spring/Summer 1976).

de Beaumont, G. and de Tocqueville, A. *On the Penitentiary System in the United States and its Application in France*. Philadelphia: Corey, Lea, and Blanchard, 1833.

Degler, Carl N. *Out of Our Past*. New York: Harper and Row, 1970.

———. *At Odds—Women and the Family in America from the Revolution to the Present.* New York: Oxford University Press, 1980.

DeMause, Lloyd (ed.). *The History of Childhood.* New York: Harper and Row, 1974.

Demos, John. *A Little Commonwealth: Family Life in Plymouth Colony.* New York: Oxford University Press, 1970.

———. "Developmental Perspectives on the History of Childhood," *The Journal of Interdisciplinary History* 2(2) (Autumn 1971).

———, and Demos, Virginia. "Adolescence in Historical Perspective," *Journal of Marriage and the Family* 31 (1969).

de Toqueville, Alexis. *Democracy in America.* New York: Washington Square Press, 1964.

Dix, Dorothea L. *Remarks on Prisons and Prison Discipline in the United States.* Philadelphia: Joseph Kite and Company, 1845.

Douglas, Ann. *The Feminization of American Culture.* New York: Avon Books, 1978.

Dublin, Thomas. "Women, Work and the Family: Female Operatives in the Lowell Mills, 1830–1860," *Feminist Studies,* 3(1/2) (Fall 1975).

———. *Women at Work: The Transformation of Work and Community in Lowell, Massachusetts, 1826–1860.* New York: Columbia University Press, 1979.

Dubofsky, Melvyn. *Industrialization and the American Worker, 1865–1920.* Arlington Heights, IL: AHM, 1975.

DuBois, Ellen. "On Labor and Free Love: Two Unpublished Speeches of Elizabeth Cady Stanton," *Signs* 1(7) (Autumn 1975).

Dugdale, Robert. *The Judes: A Study in Crime, Pauperism, Disease and Heredity.* New York: G. P. Putnam & Sons, 1877.

Eade, Susan Margaret. "The Reclaimers: A Study of the Reformatory Movement in England and Wales 1846–1893." PhD Dissertation, Australian National University, 1975.

Encyclopedia of Sociology. Guilford, CT: The Dushkin Publishing Group, 1974.

Faragher, Johnny, and Stansell, Christine. "Women and Their Families on the Overland Trail, 1842–1867," *Feminist Studies* 2(2/3) (1975).

Farber, Bernard. *Guardians of Virtue—Salem Families in 1800.* New York: Basic Books, 1972.

Feldstein, Stanley, and Costello, Lawrence (eds.). *The Ordeal of Assimilation: A Documentary History of the White Working Class.* New York: Anchor Books, 1914.

Ferri, Enrieo. *The Positive School of Criminology.* Chicago: University of Chicago Press, 1906.

Finestone, Harold. *Victims of Change: Juvenile Delinquents in American Society.* Westport, CT: Greenwood Press, 1976.

Fisher, Berenice M. *Industrial Education: American Ideas and Institutions.* Madison, WI: University of Wisconsin Press, 1967.

Flinn, Michael W. *An Economic and Social Theory of Britain, 1066–1939.* London: Macmillan, 1972.

Foucault, Michel. *Madness and Civilization: A History of Insanity in the Age of Reason.* New York: Vintage Books, 1965.

———. *The Birth of the Clinic.* New York: Pantheon Books, 1973.

———. *Discipline and Punish: The Birth of Prison.* New York: Pantheon Books, 1977.

Freedman, Estelle B. *Their Sisters' Keepers: Women's Prison Reform in America, 1830–1930.* Ann Arbor: University of Michigan Press, 1981.

Frisch, Michael H. *Town into City: Springfield, Massachusetts, and the Meaning of Community, 1840–1880.* Cambridge, MA: Harvard University Press, 1972.

Garcia, J. M. *La Colonie De Mettray.* Paris: n.p., 1870.

Gaskell, Elizabeth G. *Mary Barton.* London: J. M. Dent, 1971.

———. *North and South.* New York: J. M. Dent, 1975.

Gasparin, M. le comte de. *Discours.* Paris: n.p., 1841, 1843.

Geiser, Kenneth R., Jr. "Reform School Reform: The Nature of Change in a Social Policy Biography." PhD Dissertation, MIT, 1977.

George, Vic, and Wilding, Paul. *Ideology and Social Welfare.* Boston: Routledge and Kegan Paul, 1876.

Gillis, John R. *Youth and History: Tradition and Change in European Age Relations, 1770–Present.* New York: Academic Press, 1974.

Goffman, Erving. *Asylums.* New York: Doubleday, 1961.

Goldman, Eric F. *Rendezvous with Destiny: A History of Modern American Reform.* New York: Vintage Books, 1955.

Goodsell, Willystine. *Pioneers of Women's Education in the United States: Emma Willard, Catharine Beecher, Mary Lyon.* New York: McGraw-Hill, 1931.

Gordon, Linda. *Woman's Body, Woman's Right—Birth Control in America.* New York: Penguin Books, 1976.

Gould, Stephen J. *The Panda's Thumb—More Reflections in Natural History.* New York: W. W. Norton, 1980.

———. *The Mismeasure of Man.* New York: W. W. Norton, 1981.

Gramsci, Antonio. *Selections from the Prison Notebooks of Antonio Gramsci.* Quintin Hoare and Geoffrey Nowell Smith, eds. and trans. New York: International Publishers, 1971.

Greer, Colin. *The Great School Legend—A Revisionist Interpretation of American Public Education.* New York: Basic Books, 1972.

Grob, Gerald N. *The State and the Mentally Ill—A History of Worcester State Hospital in Massachusetts, 1830–1920.* Chapel Hill: University of North Carolina Press, 1966.

———. *Mental Institutions in America: Social Policy to 1875.* New York: Free Press, 1973.

———. "Mental Illness, Indigency, and Welfare: The Mental Hospital in Nineteenth Century America." In *Anonymous Americans,* Tamara Haraven, ed. Englewood Cliffs, NJ: Prentice-Hall, 1977.

Hahn, Emily. *Once Upon a Pedestal.* New York: New American Press, 1974.

Haller, John S., and Haller, Robin M. *The Physician and Sexuality in Victorian America.* Chicago: University of Illinois Press, 1974.

Hampel, Robert L. *Temperance and Prohibition in Massachusetts, 1813–1852.* Ann Arbor, Michigan: UMI Research Press, 1982.

Handlin, Oscar. *Boston's Immigrants.* Cambridge, MA: Harvard University Press, 1941.

———. *Commonwealth: A Study of the Role of Government in the American Economy: Massachusetts, 1774–1861.* Cambridge, MA: The Belknap Press of Harvard University Press, 1969.

———. *Boston's Immigrants: A Study in Acculturation.* New York: Atheneum, 1972.

———, and Mary Flug. *Facing Life: Youth and the Family in American History.* Boston: Little, Brown, 1971.

Haraven, Tamara K. "Family Time and Industrial Time: Family and Work in a Planned Corporation Town, 1900–1924," *Journal of Urban History* 2 (May 1975).

———. "Modernization and Family History: Perspectives on Social Change," *Signs* 1(4) (Autumn 1976).

———(ed.). *Anonymous Americans. Explorations in Nineteenth Century Social History.* Englewood Cliffs, NJ: Prentice-Hall, 1971.

Harrison, Brian. "Philanthropy and the Victorians," *Victorian Studies,* 9(4) (1966).

———. *Drink and the Victorians. The Temperance Question in England 1815–1872.* Pittsburgh: University of Pittsburgh Press, 1971.

Hawes, Joseph M. *Children in Urban Society—Juvenile Delinquency in Nineteenth Century America.* New York: Oxford University Press, 1971.

Hay, Douglas, Linebaugh, Peter, Rule, John G., Thompson, E. P., and Winslow, Cal. *Albion's Fatal Tree—Crime and Society in Eighteenth Century England.* New York: Pantheon, 1975.

Hays, Samuel P. *The Response to Industrialism, 1855–1914.* Chicago: University of Chicago Press, 1957.

Hershberg, Theodore. "The Philadelphia Social History Project," *Historical Methods Newsletter.* 9(2,3) (1976).

Hibbert, Christopher. *The Roots of Evil: A Social History of Crime and Punishment.* London: Minerva Press, 1968.

Hindus, Michael S. *Prison and Plantation: Criminal Justice and Authority in Massachusetts and South Carolina 1767–1876.* Chapel Hill: University of North Carolina Press, 1980.

Hobsbawm, E. J. *The Age of Revolution: Europe 1789–1848.* London: Cardinal, 1962.

———. *Labouring Men—Studies in the History of Labour.* London: Weidenfeld and Nicolson, 1964.

———. "From Social History to a History of Society," *Daedalus* 1 (Winter 1971).

———. *Industry and Empire.* London: Penguin Books, 1975.

Hobson, Barbara. "Sex in the Marketplace: Prostitution in an American Victorian City, Boston 1820–1880." PhD Dissertation, Boston University, 1981.

Hofstadter, Richard. *The Age of Reform: From Bryan to F.D.R.* New York: Random House, 1955.

———. *America of 1750: A Social Portrait.* New York: Vintage Books, 1973.

Houston, Susan. "The Impetus to Reform: Crime, Poverty and Ignorance in Ontario 1850–1875." PhD Dissertation, University of Toronto, 1974.

Hudson, Winthrop S. *Religion in America.* New York: Charles Scribner's, 1965, 1973.

Hugins, Walter. *The Reform Impulse, 1825–1850.* Columbia, SC: University of South Carolina Press, 1972.

Huthmacher, Joseph J. *A Nation of Newcomers: Ethnic Minority Groups in American History.* New York: Dell, 1967.

Inglis, Brian. *Poverty and the Industrial Revolution.* London: Panther Books, 1972.

Jarvis, Edward. *Insanity and Idiocy in Massachusetts: Report of the Commission on Lunacy, 1855.* Cambridge, MA: Harvard University Press, 1971.

Jeffrey, Kirk. "Marriage, Career and Feminine Ideology in Nineteenth Century America: Reconstructing the Experience of Lydia Maria Child, 1828–1874," *Feminist Studies* 2(2/3) (1975).

Johansson, Sheila Ryan. "Herstory as History: A New Field or Another Fad?" In *Liberating Women's History*, Berenice A. Carroll, ed. Chicago: University of Chicago Press, 1976.

Jones, Douglas. "The Strolling Poor: Transiency in Eighteenth Century Massachusetts," *Journal of Social History* 8 (1975).

Kaestle, Carl F. *The Evolution of an Urban School System*. Cambridge, MA: Harvard University Press, 1973.

Katz, Michael B. *The Irony of Early School Reform*. Cambridge, MA: Harvard University Press, 1968.

———. *Class, Bureaucracy and Schools*. New York: Praeger, 1971.

———. *The People of Hamilton, Canada West: Family and Class in a Mid-Nineteenth Century City*. Cambridge, MA: Harvard University Press, 1975.

———. "Origins of the Institutional State," *Marxist Perspectives* 1(4) (Winter 1978).

———(ed.). *Education in American History*. New York: Praeger, 1973.

———(ed.). *School Reform Past and Present*. Boston: Little, Brown, 1971.

———, Doucet, Michael J., and Stern, Mark J. *The Social Organization of Early Industrial Capitalism*. Cambridge, MA: Harvard University Press, 1982.

Katzman, David M. *Seven Days a Week: Women and Domestic Service in Industrializing America*. New York: Oxford University Press, 1978.

Keller, Morton. *Affairs of State: Public Life in Late Nineteenth Century America*. Cambridge, MA: The Belknap Press of Harvard University Press, 1977.

Kessler-Harris, Alice. "Women, Work and the Social Order," Center for Education Policy Research reprint, Harvard University, 1971.

———. *Out to Work: A History of Wage-Earning Women in the United States*. New York: Oxford University Press, 1982.

Kett, Joseph F. "Growing Up in Rural New England, 1800–1840." In *Anonymous Americans*, Tamara Haraven, ed. Englewood Cliffs, NJ: Prentice-Hall, 1971.

———. *Rites of Passage—Adolescence in America 1790 to the Present*. New York: Basic Books, 1977.

Kohn, Melvin L. *Class and Conformity: A Study in Values*. Homewood, IL: The Dorsey Press, 1969.

Kramer, Paul, and Holborn, Frederick L. (eds.). *The City in American Life: A Historical Anthology*. New York: Capricorn Books, 1971.

Laslett, Peter. *The World We Have Lost*. London: Methuen, 1965.

Lasser, Carol S. *A 'Pleasingly Oppressive' Burden: The Transformation of Domestic Service and Female Charity in Salem, 1800–1840*. Offprint from Essex Institute Historical Collections, Vol. 116, No. 3, April 1980.

———. "Mistress, Maid and Market: The Transformation of Domestic Service in New England, 1790–1870." PhD Dissertation, Harvard University, 1981.

Lawler, James M. *IQ, Heritability and Racism*. New York: International Publishers, 1978.

Lazerson, Marvin. *The Origins of the Urban School*. Cambridge, MA: Harvard University Press, 1971.

———, and Grubb, W. Norton.*American Education and Vocationalism: A Documentary History, 1870–1970.* New York: Teachers College Press, 1974.

Leavis, F. R. *John Stuart Mill on Bentham and Coleridge.* New York: Harper, 1950.

Leavitt, Jonathan. *A Summary of the Laws of Massachusetts Relative to the Settlement, Support, Employment and Removal of Paupers.* Greenfield, MA: John Denio, 1810.

Lebergott, Stanley. *Manpower in Economic Growth: The American Record since 1800.* New York: McGraw-Hill, 1964.

Lerner, Gerda. "New Approaches to the Study of Women in American History." In *Liberating Women's History*, Bernice A. Carroll, ed. Chicago: University of Chicago Press, 1976.

———. "Placing Women in History: A 1975 Perspective." In *Liberating Women's History*, Bernice A. Carroll, ed. Chicago: University of Chicago Press, 1976.

Lewis, David W. *From Newgate to Dannemora—The Rise of Penitentiary in New York, 1816–1848.* Ithaca: Cornell University Press, 1965.

Lockridge, Kenneth A. *A New England Town: The First Hundred Years, Dedham, Mass., 1636–1736.* New York: W. W. Norton, 1970.

Lubove, Roy. *The Professional Altruist: The Emergence of Social Work as a Career, 1880–1930.* Cambridge, MA: Harvard University Press, 1965.

Mann, Arthur. *Yankee Reformers in an Urban Age.* Cambridge, MA: Harvard University Press, 1954.

Manton, Jo. *Mary Carpenter and the Children of the Streets.* London: Heinemann, 1976.

Marcus, Steven. *Engels, Manchester, and the Working Class.* New York: Random House, 1974.

Marris, Peter. *Loss and Change.* New York: Pantheon, 1974.

Marshall, J. D. *The Old Poor Law, 1779–1834.* Dublin: MacMillan, 1974.

Marx, Leo. *The Machine in the Garden: Technology and the Pastoral Ideal in America.* New York: Oxford University Press, 1976.

May, Margaret. "Innocence and Experience: The Evolution of the Concept of Juvenile Delinquency in the Mid 19th Century," *Victorian Studies*, 17(1) (1973).

McCluskey, Neil G. (ed.). *Catholic Education in America: A Documentary History.* New York: Teachers College, Columbia University Press, 1964.

Mead, Edwin D. *The Influence of Emerson.* Boston: American Unitarian Association, 1903.

Mennel, Robert M. *Thorns and Thistles: Juvenile Delinquents in the United States, 1825–1940.* Hanover, NH: University Press of New England, 1973.

———. " 'The Family System of Common Farmers': The Origins of Ohio's Reform Farm, 1840–1858," *Ohio History* 89 (1980).

———. " 'The Family System of Common Farmers': The Early Years of Ohio's Reform Farm, 1858–1884," *Ohio History* 89 (1980).

Messerli, Jonathan. *Horace Mann.* New York: Knopf, 1969.

Midwinter, E. C. *Victorian Social Reform.* London: Longman, 1968.

Mingay, G. E. *Enclosure and the Small Farmer in the Age of the Industrial Revolution.* Dublin: MacMillan, 1968.

Mohl, Raymond A., and Betten, Neil (eds.). *Urban America in Historical Perspective.* New York: Weybright and Talley, 1970.

Muller, Norbert. "La Colonie Agricole Penitentiaire De Mettray." Unpublished memoire de L'Université de Tours, 1976.

Nisbet, Robert A. *The Quest for Community*. New York: Oxford University Press, 1969.

———. *Social Change and History: Aspects of the Western Theory of Development*. New York: St. Martin's Press, 1973.

North American Review. 44 (1837).

———. 86 (1858).

Olmstead, Clifton E. *History of Religion in the United States*. Englewood Cliffs, NJ: Prentice-Hall, 1960.

O'Neill, William L. *Everyone Was Brave—a History of Feminism in America*. Chicago: Quadrangle Books, 1969.

Parker, Gail (ed.). *The Oven Birds: American Women on Womanhood, 1820–1920*. New York: Anchor Books, 1972.

Paulian, Louis. "M. de Metz et la Colonie Penitentiere." In *Extrait de Journal des Economistes*. Paris: n.p., 1873.

Payne, P. L. *British Entrepreneurship in the Nineteenth Century*. Dublin: MacMillan, 1974.

Pearsall, Ronald. *The Worm in the Bud*. New York: Macmillan, 1969.

Peirce, Bradford K. *A Half Century with Juvenile Delinquents—the New York House of Refuge and Its Times*. New York: D. Appleton and Company, 1869.

Perkins, Linda M. "Fanny Jackson Coppin and the Institute for Colored Youth: A Model of Nineteenth Century Black Female Educational and Community Leadership, 1837-1902." PhD Dissertation, University of Illinois, 1975.

Pickett, Robert S. *House of Refuge: Origins of Juvenile Reform in New York State, 1815–1857*. Syracuse: Syracuse University Press, 1969.

Piven, Frances Fox, and Cloward, Richard. *Regulating the Poor: The Functions of Public Welfare*. New York: Random House, 1971.

Platt, Anthony. *The Child Savers—The Invention of Delinquency*. Chicago: University of Chicago Press, 1961.

Polanyi, Karl. *The Great Transformation*. Boston: Beacon Press, 1944.

Police Department of Boston. *Miscellaneous Remarks on the Police of Boston as Respects Paupers, Alms & Work House; Classes of Poor and Beggars, etc.* Boston: Cummings & Hilliard, 1814.

Powell, Aaron M. *State Regulation of Vice. Regulation Efforts in America: The Geneva Congress*. New York: Wood and Holbrook, 1878.

Prentice, Alison. *The School Reformers*. Toronto: McClelland and Stewart, 1977.

Ravitch, Diane. *The Great School Wars—New York City 1805–1973—A History of the Public Schools as Battlefield of Social Change*. New York: Basic Books, 1974.

Report of the Commissioners on the Subject of the Pauper System of the Commonwealth of Massachusetts, appointed by an order of the House of Representatives, Feb. 29, 1832. Boston: Dutton and Wentworth, State Printers, 1835

Report of the Committee on the Consideration of the Pauper Laws of This Commonwealth. 1821 (= Quincy Report).

Riis, Jacob A. *How the Other Half Lives*. New York: Hill and Wang, 1957.

Rose, Michael E. *The English Poor Law, 1780–1930*. Newton Abbot: David and Charles, 1971.

———. *The Relief of Poverty 1834–1914*. London: MacMillan, 1972.

Rosenberg, Carroll Smith. *Religion and the Rise of the American City: The New York City Mission Movement, 1812–1870*. Ithaca: Cornell University Press, 1973.

Rosenberg, Rosalind. "In Search of Woman's Nature, 1850–1920," *Feminist Studies* 3(1/2) (fall 1975).

Rosenkrantz, Barbara G. *Public Health and the State: Changing Views in Massachusetts 1842–1936*. Cambridge, MA: Harvard University Press, 1972.

Ross, Dorothy. *G. Stanley Hall: The Psychologist as Prophet*. Chicago: University of Chicago Press, 1960.

Ross, Elizabeth Dale. *The Kindergarten Crusade: The Establishment of Preschool Education in the United States*. Athens, OH: Ohio University Press, 1976.

Rothman, David J. *The Discovery of the Asylum: Social Order and Disorder in the New Republic*. Boston: Little, Brown, 1971.

———. *Conscience and Convenience: The Asylum and Its Alternatives in Progressive America*. Boston: Little, Brown, 1981.

———, and Rothman, Sheila M. *Sources of American Social Tradition*, Vols. 1 and 2. New York: Basic Books, 1975.

Rowbotham, Sheila. *Women, Resistance and Revolution*. Harmondsworth, England: Penguin, 1972.

———. *Woman's Consciousness, Man's World*. Harnmondsworth, England: Penguin, 1973.

———. *Hidden from History—Rediscovering Women in History from the 17th Century to the Present*. New York: Random House, 1976.

Ruskin, John. *Unto This Last*. London: C. Tinling, 1960.

Samuel, Raphael. "The Workshop of the World: Steam Power and Hand Technology in Mid-Victorian Britain," *History Workshop, A Journal of Socialist Historians* 3 (Spring 1977).

Sanders, Wiley B. (ed.). *Juvenile Offenders for a Thousand Years: Selected Readings from Anglo-Saxon Times to 1900*. Chapel Hill: University of North Carolina Press, 1970.

Schlossman, Steven L. *Love and the American Delinquent*. Chicago: University of Chicago Press, 1977.

Schultz, Stanley. *The Culture Factory—Boston Public Schools, 1789–1860*. New York: Oxford University Press, 1973.

Schwartz, Harold. *Samuel Gridley Howe, Social Reform, 1801–1876*. Cambridge, MA: Harvard University Press, 1956.

Seabrook, Jeremy. *The Unprivileged: A Hundred Years of Family Life and Tradition in a Working Class Street*. London: Penguin Books, 1973.

Sennett, Richard. "Middle-Class Families and Urban Violence: The Experience of a Chicago Community in the Nineteenth Century." In *Anonymous Americans*, Tamara Haraven, ed. Englewood Cliffs, NJ: Prentice-Hall, 1971.

———. *Families against the City: Middle-Class Homes of Industrial Chicago, 1872–1890*. New York: Vintage Books, 1974.

Shanahan, William O. *German Protestants Face the Social Question*. Chicago: University of Notre Dame Press, 1975.

Shaftesbury, Carl. *The Dens of London—Forty Years Mission Work among the Outcast Poor of London*. London: Exeter Hall, 1844.

Shorter, Edward. *The Making of the Modern Family*. New York: Basic Books, 1975.

Sigourney, Lydia. *How to Be Happy, Written for the Children of Some Dear Friends by a Lady*. Hartford: D. F. Robinson & Co., 1833.

———. *Letters to Young Ladies*. New York: Harper & Brothers, 1856.

Silver, Harold. "Aspects of Neglect: The Strange Case of Victorian Popular Education," *Oxford Review of Education* 3(1) (1977).

Silver, Pamela, and Silver, Harold. *The Education of the Poor: The History of a National School 1824–1974*. London: Routledge and Kegan Paul, 1974.

Sinclair, Andrew. *The Emancipation of the American Woman*. New York: Harper and Row, 1965.

Sklar, Kathryn Kish. *Catharine Beecher: A Study in American Domesticity*. New Haven: Yale University Press, 1973.

Smith, Hilda. "Feminism and the Methodology of Women's History." In *Liberating Women's History*, Bernice A. Carroll, ed. Chicago: University of Illinois Press, 1976.

Smith, Timothy L. *Revivalism and Social Reform: American Protestantism on the Eve of the Civil War*. New York: Abington, 1957.

———. "Lay Initiative in the Religious Life of American Immigrants, 1880–1950." In *Anonymous Americans*, Tamara Haraven, ed. Englewood Cliffs, NJ: Prentice-Hall, 1977.

Smith-Rosenberg, Carroll. *Religion and the Rise of the American City: The New York City Mission Movement, 1812–1870*. Ithaca: Cornell University Press, 1973.

———. "The Female World of Love and Ritual: Relations between Women in Nineteenth Century America," *Signs* 1(4) (Autumn 1975).

Snedden, David S. *Administration and Educational Work of American Juvenile Reform Schools*. New York: Teachers College Series, Columbia University, 1907.

Société Paternelle. *Statuts Constitutifs*. Paris: NP, 1832.

Solomon, Barbara Miller. *Ancestors and Immigrants*. Chicago: University of Chicago Press, 1956 (Phoenix edition, 1972).

Spring, Joel H. *Education and the Rise of the Corporate State*. Boston: Beacon Press, 1972.

Starkey, Marion. *The Devil in Massachusetts*. New York: Knopf, 1949.

Stone, Lawrence (ed.) *Schooling and Society*. Baltimore: Johns Hopkins University Press, 1976.

Strong, Rev. Josiah. *Our Country: Its Possible Future and Its Present Crisis*. New York: Baker and Taylor, 1885.

Sussman, Herbert L. *Victorians and the Machine—the Literary Response to Technology*. Cambridge, MA: Harvard University Press, 1968.

"Symposium: Schooling in Capitalist America, Functions and Fantasies: Understanding Schools in Capitalist America," *History of Education Quarterly* 17(2) (Summer 1971).

Taylor, Ian, Walton, Paul, and Young, Jock. *The New Criminology: For a Social Theory of Deviance*. New York: Harper and Row, 1973.

Temin, Peter. *Causal Factors in American Economic Growth in the Nineteenth Century*. London: MacMillan, 1975.

Thernstrom, Stephan. *Poverty and Progress—Social Mobility in a Nineteenth Century City*. New York: Atheneum, 1972.

———. *The Other Bostonians*. Cambridge, MA: Harvard University Press, 1973.

———, and Knights, Peter R. "Men in Motion: Some Data and Speculations about Urban Population Mobility in Nineteenth Century America." In *Anonymous Americans*, Tamara Haraven, ed. Englewood Cliffs, NJ: Prentice-Hall, 1977.

———, and Sennett, Richard (eds.). *Nineteenth Century Cities: Essays in the New Urban History*. New Haven: Yale University Press, 1969.

Thompson, E. P. *The Making of the English Working Class*. New York: Vintage Books, 1966.

Tobias, J. J. *Urban Crime in Victorian England*. New York: Schocken Books, 1967.

Tomalin, Claire. *The Life and Death of Mary Wollstonecraft*. New York: New American Library, 1974.

Tyack, David B. *The One Best System—A History of American Urban Education*. Cambridge, MA: Harvard University Press, 1974.

Tyrrell, Ian R. *Sobering Up—From Temperance to Prohibition in Antebellum America, 1800–1860*. Westport, CT: Greenwood Press, 1979.

Vanderwalker, Vina C. *The Kindergarten in American Education*. New York: Arno Press and The New York Times, 1971.

Verbragge, Martha H. "Women and Medicine in Nineteenth Century America," *Signs* 1(4) (Summer 1976).

Vicinius, Martha (ed.). *Suffer and Be Still—Women in the Victorian Age*. Bloomington: Indiana University Press, 1972.

Vidich, Arthur J., and Bensman, Joseph. *Small Town in Mass Society*. Princeton: Princeton University Press, 1968.

Walden, Horace G. *Relation of the Liquor Traffic to Pauperism, Crime and Insanity*. Boston: Wright and Potter Printing Co., 1896.

Walters, Ronald G. *Primers for Prudery—Sexual Advice to Victorian America*. Englewood Cliffs, NJ: Prentice-Hall, 1974.

Ware, Norman. *The Industrial Worker, 1840–1960*. Chicago: Quadrangle Books, 1964.

Warner, Sam Bass, Jr. *The Urban Wilderness—A History of the American City*. New York: Harper and Row, 1962.

———. *The Private City*. Philadelphia: Philadelphia University Press, 1968.

Welsh, Sister Mary Michael, O.P. *Catharine Maria Sedgwick—Her Position in the Literature and Thought of Her Time up to 1860*. Washington, DC: The Catholic University of America, 1937.

Welter, Barbara. "The Cult of True Womanhood 1820–1860," *American Quarterly* 18(2) (Summer 1966).

Welter, Rush. *Popular Education and Democratic Thought in America*. New York: Columbia University Press, 1962.

Wiebe, Robert. *The Search for Order—1877–1920*. New York: Hill and Wang, 1967.

———. *The Segmented Society: An Introduction to the Meaning of America*. New York: Oxford University Press, 1975.

Wilson, Jackson R. *In Quest of Community: Social Philosophy in the United States 1860–1920*. New York: Oxford University Press, 1970.

Williams, Raymond. *Culture and Society 1780–1950*. London: Penguin Books, 1975.

Wines, Enoch C. *The State of Prisons and of Child-Saving Institutions in the Civilized World*. Cambridge: Cambridge University Press, John Wilson and Son, 1880.

Wines, Frederick Howard. *American Prisons in the Tenth U.S. Census*. New York: G. P. Putnam & Sons, The Knickerbocker Press, 1888.

Wishy, Bernard. *The Child and the Republic: The Dawn of Modern American Child Nuture*. Philadelphia: University of Pennsylvania, 1969.

Wohl, Richard R. "The 'Country Boy' Myth and Its Place in American Urban Culture: The Nineteenth Century Contribution," *Perspectives in American History* 3 (1969).

Zuckerman, Michael. *Peaceable Kingdoms*. New York: Vintage Books, 1970.

———. "William Byrd's Family," *Perspectives in American History* 12 (1979).

Public Documents, Reports, and Letters

England

An Account of the Present Nature and Present State of the Philanthropic Society—Instituted in the Year 1788 and Incorporated in 1806 for the Prevention of Crimes by the Admission of the Offspring of Convicts and the Reformation of Criminal Poor Children. London: Royal Philanthropic Society, 1829.

Committee Account of the Philanthropic Society. London: Royal Philanthropic Society, 1848–1865.

Kynnersley, T. C. Sneyd. *The Law Relating to Juvenile Offenders, Reformatory and Industrial Schools, with Practical Suggestions in Reference to the Commitment of Children to Reformatory Schools, Lists*, Government Document, 1862.

Turner, Sydney. *Chaplain's Report to Royal Philanthropic*. London: Royal Philanthropic Society, 1888.

———, and Paynter, Thomas. Published letter, "To William Gladstone." In *Account of the Philanthropic Society. London: Royal Philanthropic Society, 1846.*

Unpublished case records, handwritten record books, 1795–1857, Royal Philanthropic Society.

France

Anonymous. *Status Constitutifs de la Société Paternelle*. Paris: n.p., n.d.

de Metz, August et deCourteilles, Vte. de Bretigneres. *Rapport*. 1841–1852.

de Tocqueville, Alexis. Unpublished handwritten letter to de Metz, not dated.

Massachusetts

Ames, Marcus, Brackett, L. L., Fay, Francis, Loring, Lathrop, and Peirce, Bradford. Handwritten case records, unpublished case record books for State Industrial School for Girls, Lancaster, 1856–1905.

Massachusetts, Board of State Charities. *Annual Reports*. Boston, 1865–1878.

Massachusetts. *Census*, 1860.

Massachusetts, General Court. *Acts and Resolves*, Boston.

Massachusetts, General Court, House. *Report of the Commissioners for the Establishment of a State Reform School for Girls*. House Document No. 43, Boston, 1844.

Massachusetts, General Court, House. *Report of the Committee on the Pauper Laws of the Commonwealth*. House Document, Boston, 1821.

Massachusetts, General Court, Senate, Committees. *Report of the Special Joint Committee Appointed to Investigate the Whole System of Public Charitable Institutions of the Commonwealth of Massachusetts*. Senate Document No. 2, Boston, 1859.

Massachusetts, General Court, Senate. *Report of the Joint Special Committee on* "The emigration of young women to the West." Senate Document No. 156, 1865.

Massachusetts Industrial School for Girls. *Annual Reports.* Boston, 1856–1905.

Massachusetts, Principal and Trustees of the State Primary and Reform Schools. *Annual Reports.* Boston, 1879–1894.

Massachusetts, Prison Commissioners. *Annual Reports.* Boston, 1881–1905.

Massachusetts, State Board of Charity. *Annual Reports.* Boston, 1899–1905.

Massachusetts State Board of Health, Lunacy and Charity. *Annual Reports.* Boston, 1879–1886.

Massachusetts State Board of Lunacy and Charity. *Annual Reports.* Boston, 1886–1898.

Massachusetts, Superintendent and Trustees of the State Industrial School for Girls, Lancaster. *Annual Reports.* Boston, 1856–1905.

Massachusetts, Superintendent and Trustees of the State Reform School at Westborough. *Annual Reports.* Boston, 1877–1905.

Massachusetts, Trustees of the Lyman and Industrial Schools. *Annual Reports.* Boston, 1885–1905.

Publications of the Joint Center for Urban Studies

The Joint Center for Urban Studies, a cooperative venture of the Massachusetts Institute of Technology and Harvard University, was founded in 1959 to organize and encourage research on urban and regional problems and family and social policy. Participants have included scholars from the fields of anthropology, architecture, business, city planning, economics, education, engineering, history, law, philosophy, political science, and sociology.

The findings and conclusions of this book are, as with all Joint Center publications, solely the responsibility of the authors.

Published by Harvard University Press

The Intellectual versus the City: From Thomas Jefferson to Frank Lloyd Wright, by Morton and Lucia White, 1962

Streetcar Suburbs: The Process of Growth in Boston, 1870–1900, by Sam B. Warner Jr., 1961

City Politics, by Edward C. Banfield and James Q. Wilson, 1963

Law and Land: Anglo-American Planning Practice, edited by Charles M. Haar, 1964

Location and Land Use: Toward a General Theory of Land Rent, by William Alonso, 1964

Poverty and Progress: Social Mobility in a Nineteenth Century City, by Stephan Thernstrom, 1964

Boston: The Job Ahead, by Martin Meyerson and Edward C. Banfield, 1966

The Myth and Reality of Our Urban Problems, By Raymond Vernon, 1966

Muslim Cities in the Later Middle Ages, by Ira Marvin Lapidus 1967

The Fragmented Metropolis: Los Angeles, 1850–1930, by Robert M. Fogelson, 1967

Law and Equal Opportunity: A Study of the Massachusetts Commission Against Discrimination, by Leon H. Mayhew, 1968

Varieties of Police Behavior: The Management of Law and Order in Eight Communities, by James Q. Wilson

The Metropolitan Enigma: Inquiries into the Nature and Dimensions of America's "Urban Crisis," edited by James Q. Wilson, revised edition, 1968

Traffic and the Police: Variations in Law-Enforcement Policy, by John A. Gardiner, 1969

The Influence of Federal Grants: Public Assistance in Massachusetts, by Martha Derthick, 1970

The Arts in Boston, by Bernard Taper, 1970

Families Against the City: Middle Class Homes of Industrial Chicago, 1872–1890, by Richard Sennett, 1970

The Political Economy of Urban Schools, by Martin T. Katzman, 1971

Origins of the Urban School: Public Education in Massachusetts, 1870–1915, by Marvin Lazerson, 1971

The Other Bostonians: Poverty and Progress in the American Metropolis, 1880–1970, by Stephan Thernstrom, 1973

Published by the MIT Press

The Image of the City, by Kevin Lynch, 1960

Housing and Economic Progress: A Study of the Housing Experience of Boston's Middle-Income Families, by Lloyd Rodwin, 1961

The Historian and the City, edited by Oscar Handlin and John Burchard, 1963

The Federal Bulldozer: A Critical Analysis of Urban Renewal, 1949–1962, by Martin Anderson, 1964

The Future of Old Neighborhoods: Rebuilding for a Changing Population, by Bernard J. Frieden, 1964

Man's Struggle for Shelter in an Urbanizing World, By Charles Abrams, 1964

The View from the Road, by Donald Appleyard, Kevin Lynch, and John R. Myer, 1964

The Public Library and the City, edited by Ralph W. Conant, 1965

Regional Development Policy: A Case Study of Venezuela, by John Friedmann, 1966

Urban Renewal: The Record and the Controversy, edited by James Q. Wilson, 1966

Transport Technology for Developing Regions: A study of Road Transportation in Venezuela, by Richard M. Soberman, 1966

Computer Methods in the Analysis of Large-Scale Social Systems, edited by James M. Beshers, 1968

Planning Urban Growth and Regional Development: The Experience of the Guayana Program of Venezuela, by Lloyd Rodwin and Associates, 1969

Build a Mill, Build a City, Build a School: Industrialization, Urbanization and Education in Ciudad Guayana, by Noel F. McGinn and Russell G. Davis, 1969

Land-Use Controls in the United States, by John Delafons, second edition, 1969

Beyond the Melting Pot: The Negroes, Puerto Ricans, Jews, Italians, and Irish of New York City, by Nathan Glazer and Daniel Patrick Moynihan, revised edition, 1970

Bargaining: Monopoly Power versus Union Power, by George de Menil, 1971

Housing the Urban Poor: A Critical Evaluation of Federal Housing Policy, by Arthur P. Solomon, 1974

The Politics of Neglect: Urban Aid from Model Cities to Revenue Sharing, by Bernard J. Frieden and Marshall Kaplan, 1975

Planning a Pluralist City: Conflicting Realities in Ciudad Guayana, by Donald Appleyard, 1976

The Environmental Protection Hustle, by Bernard J. Frieden, 1979

The Urban Transportation System: Politics and Policy Innovation, by Alan A. Altshuler with James P. Womack and John R. Pucher, 1979

Seasonal Cycles in the Housing Market: Patterns, Costs, and Policies, by Kenneth T. Rosen, 1979

The Prospective City: Economic, Population, Energy, and Environmental Developments, edited by Arthur P. Solomon, 1979

Discrimination in Mortgage Lending, by Robert Shafer and Helen F. Ladd, 1981

Daughters of the State: A Social Portrait of the First Reform School for Girls in North America, 1856–1905, by Barbara M. Brenzel, 1983

The Joint Center also publishes reports and working papers.

Index